Public Sector Auditing

Public Sector Auditing

Practical techniques for an integrated approach

P.C. Jones BSc (ECON), IPFA, MIIA
Chief Internal Auditor,
North Avon District Council

and

J.G. Bates BSc ACA
Chartered Accountant

CHAPMAN AND HALL

University and Professional Division

LONDON · NEW YORK · TOKYO · MELBOURNE · MADRAS

UK	Chapman and Hall, 2–6 Boundary Row, London SE1 8HN
USA	Chapman and Hall, 29 West 35th Street, New York NY10001
JAPAN	Chapman and Hall Japan, Thomson Publishing Japan, Hirakawacho Nemoto Building, 7F, 1-7-11 Hirakawa-cho, Chiyoda-ku, Tokyo 102
AUSTRALIA	Chapman and Hall Australia, Thomas Nelson Australia, 102 Dodds Street, South Melbourne, Victoria, 3205
INDIA	Chapman and Hall India, R. Sheshadri, 32 Second Main Road, CIT East, Madras 600 035

First edition 1990

© 1990 P.C. Jones and J.G. Bates

Typeset in 10/12 pt Times by
Excel Typesetting Company, Hong Kong

Printed in Great Britain by
T.J. Press (Padstow) Ltd, Padstow, Cornwall

ISBN 0 412 36260 0

British Library Cataloguing in Publication Data

Jones, Peter
  Public Sector Auditing
  1. Great Britain. Public sector. Auditing
  I. Title II. Bates, Jonathan
  657.835045

  ISBN 0–412–36260–0

Library of Congress Cataloging in Publication Data

available

Contents

Preface

The public sector accounts for about 40% of the gross domestic product of the United Kingdom. There is, however, little published literature on the auditing of these enormous financial undertakings. In any sizeable library one can find all manner of works with the private sector in mind. *Public Sector Auditing* will help redress the balance.

The book has been written in response to the major changes that are taking place in the public sector. Throughout central and local government managers are being held more accountable for their actions. The role of the auditor is changing to accommodate this. For example:

(a) The auditor must justify the service he offers his clients.
(b) He must continuously monitor and improve his technical standards.
(c) He may be subject to active competition for the supply of audit services.

For an auditor to tackle these challenges successfully he needs to be absolutely certain of his own professionalism.

This book puts forward a professional, unified approach to practical auditing based on the idea that audits of all types require the auditor to give an **opinion** to his client. The external auditor traditionally gives an opinion on a set of financial statements. An internal auditor, carrying out work on, say, internal controls, will give an opinion to managers on the strength of a financial system. Opinions can be given about future as well as past events. Value-for-money audit, an interesting element of public sector audit, although drawing upon past events, aims to improve the future.

Public Sector Auditing covers techniques required for the following:

(a) Attestation audit (audit of accounts both internal and published);
(b) Systems reliability audit;
(c) Value-for-money audit;
(d) Fraud investigation;
(e) Computer application audit;

(f) Regularity audit.

The book makes little differentiation between internal and external audit practices. All opinions result from an **essential audit process** which applies to all audit types. Audit of accounts and fraud investigation will require emphasis on different techniques. However, both opinion forming assignments will require planning, controlling and recording. Both may involve sampling of available data and both will require review of evidence before an opinion is given in a report. In these circumstances it is of little help to treat internal and external audit as separate professions. Within the public sector internal and external audit roles are often strikingly similar.

This work is intended for use by practising public sector auditors. It is hoped that it will be of use to them in their work during this period of flux. Students studying for the professional qualifications such as those of CIPFA, the other CCAB bodies and the Institute of Internal Auditors will also find the work of interest. It should assist them in their practical work as they come to grips with the nature of audit.

The book is divided into explanatory text and case examples. The main body of the text describes the techniques and underlying theory which the auditor should understand. The case studies attempt to illustrate the techniques in realistic situations. Technical summaries are also provided at strategic intervals.

In this book the case studies are as important as the text in helping the reader to understand the audit techniques and to recognize the situations in which to apply them. A basic knowledge of accountancy is assumed throughout, though not to a formal academic or professional level. Finally, Chapter 8 assumes some rudimentary understanding of statistics.

Glossary of terms

Audit

An independent appraisal of an organization undertaken in persuance of statutory requirements and/or contractual obligations. This involves forming and reporting opinions on the financial affairs and/or systems of the audited body, together with any further investigations needed to satisfy the requirements and obligations.

Audit area

A loosely used term that describes a convenient aggregation of audit work, usually relating to key figures or parts of a system.

Audit assignment

A defined part of the total audit. An assignment will form an individual audit investigation into a practically defined aspect, financial or otherwise, of the organization. Assignments have individual objectives and specific conclusions are formed.

Auditor

The person with responsibility for the audit work.

Audit instructions

These can be statutory requirements, often of a general nature, that require detailed interpretation by the auditor, usually in accordance with guidance laid down by professional bodies or the internal standards of the audit organization. Audit instructions can also be of a more specific nature as agreed between senior managers and the auditor. This is often the case with 'value-for-money' work and non-statutory assignments carried out on a negotiated basis.

Audit objectives

These are the 'high level' objectives of the audit and of individual assignments that are formulated by the auditor to satisfy the audit instructions.

Analytical review

A form of substantive testing where evidence is obtained by analysing the wider financial relationships between sets of figures. For example, payroll costs can often be analytically reviewed in relation to staff numbers, grades and pay settlements.

Attestation audit
Audit work carried out to form an opinion on the fairness of a set of figures, usually a published account.

Business planning
Long- and medium-term audit planning carried out to enable the auditor to operate in a competitive situation by matching resources to the demand for his services.

Client
The 'client' is usually taken to mean the organization employing the auditor. It is often difficult to decide who or what body forms the ultimate client for a public sector audit. In this book the term client is taken to mean the senior management or the political leaders of the audited body.

Confidence
This term is used when referring to the auditor's confidence in systems controls or in sets of figures. For statistical sampling purposes confidence is usually expressed as a percentage confidence level, e.g. the auditor may say he is 95% confident that errors amount to no more than an estimated maximum amount.

Compliance tests
Audit tests undertaken to verify that the internal controls of a system are operating over a period of time. Compliance tests help the auditor to form an opinion on the reliability of a system and the extent to which it is self-checking.

Control objectives
These are purposes of operating internal controls which usually form the test objectives of compliance tests. For example, a stock recording system will usually have internal controls designed to meet the objective of ensuring that stocks are only issued for authorized purposes.

Directional testing
A method of testing that allows a reduction in the amount of detailed work by placing reliance on the organization's double-entry book-keeping system.

Essential audit process
A fundamental process setting out the key stages of an audit. This process can be applied to most audits to provide a cohesive framework for the detailed work.

Evidence

In an audit context evidence is taken to mean facts and opinions that help to support or disprove the accuracy of figures, reliability of systems, value for money, etc., as defined by audit and test objectives. Audit evidence may arise from the auditor's own work, from third parties, or from the records and statements of the client.

Internal controls

Procedures and arrangements that are part of a wider system but are operated to ensure that the completeness, accuracy and validity of transactions and assets or liabilities are maintained. Internal controls are normally applied on a systematic basis to ensure the system operates to a reliable and acceptable standard and are evidenced in some recorded or visual manner.

Materiality

This term is used to described the financial significance of accounts balances or other values. These include the annual value of transactions processed by a system or the importance of a known error when forming an audit opinion. Materiality is an important concept in audit planning. It helps to define the level of audit effort needed for each audit area in terms of its financial significance.

Monetary unit sampling (MUS)

A statistical sampling technique that allows the auditor to express his conclusions in monetary terms. MUS is particularly useful for attestation and to some extent for systems reliability audits. Sample sizes are usually smaller than those required when using other methods for the same purpose.

Opinion

This is taken to mean the professional audit opinion formed on the basis of audit work undertaken to meet defined audit objectives.

Precision gap widening (PGW)

A stage in the process of extrapolation of the errors discovered using MUS.

Regularity

The legality, under statute and internal regulation, of the values or procedures being audited. Regularity audit work ensures that the audited body is not acting *ultra vires*.

Reliability factor

A single measure that combines the auditor's confidence level and his anticipated error rate used in MUS. The reliability factor is a key determinant of sample size.

Report
The formal written statement of opinions. This can be very brief for a satisfactory attestation audit, or can run into many pages of findings for a major value-for-money study.

Risk
Risk is the auditor's subjective assessment of the likelihood of errors. Risk, in conjunction with materiality, is one of the main determinants of audit effort taken into account in planning. Risk is also taken to mean the compliment of confidence in statistical sampling, e.g. a 95% confidence level implies a 5% risk that a statement is not true.

Sample
This is a statistically obtained selection of items to be tested by the auditor. So-called 'judgemental samples' are termed 'selections' in this book.

Strategic plan
This is a long-term plan to ensure that the totality of audit work meets the auditor's statutory duties and other instructions. The plan will usually set out relative priorities for each assignment and match these to the required resources.

Substantive testing
Audit testing undertaken to gain evidence to substantiate directly the accuracy, completeness and validity of transactions. A less direct form of substantive evidence is obtained by *analytical review* (q.v.).

Systems based audit
This is an approach to audit that relies heavily upon the ability to identify and test internal controls in a system. Such reliance will reduce the level of substantive testing otherwise required. This approach also highlights any serious lack of internal control and any preventive measures needed to make the system secure can be suggested.

Upper error limit (UEL)
The maximum predicted level of errors in a population. The prediction is obtained from analysing the results of MUS.

Chapter

1 The audit environment and current issues

INTRODUCTION

This short chapter aims to set the scene, although it can only skim briefly over what could easily form a separate book in its own right. It considers the extent of the public sector, the main groupings of public sector auditors and some of the current issues which affect them.

Public sector auditors, despite their common objectives, are often relatively isolated and others may know little about their work. This brief overview may give a wider appreciation to all concerned.

WHAT IS THE PUBLIC SECTOR?

Perhaps the most convenient listing of the public sector is the annual Public Expenditure White Paper. Despite a decade of privatization and axing of quangos most first-time readers express some surprise at the number and diversity of public bodies. A brief summary is provided in Table 1.1. CIPFA by-laws give a more generic definition of public sector bodies dividing them broadly into central and local government, public utilities accountable to Parliament, other public bodies funded mainly from taxation, bodies largely regulated, owned, or controlled by central or local government, and educational and training establishments.

No definition seems to be comprehensive or complete. Indeed, some reflection on the great changes of the past two centuries of public life can leave little doubt that, but for a solid core of activities such as defence or care of the very needy which the market inevitably fails to provide, the 'public sector' fluctuates widely according to political fashion and historical accident.

Table 1.1 Public sector organizations

Nationalized industries
British Coal Corporation
British Railways Board
British Waterways Board
Civil Aviation Authority
Post Office

Other public corporations
The Audit Commission
British Technology Group
Cable Authority
Commonwealth Development Corporation
Covent Garden Market Authority
The Crown Agents
The Crown Agents Holding and Realization Board
The Crown Suppliers
Development Board for Rural Wales
English Industrial Estates Corporation
General Practice Finance Corporation
Her Majesty's Stationery Office
Highlands and Islands Development Board
Housing Action Trusts
Letchworth Garden City
Local Authority Public Transport and Airport Companies
National Film Finance Corporation
Northern Ireland Electricity Service
Northern Ireland Housing Executive

Central government departments[1]
Defence
Foreign and Commonwealth Office
Overseas Development Administration
Ministry of Agriculture, Fisheries and Food
Intervention Board for Agricultural Produce
Trade and Industry
Export Credits Guarantee
Energy
Employment
Transport
Environment
Home Office
Lord Chancellor's
Education and Science
Arts and Libraries
Health
Social Security
Scottish Office
Welsh Office
Northern Ireland Office
Customs and Excise
Inland Revenue
Property Services Agency

Local government[2]	*Number of bodies*
England:	
Counties	39
Met. Districts	36
Non-met. Districts	296
Scotland:	
Regions	9
Districts	53
Islands Council	3
Wales:	
Counties	8
Districts	37
N. Ireland:	
Areas Boards	9
Districts	26
London:	
L.R.B.	1
London Boroughs	32
	549

Health authorities[2]	*Number of bodies*
England:	
Regional authorities	14
District authorities	191
Scotland:	
Health boards	15
Wales:	
C.S.A.	1
Health authorities	9

Northern Ireland Public Trust Port
  Authorities
Northern Ireland Transport Holding
  Company
Oil and Pipelines Agency
The Pilotage Commission
Royal Mint
Royal Ordnance plc
Scottish Development Agency
Scottish Homes
United Kingdom Atomic Energy
  Authority
Urban Development Corporations
Welsh Development Agency
The Welsh Fourth Channel Authority
Bank of England
British Broadcasting Corporation
Housing Corporation (Scotland)
Independent Broadcasting Authority
New Town Development Corporations
  and the Commission for New Towns
Public Trust Ports
Scottish Special Housing Association

N. Ireland:

C.S.A.	1
Boards	4
	235

784

---

1. Individual Departments may contain large self-administering units such as the Transport Department's Driver and Vehicle Licensing Centre. Many such semi-independent units will contain a permanent audit presence. Only the main Departments are listed here.
2. Individual local and health authorities may be responsible for numerous large units of service provision such as hospitals and colleges.

Public sector audit

At the technical level public sector audit is similar to audit anywhere. Some techniques are currently relatively underdeveloped in the public sector, for example planning techniques and statistical sampling. However, the pressures for change are already forcing some public sector auditors to catch up with – and sometimes overtake – the private sector. In other techniques, on the other hand, the public sector has a long history in the forefront of development, for example the auditor's duties in relation to fraud. Most of this text, from Chapter 3 onwards, is concerned with the techniques of audit and their practical application in the public sector. However, this introductory chapter is intended to give a broad overview and at this level, unlike at the technical level, some quite distinct features of public sector audit are apparent.

Perhaps the most striking difference is the underlying need to take account of **political** influences. At the end of an audit, particularly a value-for-money audit, the auditor will make his best objective and impartial recommendations. Unless these relate to clear-cut cases of inadequate control, improper accounting or fraud he or she may well find considerable debate ensues among management and politicians. Auditors not experienced in the public sector often express some surprise that apparently 'uncontroversial' recommendations such as to increase prices to cover expenses are met with resistance. Some examples are famous – the fees for dog licences for example. The important point to grasp is that in a clash between political 'policies' and economic 'rationale', policies usually take priority in the public sector – at least in the short run. This can be said to apply even when such policies are designed to encourage adherence to 'economic' considerations. In short, in the **private** sector the auditor's advice and recommendations are virtually guaranteed respect – anyone used only to this environment may be in for a shock.

Another important point of comparison between public and private sector auditors is the more wide-ranging remit of the external public auditors. Often work such as fraud investigation and value-for-money assessment would be considered the realm of specialist accountants in the private sector, yet such work is tackled as audit throughout the public sector. Specialized regulatory work, often of a legal nature, can also arise in most statutory bodies. A good example is the Audit Commission for Local Authorities' requirement to hear public objectors to local authority accounts. This can place the District Auditor, or the partner of a firm, in a quasi-judicial role.

The rest of this chapter discusses some of the basic characteristics and issues which identify the public sector auditor.

WHO ARE THE AUDITORS?

External auditors

The National Audit Office (NAO)

This body provides the external audit of central government and related activities and reports to Parliament and the public. It was set up under the National Audit Act of 1983 and is the successor to the Exchequer and Audit Department (E&AD) dating from the Exchequer and Audit Department Act of 1866.

The NAO is headed by the Comptroller and Auditor General (C&AG), an official post the origins of which date back to the early fourteenth century. The C&AG is a Crown appointee, rather like a judge, and he and his department are completely independent of the government bodies under audit.

The NAO is quite a small organization of around 900 staff which is often a source of some surprise considering the number of accounts audited, over 500 with turnover totalling well over £100 billion. It must be said, however, that the vast majority of accounts under audit are of a relatively simplistic cash receipts and payments structure compared to the complex consolidated largely accruals-based accounts of private companies or local authorities. Even so, the figures are often in £ billions and can represent the end product of very complex computerized systems.

In addition to its attestation role the NAO and the E&AD before it had a long tradition of value-for-money audit. This forms the bulk of reports to Parliament via the Public Accounts Committee, the main Select Committee for financial affairs. The NAO audit does not extend to Northern Ireland, where the Northern Ireland Audit Office performs a similar role in respect of central government bodies.

The Audit Commission for Local Authorities in England and Wales

The Audit Commission was set up under the Local Government Finance Act 1982 with responsibility for all local government external audit. Its reports are published generally as well as directly to local authorities. Prior to 1982 the Department of the Environment's District Audit Service fulfilled this role together with a few private firms of 'approved' auditors.

Currently, the 17-member Commission awards about 70% of local government audits to the District Audit Service which has become, in effect, its own 'practising arm', and 30% to approved private firms. From 1990 the Audit Commission will, as a result of the White Paper on the

NHS, also become responsible for the audit of health authorities which, prior to this, had been audited by the Health Service Statutory Auditors set up under the National Health Service Act 1977, and since 1987 by some private sector firms. It is not yet clear what organizational structure and arrangements will arise from this change, but something similar to the current Audit Commission District Audit Service and approved private firms looks very likely.

Apart from appointing auditors the Commission provides a measure of central support and direction for their work, much of which takes the form of publications such as *The Code of Local Audit Practice for England and Wales* and detailed volumes of guidance entitled *Local Government Auditor*. The Commission's other main role is to undertake national statistical profiles and value-for-money studies. These are usually the basis of local investigations by the DA Service or the approved private firms. The Commission's other functions include the certification of claims for government grants, extraordinary audits and very occasionally the audit of bodies not covered by the Local Government Finance Act 1982.

The external audit of Northern Ireland local government is very similar to the pre-Audit Commission situation in England and Wales. The Department of Environment (Northern Ireland) appoints a Chief Local Government Auditor and his supporting auditors. Although he is independent in practice, the Chief Local Government Auditor is ultimately responsible to the Permanent Secretary of the Department of the Environment who can direct a local government auditor to carry out an extraordinary audit. Unlike the rest of the UK no private firms are awarded local government audits in Northern Ireland.

The Commission for Local Government Accounts in Scotland

The 'Accounts Commission' was set up under the Local Government (Scotland) Act 1973, though it did not come into effect until 1 April 1975. The Commission appoints a Controller of Audit and his staff, and has responsibility for external audit for all Scottish local authorities and various boards and joint committees. Like the Audit Commission, for which it was in many ways a forerunner, it performs both attestation and value-for-money audits, though in Scotland the Accounts Commission awards a far larger proportion of audits to private firms, around 60%.

The nationalized industries

External audit of nationalized industries and public utilities is generally undertaken along similar lines to the external audit of private companies. The main differences relate to the need to ensure that the bodies have adhered to their wider enabling legislation, including any statutory instruments and directives laid down by ministers. Over the years a great many performance indicators have been set in addition to profit such as rates of return on assets employed, and the audit of these is of critical political importance to the reader of the accounts.

Internal auditors

It is very difficult to generalize about the numbers or nature of internal auditors in the public sector. Unlike the private sector, public bodies are often required by law to provide for internal audit. Though the standards of provision can vary most, if not all, public sector internal auditors attempt to comply with CIPFA statements of internal audit practice and the Institute of Internal Auditor's code of ethics and standards. (The development of auditing standards is discussed later.) Internal auditors may report directly to political office holders in serious cases, but usually report to chief officers or senior managers.

As a guide to the number of internal audit sections, all 549 local authorities and 235 health authorities have an internal audit section as do all government departments, though smaller departments may use the internal audit service of larger ones just as some of the larger local authorities may provide specialized computer and other audit services to smaller ones. In fact, almost all of the bodies listed in Table 1.1, including nationalized industries, quangos and other public bodies totalling 854 in number, at the last count can be expected to undertake internal audit. Most universities, many polytechnics, government agencies and semi-autonomous public bodies will also have internal auditors.

WHO IS THE 'CLIENT'?

External audit value-for-money (VFM) reports are often the subject of wide media coverage. This is particularly so in the current climate of controversy surrounding the size and value for money of public expenditure. Unlike a limited company where the overriding duty of the auditors is to report to the shareholders, the 'client' of the public sector external auditor is less clear cut. Ultimately the electorate can be considered the 'client' and this is reflected in both the NAO's and the AC's right to report directly to the public and press, publishing its audit reports sometimes in great detail.

In this book the term 'client' is often used to describe the audited body and its management. This practice is for convenience and should not be confused with the issue of who is the ultimate client or beneficiary of the audit.

CURRENT AUDITING ISSUES

The form of the accounts

The form of public accounts has a history of change which is likely to continue indefinitely. Most accounts formats are subject to gradual change to cater for changing legal and economic circumstances. Today there is considerable pressure for greater commercial-style accountability. Why do departments of state not have balance sheets to show the value of the assets they control? Why are health authority accounts not more like the glossy accounts of private sector health care bodies?

The one great advantage of central government's receipts and payments accounts is their simplicity and ease of understanding. For a non-accountant politician or journalist this may be more helpful than more complex accruals-based accounts. The present accounts might not tell the reader a great deal about the organization but at least he or she can easily understand what is set out. However, calls for more complex, generally commercial-style accounts that will give greater financial accountability seem to be increasing in recent years.

Audit reporting

This is another fast developing area. Not so long ago any audit report was a very unwelcome event for the manager. The external auditor signed his certificate on the accounts, and, unless serious problems arose, had little else to say. Internal audit, preoccupied with errors and fault finding, tended to write only critical reports.

Critical reports will still be forthcoming, and these no doubt will be the ones which catch the headlines. But over the past decade less critical types of audit reports have become more common. Two broad categories can be distinguished:

(a) those that seek to give constructive advice;
(b) those that seek to offer assurance to management.

Constructive advice has often been 'bolted on' to critical audit reports, more as an afterthought or in an attempt to sweeten an otherwise bitter pill. Unlike the private sector, management consultants have, until recently, played only a minor role as advisors to public bodies. The auditor's report, often in the form of a value-for-money study, is now helping to meet this need for expert and objective advice. This has been particularly so of external auditors over the past few years. For instance, the Audit Commission's auditors, when undertaking local studies based on the Commission's national studies, will invariably give advice on how recognized national good practice can be achieved in their particular localities.

Reports that **seek to offer assurance to management** may be in similar vein to the traditional attestation certificate purporting to give a 'presents fairly' or 'true and fair' type of assurance on a set of figures. Such reports may arise from special investigations into almost any aspect of the organization arising, for example, from cases of suspected fraud or misleading management information.

Much of the auditor's routine work, particularly internal audit testing of transactions such as creditors' payments and payroll payments, have traditionally resulted in a kind of 'exception' reporting – if you don't hear from the auditor you can assume he found nothing. Many line managers have been content to assume that no news was good news even to the point of considering that no news amounted to a clean bill of health. Some managements, particularly senior departmental managers in central government and those at chief officer level in local authorities, have started to question this attitude and to require assurance that:

(a) The auditor has performed a reasonable level of work in the authority's areas of responsibility (after all, the authority's budget will be paying for the audit).
(b) The auditor's review of systems and the financial information these provide are in fact reliable. The auditor may only have found a few minor errors, but how representative was his testing?

The desire of senior management to have a positive report that all is well and to know on what evidence the auditor bases his conclusions may well arise from their desire to get as much value for money as possible from audit work.

Scope of the audit

Apart from being expected to give more helpful, constructive and, if appropriate, more reassuring reports, the scope of the auditor's reporting appears to be ever widening. Value-for-money audit, though by no means a new area, has attracted increasing attention – Chapter 10 outlines this area in detail. Auditors are expected to be able to offer professional financial advice akin in many ways to a management consultant.

The prevention of fraud and corruption is still part of the mainstream of professional work for both internal and external auditors. This is largely due to the increasing level of computer-related frauds, though most auditors still see their role as a 'watchdog' rather than a 'bloodhound'. Chapter 9 deals with this area.

Independence

This is a much debated topic among auditors. In practice innumerable factors come into play to affect the auditor's independence on any given audit assignment. The most common influences come under three headings.

(a) **Statutory or other regulating provisions.** These are particularly rele-vant to external auditors and local authority internal auditors whose appointments are governed by statute. The law lays down the auditor's rights of access to evidence and the right to report.
(b) **Organizational influences.** These refer in particular to the right to make direct contact with and report to the highest levels of the organ-ization. Such influences are usually more important for internal auditors, who, by definition, form part of the internal 'command' structure of the organization.
(c) **Attitude of mind.** The auditor should maintain an independent and objective stance whatever the pressures of the assignment or the relationships he or she forms.

It is inevitable, given their expanding role, that some auditors will become concerned at being placed in a compromising position with regard to their independence. Independence is critical if the auditor is to retain credibility and avoid accusations of bias. Nevertheless, in this country, private firms have up to now generally managed to combine an audit and a consulting role for the same client. The European Community's directives might go some way to enforcing a split, time alone will tell.

Resources

In common with most of the public sector the past decade has seen the auditor's resources, particularly manpower, put under increasing pressure. This has come at a time of almost revolutionary changes in the demands placed upon auditors and the development of techniques involved in audit. Further problems have come from the increasing drain of skilled officers to private-sector firms and industry.

The techniques outlined in Chapter 3 onwards are in large part a response to pressure upon audit resources. A well planned and controlled audit will almost invariably save time by targeting resources to problem areas.

(a) **Statistical sampling** offers the auditor the chance to obtain far greater value for money for the effort usually expended on routine substantive checking. Some initial time and effort will invariably be 'sunk' into developing the expertise required, testing software interrogation packages or writing programs in enquiry languages such as 'filetab'. But the increased assurance given to management and auditors will pay back the effort.

(b) **Directional testing** can reduce the size of samples or judgemental selections often by half, providing of course that the organization's double-entry book-keeping is reliable.

(c) A **unified systems approach** involving regular compliance testing can reduce subsequent effort involved in complete systems evaluation and in forming attestation opinions.

(d) **Analytical review of data**, collected over time and from similar organizations, can provide audit assurance when detailed testing is too costly or time-consuming to perform. Similarly, **predictive testing** using physical relationships may provide assurance on the reasonableness of income and expenditure.

There is, however, a limit to the practicality of compensating for lack of resources by adopting new or adapting existing techniques.

There is often a statutory 'minimum' of audit duties in public bodies, but few, if any, auditors confine their efforts to this minimum; most see at least part of their efforts as 'demand-led' consultancy type work. This work usually involves the highest standards of auditing, for which there is stiff competition from the private sector for staff. This is further discussed in Chapter 3 as part of the business plan.

Competition

The increased demand and limited resources mentioned above call for a more competitive approach to audit. There has been much discussion about opening up central services such as internal audit to competition. With the notable exception of the audit of central government by the NAO, most other public sector external audit is already subject to significant competition between the District Audit Service and various firms.

Some private firms already offer an internal audit service and there is little doubt that the introduction of competition for all or part of the internal audit function would be possible for most public sector bodies. A measure of the current preoccupation with this topic can be seen from the fact that the CIPFA 1989 Audit Conference lasting three days was dominated almost exclusively by the theme of competition.

The more competitive approach has encouraged auditors to increase their levels of audit planning, paying more attention to long-term strategic planning and business planning.

Standards

Professional audit standards as laid down by the main professional bodies are generally being expanded and updated. To some extent this reflects the lack of attention paid to auditing standards in the past. It also reflects political and commercial pressures. Public sector auditors have been caught up in the general tide of change.

External audit

Currently the Auditing Practice Committee of the Consultative Committee of Accounting Bodies (APC) issues four types of guidance to auditors:

(a) **Auditing Standards** – mandatory, any deviation should be explained;
(b) **Auditing Guidelines** – non-mandatory but considered to be good practice;
(c) **Audit Briefs** – issued to cover controversial topics and give detailed practical advice;
(d) **True and Fair Bulletins** – articles outlining developments and trends.

The APC has, since it was set up in 1976 and started publishing in 1980, tended to give prominence to the needs of private sector auditors. Since 1987 the APC has started publishing guidance specifically for public sector audit.

Internal audit

Both the Chartered Institute of Public Finance and Accountancy (CIPFA) and the Institute of Internal Auditors (UK) (IIA) have issued standards and guidance for their members on internal audit. The APC has also issued a guide line on internal audit practice.

It is not the intention of this book to repeat the contents of professional standards which most members, including students, have available in their place of work. Nevertheless, great care has been taken in the choice of topics to select techniques that will help auditors comply with these often rigorous standards.

Data protection

The Data Protection Act 1984 has done much to codify best practice in information collection and control. It has, at the same time, opened up a potential legal minefield. The Act and subsequent guidance issued by the Data Protection Registrar has yet to be 'tested' in the courts and some interpretations already made may be subject to re-interpretation or reversal.

How is the auditor affected by this Act? At the very least, internal and external auditors should maintain an awareness of the basic requirements for registration of personal data systems and the need to collect, maintain and disclose data in compliance with the Act. In general, controls to ensure the completeness, accuracy and validity of data processed by each audited system should go some considerable way to meeting the broader requirements of the Act. But audit objectives and data protection objectives are unlikely to coincide completely.

An advantage for auditors is the ability for them to cite the need to comply with the Data Protection Act in support of their recommendations to improve internal control. Even when a system under audit does not process 'personal' data as defined in the Act, a persuasive argument can usually be put forward for internal controls to be of a consistently high standard throughout the organization.

There is a developing trend for organizations to add data protection to the duties of the internal auditor. Only time will tell if this is really a suitable home. Ideally, a separate post of data protection officer should be created, though it must be admitted that most public bodies would, currently, find it difficult to justify the extra expense. Both internal audit and data protection duties require a high level of independence and are likely to utilize similar skills. This being so, and provided no significant conflict of interests arise, this trend may become an acceptable norm.

Office automation

'The paperless office' has become a rather hackneyed phrase. For at least a generation it has been said to be almost upon us. Yet for many auditors the volume of paper seems to be increasing as office procedures become automated. Computer printouts proliferate, urgent facsimiles are followed by letters and word processing enables almost any office to perform functions previously concentrated on the typing pool.

Despite the continuing presence of paper, automation has radically altered some aspects of the auditor's work. There are profound VFM implications in hitherto straightforward management decisions regarding office procedures and records. An automation strategy to meet each organization's office needs and to take into account its wider computer development strategy may need to be formulated and periodically reviewed. Each development needs to be subject to a cost-benefit analysis.

Automation usually affects considerations of internal control, especially in respect of hard-copy accounting records. The auditor needs to consider the management and audit implications of each new development.

CONCLUDING POINTS

This chapter has raised some far reaching issues and has attempted to give an overview of public sector audit. The most important messages to be conveyed are ones of improvement and change. The reader must not consider his or her own area of audit to be the only one of importance and should be encouraged to consider new techniques and the problems and solutions faced by colleagues in other bodies.

2 The nature of audit

INTRODUCTION

This chapter describes audit in terms of an essential process applicable to most types of work. It outlines the main types of audit and points out how they can be used to provide constructive help to management. The chapter shows how the more important aspects of audit relate to both 'internal' and 'external' auditing. It seeks to convey to the reader a basic audit framework.

THE AUDIT FUNCTION

Audit is an investigatory service for which society via public organizations and their political masters is prepared to pay. It is greatly to the public's benefit that the financial dealings of public servants and elected politicians are open to independent professional scrutiny.

As we saw in Chapter 1 Parliament has laid down various levels of internal and external audit for most of the public sector, but the law rarely lays down specific audit standards. Most public sector audit consists of the audit organization's own interpretation of the law in accordance with standards and guidelines laid down by the professional accounting bodies.

Individual audits are undertaken in accordance with the statutory, regulatory or contractual arrangements that govern each particular audit organization. For instance, the National Audit Office is governed by the National Audit Act 1983. Public sector auditors typically have a wide range of duties and obligations, from certification of accounts in a way similar to the audit of limited companies, to a duty to report on fraud and corruption and value for money. Auditors cannot usually perform all these duties by way of one homogeneous piece of work. Rather, the auditor's work is

composed of distinct subsections each with defined objectives. The first
level of subdivision of the total audit is the **audit assignment**.

THE AUDIT ASSIGNMENT

An assignment is an individual audit investigation into an aspect of an
organization. Assignments tend to represent practical aggregations of
work rather than theoretically defined divisions. An internal auditor may
consider an investigation into the effectiveness of controls in a payroll
system a single assignment; the audit of controls in a stock system would be
another assignment. In contrast the external auditor would consider the
certification of a set of accounts a single assignment even if this involved
systems work on both stocks and payroll.

   But the individual assignment has a special importance in audit. This
is because audit has to be made up of individual practical tasks. Each
assignment will be individually planned and will normally be concluded by
the issue of a report. The external auditor may report on the fair statement
of a set of accounts, the internal auditor on, say, the effectiveness of
internal controls.

   This book emphasizes the point that high quality audit work is more
important at the level of the individual assignment than in any other aspect
of audit. Auditors may produce written reports that sound excellent, they
may deal quickly and politely with the public and their clients. But if the
quality of the work done on individual assignments is low the facts will not
be fully understood. Unless the auditor is consistently lucky his opinions
will be inaccurate and he will have failed. This book therefore stresses
the idea that the 'core' of audit involves forming individual opinions on
individual assignments using an **essential audit process**.

THE ESSENTIAL AUDIT PROCESS

All audits comprise planning, controlling, data collection, opinion-forming
and reporting. The idea of an 'essential audit process' adds to this the
importance of properly formulated objectives. These define the work
required and the significance of the results obtained from testing. There is
thus a progression from audit instructions to reporting, as illustrated in
Fig. 2.1.

Audit instructions

The essential audit process starts with the auditor's understanding of the
audit instructions or duties. These instructions are the auditor's duties and

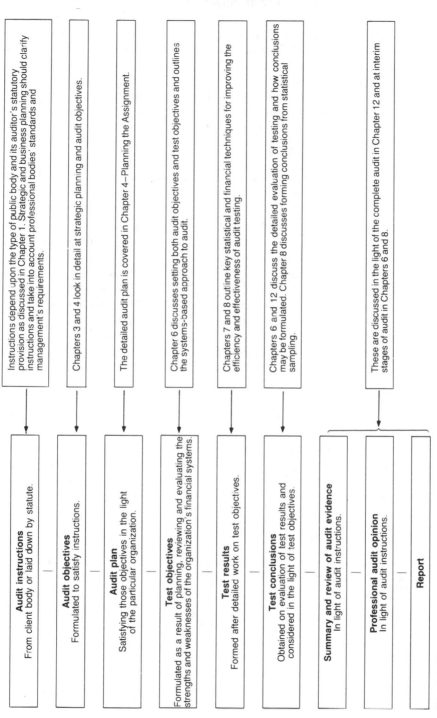

Treatment in the book

Instructions depend upon the type of public body and its auditor's statutory provision as discussed in Chapter 1. Strategic and business planning should clarify instructions and take into account professional bodies' standards and management's requirements.

Chapters 3 and 4 look in detail at strategic planning and audit objectives.

The detailed audit plan is covered in Chapter 4 – Planning the Assignment.

Chapter 6 discusses setting both audit objectives and test objectives and outlines the systems-based approach to audit.

Chapters 7 and 8 outline key statistical and financial techniques for improving the efficiency and effectiveness of audit testing.

Chapters 6 and 12 discuss the detailed evaluation of testing and how conclusions may be formulated. Chapter 8 discusses forming conclusions from statistical sampling.

These are discussed in the light of the complete audit in Chapter 12 and at interim stages of audit in Chapters 6 and 8.

The essential audit process

Audit instructions
From client body or laid down by statute.

Audit objectives
Formulated to satisfy instructions.

Audit plan
Satisfying those objectives in the light of the particular organization.

Test objectives
Formulated as a result of planning, reviewing and evaluating the strengths and weaknesses of the organization's financial systems.

Test results
Formed after detailed work on test objectives.

Test conclusions
Obtained on evaluation of test results and considered in the light of test objectives.

Summary and review of audit evidence
In light of audit instructions.

Professional audit opinion
In light of audit instructions.

Report

Fig. 2.1 The essential audit process.

obligations as outlined in Chapter 1 for the various audit bodies and determine the degree of freedom available to the auditor to set his own objectives. In practice instructions can vary from the most general of requirements such as 'to maintain an efficient and effective audit service' to specific reporting requirements on, say, the profitability of direct labour organizations in local government.

Audit objectives

To satisfy these instructions the auditor must set **audit objectives**. He may formulate a very broad statement of intent, for example to form an opinion on the fair presentation of a set of accounts, or may choose more specific objectives such as that internal controls in a stock system are adequate. Whether broad or narrow objectives are set depends both on the audit instructions and the situation encountered at the client's.

To meet the audit objectives the auditor must have a plan of action geared to the particular organization under audit. This will normally be a long-term strategic plan, but it may be a one-off plan quickly produced to coordinate an unexpected fraud investigation. Chapter 3 looks at the practical problems the auditor needs to consider in setting audit objectives and their incorporation into a strategic plan.

The audit plan

A number of short-term **audit assignment plans** will need to be drawn up as the long-term strategic plan is followed. The strategic plan will normally involve several types of audit (the different types are discussed below) and each type will normally need at least one assignment plan. These will discuss the practical details of the assignment work required to satisfy the audit objectives. Chapter 4 discusses assignment planning in detail.

Testing and test objectives

The assignment plan will invariably require the collection of audit evidence which is obtained by testing individual balances and transactions – the auditor can seldom rely to any great extent on the evidence readily available in the client's books and records. He usually needs to test items to third-party evidence (evidence provided by outside organizations such as bank statements or debtor circulars) or his own constructed evidence or prior knowledge. He may need to check similar instances to a known fraud, or may need to extract a statistical sample of, say, salary payments. The time spent testing is almost always a large proportion of the total duration of the audit.

Tests should all be undertaken for clearly defined and documented reasons – the **test objectives**. These objectives should be carefully considered to ensure they are in accordance with the overall audit objectives mentioned above. Chapters 6 to 8 cover these areas.

Test results and conclusions

Test results form the basis of the work that will eventually determine the auditor's professional opinion. This work should be clearly documented and thoroughly reviewed in the light of the original test objectives before conclusions can be drawn. Where results are unexpected or give evidence of a large number of errors great care will be needed before conclusions are drawn. Extra work may be necessary, and this may involve the formulation of additional test objectives.

Chapters 6 to 8 and Chapter 12 discuss how this is done in practice.

Summary and review of evidence

Towards the end of the assignment senior audit staff will need to review all the test conclusions and any interim summaries. This review should bring together all the audit work so that the auditor can consider all the results in the light of the overall audit objectives. By this stage the auditor will be actively formulating the professional opinions that will finally be given.

Chapters 6, 7 and 8 show how in practice different stages of the audit involving evidence obtained by using different techniques may give interim summaries and test conclusions. Chapter 12 considers how the different stages of audit work are ultimately brought together and summarized at a final review stage.

Professional audit opinions

It is important to ensure that all statutory and contractual instructions have been satisfied before the professional opinions are formed. If extra work is needed so that an opinion can be given it must be undertaken. Only very rarely will the auditor report that he cannot form an opinion. If the audit has been properly planned and controlled while the work was being done the professional opinions become a natural result of the audit process.

Reporting

Reporting communicates the professional opinions to the client. Reports can vary in size from a few lines at the end of a set of accounts to weighty tomes in glossy covers. The type of report largely depends on the purpose of the audit and the nature of its findings. Reporting is covered in Chapter 12.

General considerations and specialist topics

Chapter 5 on controlling and recording the assignment can be applied to all stages of the essential audit process. The complexity of control and re-cording techniques will depend upon the nature of the particular audit. The successful application of the essential audit process depends very much on maintaining a high standard of control and recording throughout the assignment.

Chapter 9 on fraud and corruption and Chapter 10 on value for money are specialist areas but the essential audit process still applies. Chapter 11 on computer audit is mainly concerned with techniques that will be applied to a wide range of audits at various stages in the audit process.

TYPES OF ASSIGNMENT

There are a number of different 'types' of audits. Theoretically, these types are all related in that they are designed to increase the accountability of

Checklist 2.1 Types of audit

1. **Systems reliability audit.** This type of audit forms the bulk of internal audit and a large proportion of external audit work. It also provides a basis for many of the other types of audit listed below. Table 6.3 in Chapter 6 gives an overview of the stages involved.
2. **Attestation audit – audit of accounts.** Such audits require the formation of opinions on the accuracy, fairness and proper presentation of sets of figures. These are usually published accounts but claims for major subsidies, internal trading funds and the final accounts of major contracts can also be attested. The relevant results of all the other types of audit are usually taken into account when forming an attestation opinion.
3. **Fraud investigation and prevention.** Such investigations involve a great variety of audit work with the common aim of proving or disproving a suspected fraud. Fraud prevention work is normal incorporated into systems reliability audit.
4. **Value-for-money audit.** This is an assessment of the economy, efficiency and effectiveness of an organization or its constituent parts. This work often mixes the skills of the auditor with those of the management consultant.
5. **Computer audit.** These are detailed audits of computerized systems usually as part of a wider systems, attestation, fraud or VFM audit. Computer audit is also taken to include the development of computer-assisted audit techniques (CAATS).
6. **Regularity audit.** Regularity work involves testing for and advising on compliance with statutory and internal regulations. Much of this type of work is done as part of the completion procedures of other types of audit. Regularity audit is discussed in Chapter 12.

public-sector managers. More practically they are useful functional categories, for example accounts opinion work and fraud investigation. A more precise list of audit types which this book specifically discusses is given in Checklist 2.1. The essential audit process outlined in Fig. 2.1 applies directly to all these audit types. All start with instructions, objectives are then clarified, and the process finishes only when the report is submitted.

ASSISTANCE TO MANAGEMENT

As mentioned in Chapter 1, the nature of reporting is changing so that clients are actively assisted by the auditor's work. Traditional attestation audit reassures report readers about the past. In contrast a VFM audit report attempts to improve performance in the future. In fact all audit uses evidence of past events to make statements which will be of future use. But recent developments in both private and public sector audit practice have been based on the idea that it is of importance to inform managers where

Checklist 2.2 Opportunities for assisting management

Type of audit	Practical historic opinions	Assistance to client management
1. Systems reliability	Yes, providing evidence of past control achievement.	Yes, providing advice on better internal controls.
2. Attestation audit	Yes, providing opinion on the recording of past events.	Yes, the results of systems work done to arrive at the opinion will be of use to management – see (1) above.
3. Fraud investigation	Yes, providing evidence of a crime.	Yes, providing advice on prevention of further fraud.
4. Value for money	The factual aspect of VFM work provides little more than evidence to support the improvements suggested.	Yes, providing advice on efficiency, economy and effectiveness.
5. Computer application (a specific VFM assignment)	Yes. As for VFM above.	Yes, providing advice on better computer use.
6. Regularity work	Yes, providing statements about past legality.	Yes, providing advice on how to act legally.

performance is sub-optimal as early as possible. Checklist 2.2 shows how
the types of audit discussed in this book can be used by the auditor to assist
client management in its operational procedures and decision-making.

   This book is about conducting high quality audit assignments. Consequently much of the text relates to the collection and processing by the
auditor of historic data – this is, after all, the only material available
for assessing the future. In Chapter 3 we look at the effect on business
planning of an emphasis on creative reporting. Similarly, in Chapter 12 we
discuss how reports to assist managers can be written.

INTERNAL AND EXTERNAL AUDITORS

It is the intention in this book to cut across the sometimes seemingly
alarming divide between external and internal auditors. The text differenti-
ates very little between the two groups because the techniques used by
both are basically the same. In addition, the importance of the audit
assignment is primary to internal and external auditors alike.

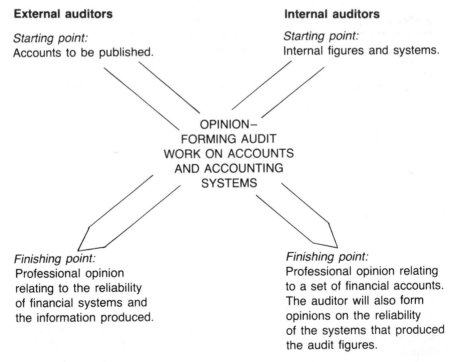

Fig. 2.2 The similarity between internal audit systems work and external audit
attestation work.

In the public sector internal and external auditors carry out a much wider range of duties than is common in the private sector. Both groups are involved in VFM, fraud, computer, regularity and systems reliability work. It is really only over the attestation functions that real divergence of interests occur. Traditionally, apart from contract bind accounts, internal auditors carry out relatively little of this work, while for external auditors it is a major duty.

However, even on this point internal and external work is remarkably similar in nature, though the audit objectives are different. Much of the external auditor's attestation work involves work on financial systems. Although the internal auditor may do little attestation work he will, like his external counterpart, carry out much audit work on systems. This similarity in work is shown graphically in Fig. 2.2. (The techniques involved in systems work are discussed in Chapter 6.)

The degree of independence is another differentiating factor. In general the internal auditor faces more obstacles to maintaining an independent stance than the external auditor. Internal employees of an organization face pressures that the external auditor can usually avoid, for instance, promotion prospects and inter-personal relationships.

Lastly, the authors would like to assert that internal auditors will probably carry out more attestation work in future. This is because if internal auditors make use of modern statistical sampling techniques for their substantive systems reliability work, they can directly inform managers of their opinions on the accuracy of financial data and on the substantive effect of weaknesses in internal controls.

CASE STUDIES

At the end of most of the chapters in this book there are case studies of practical audit. Some internal auditors may feel that the examples are slightly biased towards external audit situations. Where this is the case there is a clear reason. External audit generally looks at events within an organization less specifically and in less detail than internal audit. Consequently the external auditor is naturally better placed to provide concise cases. As an example, techniques such as cross-referencing of working papers can be more easily shown in detail using an external audit situation. But cross-referencing is of equal importance to both parties.

The reader should note that nearly all the techniques described in the chapters are equally applicable to both internal and external audit. An example from the external audit in no way invalidates the use of the technique for internal audit, and internal audit examples are just as applicable to external practitioners.

CONCLUDING POINTS

A basic framework has been outlined in terms of an essential audit process and the main types of audit. The key importance of the individual audit assignment to the wider requirements for effective audit has been stressed. Once the primacy of the assignment has been understood the rather contrived divisions between internal and external audit fall away. The audit techniques described in this book can be applied to a wide range of audits both internal and external.

3 Strategic and business planning

INTRODUCTION

Strategic and business planning are methods by which an auditor apportions his time between assignments and between clients. An auditor will have a range of statutory or other obligations to meet for each client. In order to satisfy these obligations a number of audit assignments must be undertaken. The auditor will formulate a **strategic plan** covering each client to ensure that the assignments he carries out will meet his obligations. In this chapter we show how such a plan is drawn up and provide a case example.

The strategic plan may also be part of a larger **business plan**. The auditor needs to match his own resources to his various clients, whether current or future. We will therefore formulate a business plan to match his resources to the market for the competitive audit services now developing in the public sector.

A business plan is not always relevant. For example, an internal auditor employed by one organization will only need a strategic plan. However, in this chapter we discuss the advent of compulsory tendering for audit services and in this situation a business plan is essential. With this in mind we show how a business plan could be developed.

In the context of the 'essential audit process' discussed in Chapter 2 strategic and business planning are the methods whereby auditors formulate 'audit objectives' for individual assignments. Such planning also places each assignment within a complete audit service to clients.

Parts of this chapter discuss the use of statistical parameters in formulating strategy. A reader who is unfamiliar with statistical sampling may find it helpful to return to this chapter after reading Chapter 8.

STRATEGIC PLANNING

Whereas the typical private sector auditor is primarily responsible for a yearly audit report on a set of financial statements, public sector auditors, both internal and external, typically have a far wider range of duties. As an example, the local government external auditor is responsible for a substantial number of duties as laid down in *The Code of Local Government Audit Practice*, ranging from value-for-money work to detection of fraud, as well as the accounts attestation role. Most public sector auditors, whether internal or external, have a similar range and diversity of duties.

The diverse nature of public sector practice means that a strategic plan setting out audit priorities for the medium term (1 to 3/5 years) is a very necessary tool. Only by such strategic planning can work priorities be set. Resources of staff and training can then be matched to provide the input needed to create the expected output of audit work.

Auditors may provide services to a number of quite separate client bodies. At each client the auditor may have a range of duties and each of these may necessitate a range of individual audit assignments. The strategic plan organizes the separate assignments into a coherent whole and provides a framework for an efficient and effective audit service.

When an auditor has more than one client resources will need assigning to each. A local government internal audit department may spend 80% of its time providing in-house work, the other 20% of its time may be used to assist neighbouring authorities by providing expertise in specialist areas. Alternatively a local District Audit office may be responsible for the statutory audit of four district councils and a county. In both cases resources will be allocated between clients. The basis of allocation may be straightforward: resource input is often agreed with clients in terms of man-days.

However, where an auditor has a large number of clients, wishes to maximize fee income or is in a competitive tendering situation, then this aspect of planning becomes much more complex. In this situation a business plan is required. This would set down how audit services were to be marketed using available resources. Business planning is discussed later in the chapter.

STRATEGIC PLANNING FOR AN INDIVIDUAL CLIENT

The auditor will naturally wish to direct his effort towards assignments which cover the financially significant areas of his client's activities. That is he will avoid trivia and concentrate on areas that are **material**.

Equally the auditor will be concerned to examine areas where there is a significant **risk** of financial mis-statement, poor internal control, or poor value for money. There is less pressing reason to check where the likelihood of error or 'misdoing' is low.

Some audit assignments may cover areas that carry substantial audit risk and are highly material. Clearly the auditor needs to consider all possible assignments at a client on the basis of materiality and risk before he can decide on their relative importance.

Accountability

All the auditor's duties are linked in that his prime role is to enhance accountability. Taking this view, all types of audit, whether systems reliability work, attestation or value for money, are essential components in one unified audit role. No one type of audit can be seen as of more intrinsic importance than another since it is only the total audit that is judged. As a consequence it is useful when considering a strategic plan to look at the totality of audit duties as one very large single assignment.

The concepts of materiality and risk discussed above need to be fitted into all the different types of audit work within this whole service to the client. This rather complex idea is shown in Fig. 3.1. The auditor needs to ascribe a specific quantity of audit effort to each of the empty boxes in Fig. 3.1 on the basis of a perceived view of the relative materialities and risks associated with each.

The problem now arises as to how the auditor should measure materiality and risk for each client function for each type of audit. Attestation and, to some extent, systems reliability audits are linked in that they can be undertaken using **statistical sampling** as a basis for the collection of audit evidence. We will therefore look first at the measurement of materiality and risk in these types of audit.

Before continuing to the next section some readers may find it useful to look at Chapter 4 where materiality as a concept is further discussed. In Chapter 8 materiality is looked at as an input into statistical sampling techniques.

Attestation, system reliability and fraud audit

If the auditor obtains his evidence using a form of statistical sampling known as 'monetary unit sampling' (MUS) (covered in detail in Chapter 8), then measurement of materiality and risk is made relatively straightforward. Using MUS the amount of audit work required is controlled by three variables:

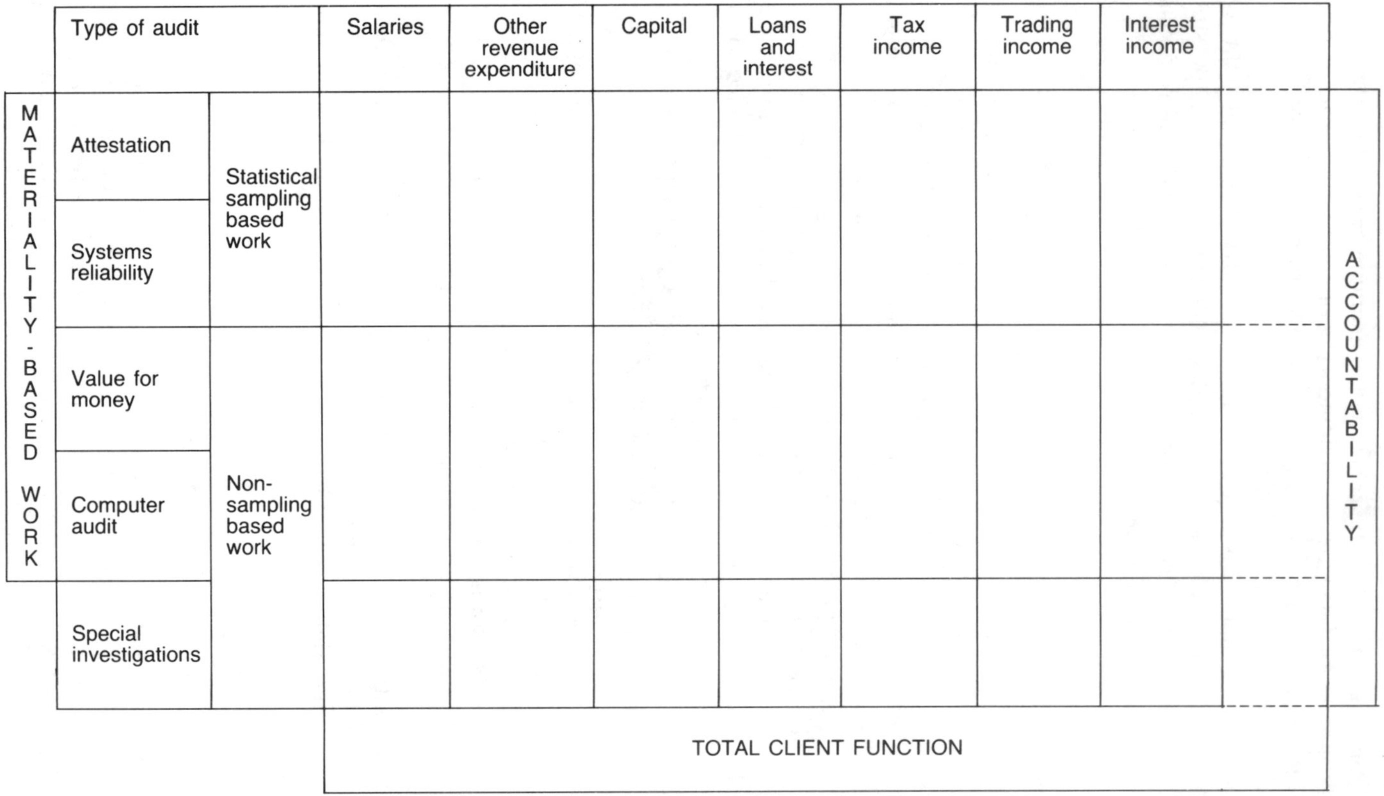

Type of audit	Salaries	Other revenue expenditure	Capital	Loans and interest	Tax income	Trading income	Interest income	ACCOUNTABILITY
Attestation — Statistical sampling based work								
Systems reliability								
Value for money								
Computer audit — Non-sampling based work								
Special investigations								

MATERIALITY - BASED WORK

TOTAL CLIENT FUNCTION

Fig. 3.1 Strategic planning and the total audit.

(a) Confidence (or risk);
(b) Population size;
(c) Materiality.

The auditor will probably require the same **confidence** about the possible accumulated value of errors for all audit areas – perhaps 95% confidence (or 5% risk). That is, he judges it adequate to be 95% confident that errors do not amount to a material level. Using MUS the perceived level of risk in an individual audit area is of little importance. Almost regardless of the actual circumstances, the auditor will need to carry out a set level of testing to bring confidence up to his preset level of, say, 95%. The mechanics of monetary unit sampling ensures that risk only becomes an issue in strategic planning if poor test results are anticipated.

Population size in MUS refers to the monetary value of the client under audit. It is therefore a constant. The only variable that affects selection of areas to audit is **materiality**.

Using MUS a practical and cogent framework exists to help the auditor to decide the basis of his strategic plan. Auditors employing statistical sampling use this method of deciding which account areas need the most coverage.

Statistical sampling of internal controls does not involve monetary unit sampling. Rather, each key control that is tested in an organization is usually considered to be equally important. Using the statistical approach described in Chapter 8 the only strategic planning issue is which controls should be tested. Such decisions are bound up with the materiality of the account area the control serves. Consequently, strategic planning for testing of controls needs to be decided at the same time as work involving MUS is planned.

Fraud work may occasionally involve statistical sampling, though not usually monetary unit sampling. Prevention of fraud is effectively covered by systems reliability work. Work on specific frauds by its nature cannot be planned for. Estimates of the likely time that will be spent on this type of fraud work need to be made for the strategic plan but will have to be based on past experience.

Value-for-money and computer audit

Value-for-money audit is not generally amenable to monetary unit sampling since non-monetary data is often just as important in value-for-money work as monetary data. In addition, much VFM work is based on 'sub-optimal' levels of data. Many of the conclusions in VFM work are not objectively provable. For example, ineffective provision of highways can only be asserted in a VFM opinion, since the data used to back the assertion, even in the best work, can rarely be described as 'statistically valid'.

This lack of a statistical framework makes it difficult to insert VFM work into a strategic plan. We have seen how with attestation and systems reliability work we can plan on the basis of materiality assessments of risk being covered by a preset and generally constant statistical confidence level. With VFM work we are faced with the problem of making non-mathematical assessments of both materiality and risk. A further consequence of this is that whatever assessments we make of these two variables no theoretical integration with our attestation and systems reliability work is possible for strategic planning purposes.

What then is the auditor who is seeking to provide an effective and economic service within an appropriate timescale to do when planning his strategic approach to a client? At the present level of technical understanding of strategic planning the auditor has to replace the mathematical objectivity of MUS with a purely subjective assessment. The relative levels of materiality and risk governing his value-for-money work can only be judged using past experience.

Computer audit, as will be made clear in Chapter 11 is made up of a number of diverse elements which include value-for-money work, systems reliability work and technical improvements to audit. Strategic planning for computer audit work will therefore require an assessment of the type of work likely before planning can take place.

Subjective assessments of materiality and risk

For 'non-statistical' audit work the amount of work needed to give adequate confidence in a given audit area can only be assessed subjectively, using past experience as a yardstick.

The materiality of an audit area can be assessed arithmetically (e.g. as a percentage of total expenses), but the amount of audit work required in a non-statistical audit environment is a subjective decision. Some of the more likely factors to be taken into account in a subjective assessment of risk are given in Checklist 3.1.

In a subjective environment risk and materiality must still be positively planned for. Although subjective, such assessments of materiality and risk should be recorded and used as the basis for the plan. Materiality is further discussed in Chapter 4.

Producing the strategic plan in practice

Before the strategic plan can be made, the auditor must analyse his staffing resources for the period so that he knows the workable staff hours available to him. This is discussed below under business planning. The next

Checklist 3.1 Factors to consider in a subjective assessment of risk

1. **The monetary value of the transactions under audit.** This risk associated with large transactions is clearly greater than for small sums.
2. **Past occurrences of errors and losses.** These may have occurred in either the body under audit or similar organizations.
3. **Other systems and figures affected.** Small errors in loan interest, for example, may signify very large errors in loan capital.
4. **The sensitivity of any error or loss to management and politicians.**
5. **Known staff shortages.** Internal controls are often overlooked when staff are short. Errors often result.
6. **Changes in a major system or in key personnel.** Changes to an organization cause uncertainty for a period and errors can be made.
7. **The client management's assessments of risk.**

requirement is to apportion this total resource between the categories discussed above and illustrated in Fig. 3.1. The auditor may also wish to leave some time for schedule slippage.

This division of time into the three or more audit types is subjective to the auditor. He makes the split on the basis of his past professional experience and client characteristics. Even his time allocation to the statistical sampling based work is subjective because, for a given materiality, the auditor can only judge how fast his staff will be able to complete the work. Statistical assessment of materiality and risk gives the **relative** time one piece of work should take compared to another, not the absolute resource required.

Having decided a time allocation for the three major categories of audit, time must now be split up into specific projects within each category.

The case study at the end of the chapter shows a strategic plan worked out in practice.

The planning cycle for attestation and systems reliability work

All auditors, both internal and external, should aim to cover all material areas of their client's organization every year. When an opinion is required on a set of published financial statements, the reason for the need for yearly coverage is clear: work on last year's transactions gives very little evidence about this year's. External auditors must, therefore, plan to test substantively all audit areas every year on the basis of their materiality as modified by clear and reliable internal control. Similarly, where internal controls are relied upon these too must be tested every year. However, systems records such as flow charts only need adjustment as accounting and control systems change.

The internal auditor's workload is governed by similar reasoning.

Evidence on last year's transactions gives little evidence about this year's. Consequently, if an auditor is to provide any service to his client in a particular year, he must audit transactions in that year. Internal auditors should, therefore, audit all material areas of their client in a yearly cycle.

Major reviews of specific financial systems and measures to guard against fraud are needed only when systems change or previous years' system notes have become difficult to use through excess of minor amendments. Every three to four years is usually sufficient in practice.

The planning cycle for VFM work

As described in Chapter 10, value-for-money work involves reviews of audit areas which are relatively lengthy and time-consuming, though these reviews do not need repeating on a yearly cycle. However, VFM work should be carried out on all material and risky audit areas every year by means of a review of the implementation of earlier audit recommendations.

As an example, a review of staffing at an organization may find that the staffing structure is highly inefficient, perhaps because outmoded job descriptions and responsibilities require substantial overmanning. In the year following this review the auditor, either internal or external, should ensure that changes are being made to all staff structures. In the same year and subsequently, he should carry out some brief financial analysis to ensure that costs are falling as projected. He should also monitor quality of services to ensure that effectiveness is maintained or is improving.

Just as for systems reliability work where the system is originally recorded and then subsequently tested, so for VFM work. An initial project is carried out which needs yearly follow-ups. The auditor does not only promote accountability when a major project is completed. Rather, he assesses the position in detail, and makes yearly assessments thereafter where materiality and risk demand.

The planning cycle for computer audit will normally be determined in a similar manner to VFM cycles, subject to any large or unanticipated changes in hardware or software.

LACK OF RESOURCES

Some general considerations for dealing with limited resources were outlined in Chapter 1. Here we consider how to incorporate such considerations into the strategic plan.

Audit work based on statistical sampling

The auditor facing a lack of resources for attestation and systems reliability work based on statistical sampling is in a simple, yet not totally enviable, position. When time becomes limiting he can do two things:

(a) Raise the monetary unit sampling testing materiality level, and
(b) Reduce the confidence level for both the substantive and compliance work.

Both these changes to his planning will reduce sample sizes and thus reduce audit time required. The corollary of reducing sample sizes in this way is that the auditor must base his audit opinions and reports on less statistical evidence. Whereas he might originally have planned to report, perhaps, 'that I am 95% certain that an internal control operates with an error rate not exceeding 2% of all transactions', he might be forced to say that he is only 90% certain of an error rate no higher than 5%.

Materiality and confidence levels can be adjusted from optimal levels. However, after a certain point the auditor will consider that the quality of opinion he is forming is too low to be consistent with his professional standards. At this point auditors involved in attestation audit must ask the client for an additional fee so that an adequate amount of work is done. If the client refuses, the auditor must consider resigning.

Internal auditors involved in systems reliability work are in a slightly different position. Rather than resign or reduce materiality and confidence levels further, they can try and agree with their clients a reduced level of audit coverage. However, the auditor must judge for himself the point at which both professional and statutory obligations for audit are breached. When under pressure due to lack of available staff hours and experience, the 'planning cycle' can often be extended. The auditor must be clear, though, that audit coverage is not being provided for those periods when no testing is done.

VFM work

We have already said that major pieces of value-for-money work need to be backed up by yearly reviews to ensure improvements are being made. In this way continuous audit coverage is provided.

Where the auditor finds he is unable to carry out the initial major review or follow-up review, his first option is to consider how he might carry out a smaller, less probing review. By carrying out a reduced size audit he is effectively increasing the materiality and risk he is prepared to accept.

When time is cut to such an extent that even a reduced review is not possible, the auditor is in the position of giving intermittent audit coverage.

As with systems reliability work for internal auditors, external and internal value-for-money auditors should inform their clients of the situation. Where audit coverage drops below that judged as consistent with statute and the auditor's own professional standards, he should consider resignation.

BUSINESS PLANNING

The present emphasis on compulsory competition and internal markets within the public sector means that many auditors need more than a good strategic plan to control and order their work. Where auditors have actively to sell their services a **business plan** is needed. Such a plan describes how a quantifiable resource of audit expertise may be marketed to likely customers within a given cost. It is worth reviewing some of the most recent changes in central and local government which are making business plans essential to all auditors interested in tendering for audit work.

Legal changes

There are three large areas of the public sector which have been or are likely to be affected by legal changes to the requirement for audit. They can be divided into local government, education and health.

Local government

At present compulsory tendering for internal audit contracts is not a statutory requirement in local authorities. However, statutory tendering is required for street sweeping, refuse collection, highway repair and capital work, housing repair and capital work and other functions. Whilst remaining outside the current political debate on the value of competitive tendering, it must be said that, even if a statutory basis is slow in coming, members of authorities may require competitive tendering for audit work as some did regarding direct labour organizations (DLOs) prior to legislation.

The methods used to account for internal services provided within local authorities is, however, subject to immediate change. CIPFA guidelines will mean that services such as personnel, legal and accountancy functions that exist only to serve other local authority functions will be charged out to specific users so that greater accountability will be obtained.

Education

Education is a local authority responsibility. However, the sheer size of education provision and the recent changes in legislation make it a special case. In addition to the points raised for local authorities recent changes affecting auditors in education authorities include 'Local Management for Schools', a system whereby individual schools manage their own budgets, autonomy for polytechnics and further education colleges and the possibility that a number of schools will opt out of education authority control and become self-governing.

All these changes are designed to encourage accountability in individual education establishments. Clearly a free choice of auditor is very much part of this accountability process.

Health

For some time central government has been encouraging specific health authorities to experiment with putting internal audit out to tender. A number of private accountancy firms appear to have successfully carried out these duties. It may, therefore, only be a matter of time before tendering becomes mandatory. This is very much in line with the increased accountability advocated in the government's recent proposal for the health service.

External audit of health authorities is now controlled by the Audit Commission. It is likely that audits will be open to private sector firms to bid for. This will make changeover to the District Audit Service less onerous whilst providing competition and an 'internal' audit market.

These far-reaching changes in the public sector open up enormous opportunities for 'strong players' in the audit services market. A big firm of accountants could consider tendering for internal audit work in local government, education establishments and health authorities. They might consider tendering for external audit of health authorities as well. These are massive markets and all are likely to grow in the future.

Client view

Whilst the legal framework for public sector audit is changing, the views of managers in public-sector organizations are undergoing no less a change. This is not surprising since the legislation is designed to increase managerial accountability.

If a manager now has to seek competitive tenders for refuse collection, he sees little reason why he should not obtain a good 'deal' for audit services. This is particularly the case when his cost centre is directly charged for audit. In the past a manager might seek to 'pad' his budget so that he was relatively immune from high costs. Competitive tendering is making this much more difficult. Consequently the modern manager is unlikely to show particular mercy to high audit charges unless he feels he receives corresponding benefits.

This change in the client's view will have a profound effect on internal auditors. Managers will need to have confidence in all professional audit work, whether it is critical or otherwise. Only in this way will managers tolerate audit charges.

Professionalism and audit credence are discussed in Chapter 5 in some detail. As well as being professional the service given must be relevant to both the manager's needs and the auditor's statutory responsibilities. In general managers are less concerned with past events than auditors. This means that a strategic plan should emphasize value-for-money work and systems work backed by substantive testing designed to warn against realistic failures in internal control. Whilst, at the moment, many managers request auditor assistance on petty frauds and control problems, in future there is likely to be much more demand for audit assurance on major items in accounts and budgets.

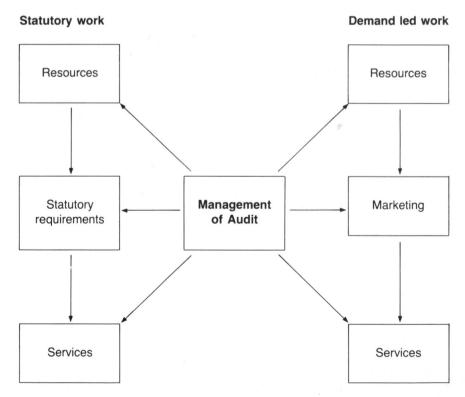

Fig. 3.2 The components of planning.

COMPONENTS OF A BUSINESS PLAN

A business plan has four major components. A **service** is **marketed** using available **resources** controlled by a **management organization**. The relationship between these is shown in Fig. 3.2.

Resources relate to staff numbers and expertise. Staff are usually the only limiting factor in an audit. There are usually no other key resources which are likely to limit the service given to clients. By combining information on resources with estimations of how much various markets are likely to pay for services, some basic costings can be worked out. There are two constraints on marketing. These are the client's needs and the auditor's statutory duties.

With regard to planning services, the service provided must match the market and statute. It must also make the best possible use of resources.

Lastly, there is the plan for the management organization of audit. The audit management structure chosen will affect all the areas already mentioned – resources, marketing and the service provision.

Resources

We will assume for simplicity that a new business plan is being made for an existing client organization. Resources available are, therefore, the present staff plus likely recruitment, less staff loss.

The first job is to analyse available staff time for the next year in detail, and the next two years or more as precisely as possible. Analysis of staff resources will take into account leave, training and time spent on administration. It will also look at when these time losses are likely to occur so that heavy reductions in staff, particularly due to training, are recognized. Resource budgeting, therefore, has a number of steps as shown in Checklist 3.2.

Before the beginning of each financial year, it is necessary to produce a **calendar** for each existing or projected staff member showing the timing of training, statutory holidays and leave. Where estimates are required for such time losses as sick leave or possible exam retakes realistic estimates should be made on the basis of past experience. The object of individual staff member calendars is twofold:

Checklist 3.2 Steps in resource planning

1. **Staff calendars** – individual staff members.
2. **Staff calendar** – whole audit department (planning board).
3. **Time summary** – whole department.
4. **Calculation of minimum charge-out rates.**

Staff grade–Part qualified trainees

Name	Salary £	1	2	3	4	5	6	7	8	9	10	11	12	13	14	15	16
J. Smith	14,600					P	P	P	P								
S. Brown	14,600					P	P	P	P								
F. Pritchard	15,100	P	P	P	P	S							P	P	P	P	
	£44,300																

Name	Weeks 34	35	36	37	38	39	40	41	42	43	44	45	46	47	48	49	50	51	52
J. Smith			L	L					P	P	P	P				S			
S. Brown							L	L	P	P	P	P							
F. Pritchard		L	L																A

Name		(Total)	Statutory holiday (H)	Training (P)	Leave (L)	Sickness (S)	Admin. (A)	Total non-audit time
J. Smith		52	2	10	3	1	—	16
S. Brown		52	2	10	3	1	—	16
F. Pritchard		52	2	9	3	1	1	11
	Total non-audit time (weeks)	156	6	29	9	3	1	43
	Hourly equivalent	5460	210	840	315	105	35	1505

Fig. 3.3 Individual staff member calendar.

A = Systems work, B = Special investigation, C = Contract Audit, D = Computer Audit.

(a) The most accurate estimate possible of 'chargeable' hours for staff is made.
(b) The relative timings of lost hours is clearly seen.

Figure 3.3 shows a possible format for a calendar for individual staff members. For small audit departments the individual calendars will not need additional summary. For large departments a summarized calendar of all staff on a planning board or computer spreadsheet kept in the audit department will be of help. The planning board will not only show lost time, but also the timing of important work. Planning boards may involve cards being set in slots, each slot representing a week's work. Cards can be written on and they can be colour-coded to hold additional information. They show at a glance the resources available at any one time to meet work commitments.

The individual staff calendars need a summary so that total chargeable hours for the department, as split between staff grades, can be calculated. At this point it is useful to include some financial data on running the department so that a minimum charge-out rate for different staff grades can be calculated. Figure 3.4 shows an example of a staffing summary document together with a calculation of minimum charge-outs. Overheads have been absorbed on the basis of salaries. However, any reasonable system of absorption can be used to ensure costs are fully recovered.

The examples given are designed to show that quite detailed analysis of resources is needed if a business plan is to be useful. Charge-out rates based on analysis of expenses form an instructive basis on which to recover costs. At about £30 an hour a qualified auditor is potentially a valuable asset. Auditors and clients will think twice about wasting his time on petty affairs if this charge-out rate is recognized. Even at the first stage of a business plan very useful information has been obtained which will help to make audit much more efficient and effective.

Marketing

Who is going to buy audit at the likely price you are going to charge? The marketing stage of the plan analyses this.

The existing market is the most likely market in the near future. However, this market can be increased by new clients and reduced by loss of old clients, perhaps due to failure in competitive tendering.

In addition, special audit 'products' can be devised and profitably sold. If selling to outside clients, that is to clients who are not also employers, charge-out rates may be raised significantly to whatever the market will bear. Profit from these clients should not be turned down unnecessarily.

Having decided what clients are likely in a period and how much work they will require, a sales budget should be drawn up. Sales budgets should

Staff grade	Total lost hours	Available hours per year	Total salaries £	Overheads absorbed on total salaries £	Total costs £	Rate per hour £
Audit Manager	315	1,505	27,500	39,399	66,899	44.45
Senior Auditor	665	2,975	38,800	55,588	94,388	31.73
3rd Year Trainee	1,505*	3,955	44,300	63,468	107,768	27.25
2nd Year Trainee	1,575	3,885	32,100	45,988	78,086	20.10
1st Year Trainee	2,275	5,005	34,800	49,857	84,657	16.71
	6,335	17,325	£177,500	£254,300	£431,800	

Fig. 3.4 Calculation of charge-out hourly rates for a complete audit group.

*taken from Fig. 3.3.

Staff grade	Core client Hours	£	Contact with DHA Hours	£	Contract with polytechnic Hours	£	Work i.e. computer consultancy Hours	£	Special projects Hours	£	Total Hours	£
Audit Manager	1,000	44,450	150		75		100	4,445	180	8,001	1,505	
Senior Auditor	2,100	66,633	300	50,000	100	20,000	300	9,519	175	5,553	2,975	458,347
3rd Year Trainee	3,000	81,750	400		155		300	8,175	100	2,725	3,955	
2nd Year Trainee	300	60,300	250		—		100	6,030	535	11,289	3,885	
1st Year Trainee	3,500	59,185	305		—		1,000	16,910	200	3,382	5,005	
Total	—	£312,318	—	£50,000	—	£20,000	—	£45,079	—	£30,950	—	£458,347

Fig. 3.5 Sales budget for internal audit department.

show both time and revenue, as shown in Fig. 3.5. Revenue may not be linked to time put into a job, but clearly it is not possible to devote more time to a client than there are chargeable hours available.

The planning board can be used to assist time budgeting in sales budget preparation. A strong visual link can then be made between available time and resources and market requirements.

When considering markets it is important to realize that what is being sold is expertise. The markets that can be obtained are those in which you hold expertise. For example, an audit department may have devised an audit package for housing maintenance at housing authorities. This expertise could then be actively sold.

The same applies when devising internal audit work for a whole public sector body so as to comply with any statutory requirements for internal audit. Rather than simply agreeing to do the job, it is much better to state that in undertaking the statutory duties ten major projects will be undertaken in the year covering the majority of the authority's functions. These can then be itemized and the likely benefit of the work described. Clients, as well as auditors, will be interested in the most material and risky audit areas. It will be very difficult to sell a client a minor fraud investigation concerning £10 of sundry income if the cost of the work will be £1,000. A £10,000 piece of work on improving maintenance of buildings costing £5,000,000 a year, even if no direct financial savings are likely, will be much more useful audit work and much easier to sell to a client who is directly charged for internal audit.

Public sector organizations often have a fear that they will receive less than expected when they contract for a service. Indeed, sometimes unscrupulous dealers have provided 'consultants' reports' which have very little substance and are in all probability little more than a brief re-write of a project done for another, superficially similar, organization.

Auditors contracting for work in the public sector should seek to convince their potential client that audit work done will be expressly tailored to their needs and organization. They can do this in a number of ways as set out in Checklist 3.3.

Marketing, finally, is concerned with selling the external presentation of an audit function. Normally this is only possible if the audit department is fully professional in the way it carries out its everyday work.

Management and organization

A business needs a management. Audit 'businesses' are normally run by senior audit staff supported by clerical assistance. Here we discuss briefly the management requirement of an audit organization which is working to a business plan. There are three important points to address:

Checklist 3.3 Quality assurance for use as a marketing aid

1. **Agreed measurement of audit performance.** The output from the audit work should be agreed in some detail with the prospective client. Work coverage and reporting may be set down in a 'memorandum of understanding' covering man-hours and reports expected. In this way audit **input** and **output** are agreed in advance by both sides.
2. **Quality control.** The auditor will carry out his own quality control as described in Chapter 5. However, for the benefit of his prospective client and himself he may agree to the following:
   (a) A yearly review with the client of all reports produced.
   (b) A yearly review with the client of recommendations implemented to assess their performance.
   (c) An agreement on specific audit standards and client assistance.
3. **Access to working papers.** The auditor normally has the right to withhold his working papers from review by client management. However, where the auditor feels that the working relationship might benefit from client access to working papers, such access may be used as a marketing point. Most clients will welcome a sight of the evidence on which reports are written. This is particularly the case in respect of major systems and VFM evaluations.

(a) Time recording systems and control;
(b) Quality control;
(c) Staff performance related pay.

When working to a business plan there are severe financial penalties for spending more time on a project than budgeted. Extra time spent does not mean additional fee income and the whole audit department needs to understand this point from the start. Since time is so important there must be a simple and reliable system for recording time spent on specific jobs. Timesheets will naturally be a necessity. Just as important is a processing system which turns timesheets into costs, by multiplying time by the appropriate charge-out rate. Such a time-recording system needs to be fully operational before the business plan is put into operation.

A strong system of quality control instituted by the audit management is required to prevent the release of substandard reports and superficially good reports based on poor audit work. The techniques outlined in Chapter 5 need to be put into operation so that all work is double checked for quality before release. In addition to review procedures on each individual assignment, overall quality control checks on the department as a whole are needed. This is done by periodically reviewing the total output of a department, and assessing its effect on the client. Audit departments will need to develop their own quality control procedures on total output in association, perhaps, with their client as suggested in Checklist 3.3.

It is the staff working to strict deadlines which ensures that a business plan is a success. The staff should be rewarded for this success and appreciate that quality and productivity on their part will result in extra pay and enhanced promotion prospects. In this respect audit managers will have to devise their own flexible remuneration procedures to fit their own specific organizations.

Services

Once a market has been secured and a fee agreed, the auditor must decide on the specific audit assignments he should carry out. Normally the services stage of the plan will be done in conjuction with the marketing since, as we have said, the auditor will wish to market specific services so as to attract the client. However, once the nature of specific services has been decided the size and mix of individual audit assignments is then subject to the strategic planning we have already discussed.

SUMMARY

In this chapter we have reviewed strategic planning and business planning for both internal and external auditors. We have discussed competition with an emphasis on internal audit. Business and strategic planning allow for tight control over the functioning of an audit department. In the context of this overall control, in the following chapters we look at the skills and techniques needed to carry out opinion-forming assignments.

This chapter emphasizes the use of planning documentation which in one form or another is needed as part of any strategic or business plan. Staff calendars, calculation of charge-out rates, sales budgets and a strategic planning summary document are some of the more important. The case study that follows indicates how these and others might be built up in practice.

CASE STUDY 3.1 STRATEGIC PLAN FOR INTERNAL AUDIT OF WORRAH COUNTY EDUCATION AUTHORITY

This case study shows how an internal auditor might produce a strategic plan for education. In practice the auditor would integrate all the council functions into this strategic plan but the other county council committees have been left out of this example for simplicity. The plan is for one year only and provides the minimum coverage that the auditor would feel is consistent with his statutory duty to provide internal audit. The auditor would consider value-for-money audit to be an important part of his work.

Since audit plans are based on assessments of materiality and risk, the auditor would use the most recent revenue and capital budgets for education as his starting point. In practice more detail would be needed than the simplified plan shown below.

Strategic audit plan

1. **Attestation and systems reliability audit.** The auditor intends to use statistical sampling wherever relevant. To comply with auditing standards and guidelines he will back all his work on internal controls with substantive testing. In this way he can be sure that internal controls actually do control. Where there is a lack of controls the effect of this can be substantively measured.
2. **Value-for-money work.** The auditor has decided that a significant proportion of his staff hours will be devoted to value-for-money work – see Time Budget below.
3. **Fraud.** The auditor has set aside time to cover special fraud investigation work as it arises. Other work to cover the adequacy of measures to guard against fraud and corruption is included within his systems reliability work.
4. **Computer audit.** Time has been budgeted for a special project on a new computer system designed to control jobbing repairs. Other valuable computer audit work is included under statistical based work in (1) above.
5. **Regularity audit.** No special budget has been assigned to regularity audit since regularity has been included in the budget of the other audit types. (See Chapter 12 for a discussion of regularity techniques.)

The following documents drawn up by the auditor are given below.

1. **Summary of education budget.** This is the starting point for the strategic plan. It clearly shows the significant areas in the education authority.
2. **Audit staff budget.** The auditor needs to know his resources available before he can draft his plan.
3. **Summarized time budget.** Using the staff budget the auditor apportions the available staff time between the various types of audit work. This is done on the basis of experience and professional judgement.
4. **Statistically based work plan.** The auditor now divides up his time allocation for statistically based work, that is his attestation and systems reliability work, on the basis of materiality. Subjective adjustments are made to take account of reliance on internal controls.
5. **Adjustments to statistically based work plan.** The auditor sets down his reasons for subjective adjustments to the plan.
6. **Creditor payments work plan.** In this case study we show an example of the detail for the strategic plan for creditor payments work.

7. **Notes on creditor payments work.**
8. **VFM based work plan.** This is similar to the statistically based work plan. Note, however, that it includes assessments of both materiality and risk.
9. **Adjustments to VFM audit plan.** The reasons for the actual time allocations chosen are given.
10. **Planning board.** The format for a planning board is shown. The auditor may wish to display the results of his strategic planning on a board for his own benefit and that of his staff.

Document 1 Summary of education budget

	£m	£m
Revenue budget:		
Salaries:		
Teachers	127	
Other employees	16	
		143
Property costs:		
Maintenance	8	
Heat and light	6	
Rates	6	
Cleaning	5	
Pupil costs:		
Transport and bus passes	8	
Exam fees	2	
Teaching materials	7	17
		185
TOTAL COSTS		
Less: Other income		(1)
NET EXPENDITURE ON SCHOOLS		£184
Capital budget:		
New schools		3
Replacement accommodation		2
Major maintenance		4
		£9

Document 2 Audit staff budget

	*Chargeable hours**
Audit Manager	1,475
Senior Auditors	2,710
Trainees	5,780
	9,965

*****Note:** These figures for chargeable hours are calculated using staff calendars such as that shown in Fig. 3.3 in the text.

Document 3 Summarized time budget

	Manager	Senior auditors	Trainees
Statistically based work	320	1,135	7,550
Value for money	420	735	420
Special fraud investigation	210	210	420
Computer project	105	210	–
	1,055	2,290	8,390
Non-audit work	420	420	1,575
	1,475	2,710	9,965

Document 4 Statistically based work plan

	Total	Salaries	Creditors payments	Capital payments	Income
Budget figures:*	£195m	£143m	£42m	£9m	£1m
Staff grade	Total hours / Materiality**	73%	21%	5%	1%
Audit Manager	320	234	67	16	3
Subjective adjustment	320	194	100	13	13
Senior Auditor	1,135	829	238	57	11
Subjective adjustment	1,135	695	350	45	45
Trainees	3,550	2,590	745	177	38
Subjective adjustment	3,550	2,176	1,088	142	144

* Composition of budget figures:

	£m
Expenditure	185
Capital	9
Income	1
	£195

** Percentage of total.

Document 5 Adjustments to the statistically based work plan

1. **Salaries.** Work hours have been reduced from those projected. This is because set-up time and testing of internal controls does not vary quite in proportion to the size of the audit.
2. **Creditor payments.** Work-hours in this area have been increased to take account of the complex systems involved for recoupment costs paid to neighbouring authorities, DSO contract, maintenance, pupil transport, etc.
3. **Capital payments and income.** These relatively immaterial areas will be covered in the time originally projected.

Document 6 Creditor payments work plan*

Project	Manager	Senior auditor	Trainee
1. Transport and buses (£8m)	19	67	220
2. Heat and light (£6m)	10	20	106
3. Exam fees (£2m)	5	17	50
4. Central purchasing system	30	180	590
	100	350	1,088

*For simplicity work plans for the other main audit areas are not included in this case study. These projects can also be shown on the planning board (see Document 10).

Document 7 Notes on creditor payments work

1. **Transport and bus passes.** This is an expensive and complex area. Rules of entitlement for help with transport costs appear not always to be properly enforced. In addition, billing by the local bus and taxi companies is difficult to tie in with the services expected.

   A detailed review of the existing system is needed, backed by plenty of substantive evidence on the actual completeness and accuracy of payments made.
2. **Heat and light.** After last year's review of this area we must ensure full compliance and substantive testing. Last year's system notes will need updating for the amendments we suggested in last year's report.
3. **Exam fees.** These are one of the single largest expenses the authority has to bear. The system for paying exam fees needs recording and fully testing both for compliance and substantively.
4. **Etc.**

Document 8 VFM based audit work

	Total	Salaries of teaching staff	Cleaning costs	Other employees	Maintenance (capital and revenue)	Energy	Transport and bus passes	Other
Budgeted*	£195m	£127m	£5m	£16m	£12m	£6m	£8m	£21m
Materiality (% of total)	100%	65%	3%	8%	6%	3%	4%	11%
Risk assessment	—	33%	33%	50%	100%	33%	50%	say 50%
Composite (Materiality × Risk)	Value% / % of total	21% / 52%	1% / 2%	4% / 10%	6% / 15%	1% / 2%	2% / 4%	6% / 15%
Audit Manager (prorata) hours	420	218	8	42	63	8	18	63
Adjusted	420	270	—	—	100	50	—	—
Senior Auditors (prorata) hours	735	382	15	73	110	15	29	111
Adjusted	735	435	—	—	200	100	—	—
Trainees (prorata) hours	420	218	8	42	63	8	18	63
Adjusted	420	320	—	—	100	—	—	—

* Composition of budget figures:

	£m
Expenditure	185
Capital	9
Income	1
	£195

Document 9 Adjustments to VFM audit schedule

1. **Teacher salaries.** This is the first time a value-for-money study has been carried out on teacher employment costs. This will be the major piece of work in the year.
2. **Maintenance.** This is a high risk area since the cost of repairing a large stock of poorly maintained buildings can be extremely high. A major project will be carried out this year.
3. **Energy.** The improvements were suggested by the Audit Commission in their report on this area. A short study to review implementation of their recommendations will be carried out.
4. **Other areas.** Studies on low materiality/risk areas will be carried forward to a future year so that a sufficient time for meaningful work can be obtained.

Document 10 Planning board

Grade	Weeks						
	1	2	3	4	50	51	52
Manager	V F M	V F M	V F M				
Auditor 1	A	B	Fraud				
Auditor 2	A	A	A				
Trainee 1	A	A	A				
Trainee 2	B	B	B				
Trainee 3	C	V F M	C				
Trainee 4	B	B	D				

CONCLUDING POINTS

This chapter has covered an area that is currently subject to rapid development and considerable controversy. These developments cannot be ignored but neither can any response be fully prescribed in a case study. It is hoped that the ideas put forward in the text and case study will provide a sufficient framework for a business and strategic plan to suit most audit situations. Particular attention should be paid to accurate costing of audit manpower and realistic time-budgeting for individual assignments. The importance of presentation should not be underestimated; well documented and presented plans provide a useful management control and an impressive part of any presentation to a client.

4 Planning the assignment

INTRODUCTION

This chapter introduces audit planning of individual assignments by out-lining the benefits of a good plan for all types of audit. We analyse the plan in terms of the audit work objectives, the amount of work relevant to the assignment and a concise audit strategy. We stress the importance of the plan as an audit working paper. Practical aspects of planning are discussed, and we give full-length sample audit plans for short and long assignments. In terms of the 'essential audit process we show how formulating objectives and assignment planning are essential prerequisites to testing in the field.

When an auditor starts an assignment his first action should be to plan that assignment. The nature and quality of this planning can vary greatly. Some auditors would claim to do no planning; they use a combination of experience and trial and error. The most effective auditors, however experienced they are, plan their work in detail. They ensure that the work is aimed at the objectives given in the original audit instructions and provide 'an effective and economic service within an appropriate time-scale' (Audit Practices Committee Guideline – Planning, Controlling and Recording).

Audit planning should be looked at as that part of the audit which translates the objectives of the assignment into the detailed testing carried out in the field. It is not possible to know what tests to do in an audit unless the objectives of the audit are understood and specific tests have been planned. For example, an auditor may check a file of goods-received notes for completeness and the value of this exercise may appear to be self-evident. But what is its value? If the objective is to test that all expenditure represents real purchases then this particular test is of no use at all. The planning stage of this audit failed. The test described ensures that pur-chases have not been left out of the accounts and not that purchases in the accounts are valid (see Chapter 7 for details). The danger is that repetitive audit tests are done without thought. Bank reconciliations are always checked, bad debts are always reviewed, and normally these exercises are of value. But what proportion of time should be spent on bank reconciliations compared to testing of purchases or testing of internal controls? It is the job of the audit plan to make issues such as this clear to senior and junior staff alike.

THE NEED FOR PLANNING

There are a number of diverse obstacles to effective auditing which a good plan anticipates and negotiates.

Nature of the client

The audit plan anticipates the likely nature of an assignment and allows the auditor to match his staff expertise to the specific client in the most efficient manner.

Expertise may be divided into two categories. There is expertise enjoyed by individuals as a result of their training and general experience. But just as important for the audit plan is knowledge of the client's activities and administration. Without this knowledge an assignment might be considered straightforward when on proper analysis it would have been clear that considerable computer expertise would be required. Similarly a value-for-money audit of a service may require substantially more staff input than expected due to specific problems in the collection of raw data.

Direction and control

Once an audit has started it needs guidance. The audit plan guides the audit staff through the audit showing relationships between different pieces of audit work and their relative importance.

Controlling the audit is discussed in detail in Chapter 5 but the audit plan is the first step in controlling the assignment.

Critical aspects

In any assignment some aspects of the work will be more sensitive, complex or difficult to resolve than others. Any reasonable plan will highlight these areas so that proper attention can be given to any special problems. For example, a local authority may have caused few audit complications for many years. If one year the Treasurer tells the auditor well before the year end that a complicated creative accounting scheme has been arranged, then the auditor must highlight this scheme in the plan. This ensures that the scheme is properly investigated by the audit team when undertaking the audit, and expert help, if required, can be obtained once the details of the scheme are clearly known. It is surprising how often important audit problems are dealt with in a hurry after the rest of the audit work has been completed. This practice weakens the auditor's position in relation to the client as well as being poor audit practice. Full planning for critical areas in an audit induces clear thinking in the preliminary stages when there is plenty of time for finding solutions.

Timescale

Auditors will usually report within a timescale which may be explicitly agreed before the work begins, may be set by statute or is set by established practice. In any event the auditor will wish to spend the minimum time consistent with effectiveness and economy on an assignment.

The time taken to carry out an audit depends on the amount of work to be done and the expertise of the staff used. Consideration of the timescale brings together the other planning points considered above so that from all the possible ways of completing an audit one particular option is chosen.

Summary

The auditor plans his assignment before he starts the field work. He does research on his client even if he is already familiar with the body under audit. He assesses his personnel and their expertise and he decides on a time when he should be finished. The consequence of all this work is an economic, efficient and effective audit.

THE AUDIT OBJECTIVES

In the public sector most audits have more than one objective. It is particularly important when there are a number of reasons for an audit that the nature and priority of objectives are clearly agreed and stated before work begins.

The Code of Local Government Audit Practice provides a good example of the wide range of audit objectives common in the public sector. A variety of additional objectives may also be agreed between the auditor and the client.

The Code includes the following:

(a) To give reports in the public interest where necessary;
(b) To produce a management letter every year for members;
(c) To provide an audit opinion on the statement of accounts every year;
(d) To review measures taken by an authority to prevent fraud and corruption;
(e) To be satisfied that the authority has taken proper arrangements for securing economy, efficiency and effectiveness.

Additional objectives could include evaluation of a computer installation, the certification of memorandum trading accounts or the provision of a stock certificate.

In any audit assignment a number of such objectives will apply. For example, an auditor carrying out work designed primarily to provide an audit opinion on a local authority statement of account will have subsidiary objectives relating to reports in the public interest, the management letter, fraud, corruption and to some extent economy, efficiency and effectiveness. The nature of the work done will vary greatly depending on the relative importance attached to all the objectives mentioned. If fraud is considered important, work on areas involving, say, cash may be greatly extended beyond the requirements for a 'presents fairly' opinion. A central government department internal audit section may be requested to review a system for processing licence applications. Several objectives will apply in such a situation. The primary objective may be evaluation of internal controls, particularly over fee-handling procedures. Subsidiary objectives might include the detection of fraud and corruption, legality and regularity and ensuring good value for money.

Whatever the combination of objectives, a clear statement of their nature and priority is required before the rest of the planning work can begin and audit testing started.

MATERIALITY AND RISK

Once objectives have been defined, a **planning materiality** level needs to be set for the values under audit. The auditor is unable to check all items to ensure they are properly dealt with by the system or appear in the accounts. He must decide what level of checking is appropriate to his objectives, and this is where the concepts of **materiality** and **risk** come in.

An audit opinion has only a probability of being correct. The reader gives credence to the opinion on the basis of where he believes the probability to lie. Assuming auditors of equal skill, the probability of an audit opinion being correct depends directly on the depth of search conducted, and this is conveyed in the values attached to 'materiality' and 'risk'.

Risk

Broadly speaking risk is the auditor's assessment of the likelihood of errors. Where a non-statistical approach to audit is used risk needs to be considered in conjunction with materiality. As we saw in Chapter 2 statistical methods do not require risk assessment to be a major issue in planning since normally materiality is the major determinant of sample size. This is further discussed in Chapter 8.

The auditor therefore will normally only need to plan actively for risk in three situations:

(a) In planning non-statistically based audit work;
(b) When error rates in sampling are expected to be high (see Chapter 8);
(c) Assessing reliance on internal control (see Chapter 8).

When non-statistical assessments of 'depth of search' are made risk and materiality will need gauging on the basis of experience. Here we need only say that where risk is judged to be above average a greater depth of search is required compared to other audit areas of similar size but less prone to error. Value-for-money work is the major area where risk assessments affect planning in modern audit and these assessments tend to be highly subjective.

The nature of materiality

Materiality signifies two aspects of auditing. The more common use of the word relates to the size and sensitivity of errors that may affect an audit opinion. The other aspect was touched on above and relates to the 'depth of search' in an audit. The two concepts are linked since the depth of search will govern the likelihood of errors being discovered.

In essence materiality relates to those monetary values above which the auditor believes that his objectives are directly affected. As such, materiality is subjective to the auditor and it may be varied from one audit situation to another. Using modern audit techniques materiality rather than risk is the main determinant of 'depth of search'.

Examples of materiality in action

Let us assume that an internal auditor has been asked to ensure that council house rent voids for empty property are correctly presented in the housing accounts. How does an auditor decide on materiality for such an assignment?

The following points require consideration:

(a) Size of figures under audit in the context of the total strategic plan;
(b) The level of assurance required by the persons requesting the audit work;
(c) The level of assurance assumed by the other readers of the report, including politicians;
(d) The resources available to the auditor;
(e) The auditor's own professional standards.

By working through an example in more detail we can demonstrate what each of these considerations involve. Consider a housing account.

Size of figures

The auditor will consider the materiality relevant to this work in the context of his general strategic plan and the size of the specific figures he has been asked to look at.

Housing A/c

	£		£
B/fwd	480,000	Cash	9,457,000
Housing subsidy	4,500,000	Voids	570,000
Rents	5,600,000	Write-offs	33,000
		C/fwd	520,000
	£10,580,000		£10,580,000

Rents with housing subsidy total £10.1m of which voids are 5.6%. Thus compared to total housing income voids are relatively small – one-twentieth. However, £570,000 is a considerable sum when compared to the normal surplus on a housing revenue account of perhaps £½m. It would also represent a substantial proportion of the housing repairs budget of, say, £3 million. The level of voids is therefore a serious matter.

The assurance required by those requesting the work

The audit work was requested by the Treasurer who had noticed, when considering next year's budget, that voids were up 30% in the previous year and were responsible for negating the effect of the 2% rent increase.

In 1986 rent voids were £438,000. In 1987 they were £570,000. The reason for the rise of £132,000 is the main concern of the Treasurer.

The assurance required by the readers of the audit report

The report will be read by the Treasurer since he commissioned it. However, it will also be read by the director of housing, the rent officer, the housing repair officer, possibly the head of the direct labour organization and the housing accountants. As in most public sector organizations a variety of political interests may be affected by the report. These people will all have different concerns ranging from mild interest to great concern over the speed in which houses are renovated before they are re-let.

The auditor should plan for the most stringent user of his report. The career of the housing repair officer may be damaged if the report is misleading or factually incorrect concerning repair times.

Resources available to the auditor

The auditor may be in a position to devote substantial resources to this project, perhaps a senior auditor, or he may have two juniors he could supervise himself. Alternatively, the audit department might be involved in a major review of tendering procedures, an audit of DLO accounts and many other pressing projects of importance involving millions of pounds. Clearly it is inefficient to take staff off important work to audit small figures which appear to be, perhaps, £100,000 over what is expected.

Auditor's own professional standards

The auditor could, perhaps, write a report which satisfied the Treasurer, did not embarrass the repairs personnel, but which nevertheless was not written on the basis of proper professional audit work. For instance, he might simply state that voids were affected by empty flats in a high-rise block due for demolition. Probably this was a cause of voids, but it may not be the main reason and it may have been true in 1986 as well.

When investigating voids a materiality figure of £50,000 may be acceptable to the auditor taking all the above into account. For an attestation audit of the housing account £100,000 would be likely to be more realistic.

Use of materiality figure

Once a materiality figure has been set, how does the auditor use it? In Chapter 8 we explain how the materiality figure chosen as part of the planning process is used to calculate sample sizes for testing. Using the technique of 'monetary unit sampling' materiality figures are used to define the level of testing for the whole audit. This is ideal for many audit situations and is at the forefront of modern audit practice. Even when statistical audit methods are not appropriate on a particular assignment, planning materiality must still be judgementally linked together with an assessment of risk to levels of testing.

Until a materiality figure is decided upon, the level of testing required in an audit is, of necessity, unknown.

Materiality and the rest of the audit plan

The auditor should now have arrived at the position where he has clearly defined audit objectives and has a materiality figure or set of figures appropriate to them. In other words, he knows exactly what he has to achieve, but has not yet said how it will be done. By deciding upon a materiality figure he has implicitly indicated the amount of work required to achieve the audit objectives. A low materiality level signifies a lot of detailed work; a high figure and less detail is thought necessary.

By not deciding a materiality figure before moving on to detailed audit planning, an auditor will be assuming he already knows all the requirements of interested parties and all the likely results of the audit. Few auditors are, in fact, endowed with such formidable brain-power.

PREPARATIONS FOR PLANNING

The detailed audit plan cannot be assembled until preparatory work on the practical problems of the audit have been finished. The preparatory planning procedures represent the research necessary before the audit can be put together.

The extent to which preparatory procedures are necessary varies with the familiarity of the auditor with his client and his level of expertise in the particular area he is concerned with. However, a degree of preparation is always required. The organization under audit will change with time. Legislation changes, personnel change and the memory fades. Time spent planning is seldom wasted, however familiar you are with the organization or the circumstances. Figure 4.1 shows the structure of the planning process.

Preparation for an audit of an established client

When an auditor is asked, or decides for himself, to carry out an assignment there are a number of possible reasons for the choice. Many audits are performed yearly often as a result of statute. Other audits are not based on statutory requirements and are irregularly performed. Client staff are often alarmed by these audits and courtesy as well as expediency requires some explanation of the cause and nature of the audit. Failure to put client staff at ease obstructs both the planning process and the subsequent audit work.

Before the first meeting with the client, preparation is required so that the auditor is well informed about the history of the client and their recent work. Many clients are naturally upset and annoyed if an auditor

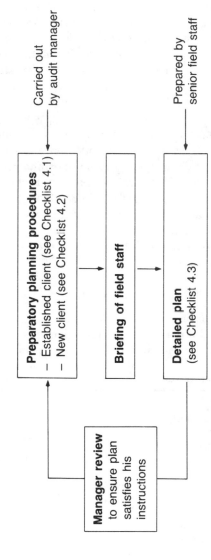

Fig. 4.1 Planning an assignment.

remembers nothing of previous years' hard work and successes. Apart from this, a good meeting with senior management before the audit begins can provide useful information which may be difficult and perhaps costly to obtain once the audit has started. Encourage a manager to talk of his successes and problems during the year. Show sympathy at the right moment and congratulations where this appears appropriate. In this manner very little of importance to the audit will be missed. A new housing project may have involved some creative accounting. Is it in the accounts? You can check later. Problems may have been experienced over staffing or the new computer. These areas will need special attention in the audit. Ask about what has changed in the year and a manager will usually say 'very little'; ask what his hopes for next year are, and he will speak at length on the schemes he is hatching, many of which may affect the audit.

But of course there are a number of important questions that must be answered at this first meeting. The most important relate to when the accounts or material under audit will be ready and when the final report will be needed. If the report is required by a deadline not set by the clients then timetables for the audit must be agreed at the first opportunity so that problems are avoided later.

Key points in a good planning preparation process are shown in condensed form in Checklist 4.1.

Preparations for the audit of a new client

Auditors should be well practised at understanding new situations rapidly. It is part of their job. Preparations for new clients, therefore, only differ from that of established clients in their thoroughness.

Checklist 4.1 Preparation for established clients

---

1. Review files on previous audits and correspondence.
2. Obtain management accounts/revised budgets and other topical management information.
3. Talk to senior management:
   (a) Out of courtesy and about reasons for audit if these are not obvious;
   (b) About major system changes;
   (c) About changes in key officers;
   (d) About regulatory changes (changes in legislation, financial regulations and departmental circulars);
   (e) About major new contracts;
   (f) Substantial law suits/contingent liabilities.
4. Then discuss:
   (a) When the client will be ready for the auditors to start work;
   (b) When any report is required;
   (c) Work required by the client's employees including, if applicable, internal audit.

With new clients proper preparation and research concerning the new proposition is needed. The usual place to start is with the estimates or accounts of previous periods. It may be possible to obtain audit working papers from a previous auditor. These can be a valuable source of information and most auditors will allow other auditors to review selected papers under supervision.

For large jobs planning cannot be completed until some detailed research into the accounting and control systems operated by the client has been done. This will involve systems evaluation and flowcharting. It is not until this basic work has been done that an informed opinion of the likely strength of internal controls and availability of audit trials can be formed. These ideas are raised fully in Chapters 5 and 6.

Checklist 4.2 Preparation for a new client

1. Obtain previous period's figures and review in detail.
2. Obtain, if possible, other auditor's working papers.
3. If unfamiliar with new client's activities research is required into:
   (a) Operations in general. What does the client do?
       – Read books.
       – Consult other auditors.
   (b) Legislation peculiar to the organization.
   (c) Common problems associated with such organizations.
   (d) Service users or clients of the organization.
   (e) Suppliers to the organization
       – Own workforce.
       – Bulk purchasing.
4. Discuss audit with senior management:
   (a) Reason for audit – courtesy.
   (b) General operational background as in (3) above.
   (c) Administrative set-up.
   (d) Talk to senior management:
       – Out of courtesy and about reasons for audit if these are not obvious;
       – About major system changes;
       – About changes in key officers;
       – About regulatory changes (changes in legislation, financial regulations and departmental circulars);
       – About major new contracts;
       – About substantial law suits/contingent liabilities.
5. Then discuss:
   (a) When the client will be ready for the auditors to start work;
   (b) When any report is required;
   (c) Work required by the client's employees including, if applicable, internal audit.
6. For a major audit, research into the detailed systems operation will be required before detailed planning is possible. This will involve systems evaluation and flowcharting. (See Chapters 5 and 6.)

Checklist 4.2 suggests a planning preparation process for new clients in a condensed form.

THE DETAILED PLAN

The Audit Practices Committee Guideline on Planning, Controlling and Recording states, 'Audit working papers should always be sufficiently complete and detailed to enable an experienced auditor, with no previous connections with the audit, subsequently to ascertain from them what work was performed and to support the conclusions reached.'

The audit plan is the first working paper that such an 'experienced auditor' would look at when reviewing an audit file. It is from the plan that he obtains background information about the client and learns concisely what the audit strategy for the client was. It is rather hopeful to imagine that the audit strategy for a large client can be gleaned from the detailed working papers alone. It is important then that the detailed audit plan is placed at the front of the audit working papers and is available for reference by all staff grades at any time during the audit work.

Who prepares the plan?

Depending on the type of organization, senior audit staff will have decided independently or will have been asked expressly to carry out a particular audit. Auditors of 'management' grade will have to brief field staff so that work can begin. Senior operational or 'field' auditors can be expected to contribute to the plan. In fact it is normally appropriate for the detailed plan to be drafted by senior operational staff as they are in regular contact with client staff and more fully aware of the day-to-day arrangements and problems.

The audit manager will brief the senior staff on the audit work he has in mind. The manager will have done the preparatory work on the scope of the audit as described already and will know how long he expects it to take. However, the manager now needs more information on the detail of the audit. He will receive this from the senior auditor's draft.

Manager's review

The manager reviews the draft audit plan using two main criteria as follows:

1. Does the senior auditor understand what I require from the audit?
2. Have I understood the full implications of my instructions?

Both these questions should be applied to each technical point referred to in the audit plan. The field auditor is often away from direct contact with management. It is helpful for the field staff to have the audit plan and any amendment agreed in writing.

The form and content of the plan

Much of the contents of the audit plan have been referred to already in this chapter. The importance of objectives, materiality and means and resources have been discussed in detail. All these aspects of an audit require mention in the plan.

Form

The plan is effectively a statement of intended audit quality and is one of the most frequently read pieces of audit documentation. It should be kept at the front of the audit working papers file for reference **during** and **after** the work by the following people:

1. The head of audit department/District Auditor/Director of Audit/ Partners
2. Audit manager
3. Senior auditors
4. Junior auditors
5. Peer reviewers/Other audit organizations

It is important that it has the following attributes:

1. It should follow a standard logical 'house' style.
2. It should be typed.
3. It should bear evidence of manager review.
4. It should be a precise, considered document detailing all the important aspects of the work.
5. It must be well laid out with clear titles and subtitles.
6. It should be as short as possible.

Contents

Every audit plan will cover between, say, eight and ten detailed headings. Suggestions have been summarized in Checklist 4.3. They are applicable to every type of audit whether it is a fraud investigation, the external audit of a major public body, a VFM study or a day spent certifying a small grant claim. These headings are discussed further briefly below.

(a) **Client/Title/Date.** This information is clearly essential (see also Chapter 5 on recording and controlling work for the importance of such details).

Checklist 4.3 Audit plan headings

1. Client/Title/Date.
2. Objectives.
3. Ranking of objectives.
4. Brief details of reporting format.
5. Administration points:
   (a) Staff
   (b) Client staff
   (c) Timetable.
6. Important points specific to the audit.
7. Figures under audit.
8. Materiality.
9. Detailed audit overview.

(b) **Objectives and ranking of objectives.** The importance of a clear statement of audit objectives has already been discussed.
(c) **Reporting format.** Sometimes the reporting format is clear from the audit objectives. For instance, audits of local authority statements of account have a reporting format prescribed by *The Code of Local Government Audit Practice*. For many audits, however, there is no set method of reporting. Where there are a number of audit objectives, as is common in the public sector, reporting may be particularly complex. This element of the audit plan should detail the reporting system consistent with each audit objective. Some secondary audit objectives will not be specifically reported upon unless there is cause for management concern.
(d) **Detail of audit staffing.** It is useful to list audit staff to be used on the audit together with a brief note of their experience of the work required of them. Any lack of experience can be catered for in the detailed plan; the manager is also made aware of the resources available for the audit.

   The time expected to be spent on the work by each staff member should also be stated. However, this aspect of the plan is not a time budget for the audit and information should be kept to a minimum. It acts only as a guide to the resources required for the work.
(e) **Client staff.** A note is required of the staff audit personnel will be dealing with, together with details of their responsibilities. This aspect of the plan can be important. For some audits very senior client staff may be involved; their time is costly and should not be wasted. This will affect the seniority of audit staff employed and perhaps the detailed audit strategy.

   Junior staff benefit from seeing details of client staff early on in the audit. They must know who is important within the organization under audit to avoid possible antagonism and to give credibility to their work.

(f) **Timetable.** Managers need to know when audit work will be done and they need to know reporting deadlines. Field staff also require the same information. Once the plan has been cleared by the manager, they can work to deadlines with confidence.

(g) **Important points specific to the audit.** This has been discussed already in this chapter. The written audit plan should raise points important to the audit only in brief. Details will be held on correspondence files or previous audit files and the audit working papers for the current audit. Such points can range from known systems weaknesses to major spending programmes.

(h) **Figures under audit.** It is important that those making the plan and those reading it have a clear conception of the magnitude of the department or authority under audit. Summarized figures of estimates, revenue accounts and balance sheets for the current and previous years are helpful. Again detail is not important; this can be obtained from the accounts and books of the organization.

(i) **Materiality.** For systems and attestation work materiality and confidence levels must be clearly discussed in the plan. Likely reliance on internal controls and the level of substantive testing will also be dealt with here.

For VFM work risk as well as materiality is important. Within a particular area under study different aspects will need different levels of analysis relative to one another. For example, a study on a relatively low materiality low risk area such as the heating of school buildings would be far less comprehensive than work on teacher employment costs. The materiality section of the plan is where this aspect of the audit is dealt with.

(j) **Detailed audit overview.** This is the most comprehensive element of every audit plan. It is the essence of the planning work where the points raised already in the plan are brought together and the audit testing necessary is worked out.

The reader of the plan should be able to conceive the entire audit from the detailed overview. He or she will have understood the following aspects of the projected audit:

1. The depth of audit work anticipated.
2. The likely sources of audit evidence.
3. The audit methods to be used for specific problems anticipated in the work.
4. Details of how other work already under way or already completed will be used to support or modify planned methods.

5. The nature of the more important audit tests planned for each area of the audit.

The total of this information allows the reader and the planner to judge the theoretical integrity of the intended audit approach. Having read and understood an audit plan much of the final audit output can be accepted or rejected with very little additional work.

It is no exaggeration to say that the detailed audit overview will show up the holes in weak audit work within a few minutes of the audit file being examined. It is also no exaggeration to say that audit files with detailed audit plans are far less likely to lead to poor audit work.

TIME NEEDED TO PLAN

The length of time needed to plan an audit varies greatly with the type of assignment. Very short assignments such as stock checks or cash counts need perhaps one to two hours of staff time. Major systems reliability audits take longer to plan depending on previous experience of the client.

Attestation audits of complete organizations require substantial planning. New assignments will need systems documentation before much of the plan can be written. The size of the body under audit will be another factor affecting planning time. An established client the size of an average shire district council (that is total expenditure of about £30m and 800 staff) will require one or two days of planning for external attestation audit. This remarkably short period is possible because of the similarity of many public bodies. An organization of the same size but new to the auditor might typically need three or four days' planning excluding systems documentation. A body with expenditure of £500m might require a week's planning time if it were an established client.

VFM audits take longer to plan. Research is often needed into a specialist field. For many audit topics this planning can be partially bypassed using Audit Commission, NAO or other published statistics, and booklets and reports on material and risky areas. In Chapter 10 use of published material for VFM audits is further discussed.

Planning is not generally particularly time consuming. As a general rule less than 5% of total audit time is spent at the planning stage. Considering the benefits, planning is very seldom worth cutting.

SUMMARY

The assignment plan is the first working paper in an audit file. It states the reason for the assignment and how the assignment ties in with strategic or business planning. Planning is that part of audit work which translates audit instructions into objectives and then into details of the audit testing needed. In setting out the basis of testing, the plan addresses the issues of materiality and, when appropriate, risk. Each audit assignment will require a different emphasis on the various aspects of planning.

However, all assignment plans will be based on the points raised in Checklists 4.1, 4.2 and 4.3. These outline the key aspects of preparation for planning of the actual audit plan.

In following sections of the chapter we give three examples to illustrate successful assignment plans drawn up for different types of public-sector organizations. The first shows the plan for a stock check carried out by an internal auditor at a district council. Although the work is expected to take only two man-days, the plan has highlighted a number of important points that might otherwise have been overlooked. The auditors have addressed the issues of reliance on internal control and checking for both over- and understatement of stock. The assignment has been tied in with the internal audit department's strategic planning both as regards materiality and the effects on other areas of work.

The second example illustrates a purchases audit in a district health authority. The assignment is substantially larger than in Case study 3.1. However, the planning process is very similar. Again, note how the plan ties the work into the department strategic planning process. Some of the results of this audit are shown in Case study 10.1 in Chapter 10. Significant value-for-money issues arose as part of the work and are raised in the report issued.

The last case study looks at the VFM audit of a small central government agency. The plan forms the first major working paper of the assignment. The reviewer is told at the start of his review work the objectives of the work, the administrative details and is given a succinct overview of the work done. The case is also continued in Chapter 10 in Case study 10.2.

The assignment plan for the attestation audit of a complete set of accounts for a district council is contained in Case study 7.2 in Chapter 7.

CASE STUDY 4.1 NOVA DISTRICT COUNCIL – INTERNAL AUDIT

Attendance at year-end stock-take of main stores

1. Objectives:
   Primary:
   That stock-take figures included in the year-end accounts are a fair record of stock held.

Secondary:
That the stock-taking system is free from fraud and corruption.
2. Staffing:
   Senior Auditor   J. Smith   (1 day)
   Audit Assistant   S. Jones   (1 day)
3. Departmental staff:
   J. Barrett, the Technical Services Department administrative officer, is well known to Internal Audit, but he has not been warned of the visit.
4. Timetable:
   Date of stock-take   31 March 1989
5. The main stores stock-take has not been attended for a number of years. No major problems involving stock have come to Internal Audit notice recently.
6. Recent figures:

	1989 *estimate*	*1988*	*1987*
Book value	£350,000	£337,750	£329,306
Estimated no. of stock lines	5,000		

7. Materiality:
   £20,000 to be consistent with our overall strategic plan.
   A confidence level of 95% is considered appropriate.
8. Audit overview:
   Stock-taking instructions are always sent to Internal Audit before counts take place. These have been reviewed. They form a sound basis on which to carry out a stock-take.
9. A monetary unit sample of 52 items* has been selected from the stock ledger using the computer department's interrogation program. (In previous years samples were calculated manually.)
10. Items selected from the ledger will be agreed to counters' stock sheets and stock items will be recounted.
11. No formal audit reliance is placed on internal controls for this brief assignment.
12. Understatement of stock in the accounts will be only partially covered by selecting from the stock ledger. Other audit evidence has been obtained from Internal Audit work on creditor purchases. Additional unquantifiable audit assurance will be obtained by selecting 10 high value lines from the shelves and agreeing quantities to count sheets and the stock ledger.

*See Chapter 8 for calculation of sample sizes.

CASE STUDY 4.2 RIBSTONE DISTRICT HEALTH AUTHORITY – INTERNAL AUDIT

Audit of purchases and creditor payments system

1. Objectives:
   Primary:
   (a) That figures recorded in the accounts are a fair record of purchases and payments made.
   (b) That effective internal controls exist throughout the system and are in effective operation during the year.
   Secondary:
   (c) That purchases and payments have been made free from fraud or corrupt practices.
   (d) That the purchases and payments system is run in an efficient and economic manner.

2. Ranking of objectives:
   Internal Audit have agreed with service managers and the Deputy Treasurer that audit work should aim to provide significant quantifiable confidence on accounts figures. Effective operation of internal controls is an important aspect of being able to provide this assurance. Consideration of fraud, corruption and efficiency are secondary and may form a 'by-product' to the audit if matters of significance arise.

   After the audit monthly checking of small samples is planned to give continuous up-to-date audit assurance.

3. Reporting format:
   Standard report in 'house' style concluding on the accuracy of accounts figures output for the period and the system's internal controls. Attention will be drawn to any control weaknesses found.

Administration

4. Staffing:

Senior Auditor	J. Smith	(5 man-days)
Audit Assistant	S. Jones	(10 man-days)

   The majority of detailed testing work will be performed by S. Jones. He is familiar with many aspects of the creditors system from other work.

5. Department staff:
   Paymaster's Department:

Paymaster	H. Clarke
Assistant Paymaster	S. Berkeley

   Both report to the Assistant Treasurer.

Service Departments:
Various senior officers and clinicians acts as budget controllers and
these are listed in the internal telephone directory.
6. Timetable:
The Treasurer wishes to give a brief report on the results of this work
to a meeting with the Audit Commission appointed external auditors.
(a) August 19XX   Basic audit work
(b) 1 September 19XX   Draft report to Deputy Treasurer
(c) 7 September 19XX   Report to Service Managers
(d) 20 September 19XX   Treasurer's Report

Audit strategy
7. Points specific to the Creditors' Department:
Recently a number of duplicate payments of invoices have been picked
up by service managers on review of their detailed budgets.
8. Since the last audit review an on-line VDU input system has been
added replacing the old batch system. This aspect of the system will
require special attention.
9. Recent figures:

| | *19XY* | *19XX* |
| | *estimate* | |
	£000	£000
Administration and property costs	2,410	2,390
Drugs	5,165	4,910
Equipment	2,771	2,571
Capital expenditure	1,305	1,211
Consumable materials		
(Operating theatre + Radiology)	6,326	6,588
	£17,977	£17,670

10. Materiality:
Set at £100,000. This materiality level was set in the strategic plan for
the year and has been agreed with service managers. This will form our
reporting basis.
A 95% confidence level will be used in conjunction with this level of
precision.

Detailed audit overview
11. The Internal Audit Department have flowcharts and systems notes for
the creditors system. These will be updated for the new on-line input
system.
12. Systems notes will be subject to a 'walk-through test' and will be
updated before testing begins.
13. Some reliance is expected to be placed on internal controls following
compliance testing of key areas. Authorization of orders and evidence

of receipt of goods and services prior to invoice certification are two areas where significant compliance test evidence is expected.

14. Audit samples for both compliance and substantive tests will be selected using a transactions interrogation program attached to the main accounting software system.

   The same samples will be used for both compliance and substantive tests.

15. Items will be sampled from the main accounting ledger system and will be traced to invoice, delivery note or equivalent, and authorized order.

16. There will be no testing for understatement. Understatement errors would involve overstatement of other accounts or understatement of income. Both eventualities have been satisfactorily covered by other Internal Audit work. Transactions not entering the accounts would not receive payment. In this instance suppliers would be expected to complain. The only likely error is that items are recorded in the incorrect accounting period.

17. In the event of very poor compliance testing, results tests will be continued so that the possibility of fraud can be investigated.

18. For details of testing see Audit Programme.

CASE STUDY 4.3 URBAN POLLUTION INSPECTORATE – EXTERNAL AUDIT

Building maintenance VFM audit

1. Objectives:
   Primary:
   (a) That the provision of building maintenance by the Inspectorate is made economically and efficiently and is effective.
   Secondary:
   (b) That building maintenance is provided in such a manner that fraud and corruption are unlikely to occur.
   (c) That the accounting records of the Inspectorate with respect to maintenance form a fair record of their activities.

2. Ranking of objectives:
   The primary objective of the work is an analysis of the VFM of the Inspectorate's building maintenance. Only when work uncovers points of importance relating to fraud and corruption or the accounting records will specific work be undertaken.

3. Report format:
A detailed report on the existing VFM of the building maintenance provision together with specific recommendation on improving the service will be sent to senior officials.

Administration
4. Staffing:

Audit Senior	J. Smith	(15 man-days)
Audit Semi-Senior	S. Palmer	(10 man-days)

J. Smith has been on our building maintenance VFM course and has carried out similar work at other client bodies.

5. Client staff:

Building Maintenance:	Building Repair Manager	– S. Brown
	Building Repair Assistant	– W. Andrews
Accounts:	Chief Accounts Officer	– B. Wood
	Assistant Accounts Officer	– T. Glover

The Accounts Department is well acquainted with external audit staff. The Maintenance Department have been contacted and were present at a preliminary meeting with both accountants and auditors present.

6. Timetable:
(a) August/September 19X2 – Basic audit work
(b) 20 September 19X2   – Draft report to be sent to
                           Building Repair Manager
(c) 10 October 19X2   – Final report to Chief Officers

Audit strategy
7. Points specific to the Inspectorate:
Three years ago the Department of the Environment and the Welsh Office set up the Inspectorate to monitor pollution from industrial installations over the whole of England and Wales.

8. The Inspectorate took over offices, transport depots and testing stations from various public sector bodies. Building maintenance is thus a continuation of that provided by the previous users. Few of the buildings are new or in particularly good condition. Much of the Inspectorate's work involves visiting locations using specialist vehicles, taking samples and readings, and returning to the regional offices and testing stations where analysis and follow-up work is carried out. The Inspectorate thus has a surprisingly large stock of buildings in need of repair.

9. The vast majority of maintenance work is carried out by private sector contractors. The larger testing stations may have an 'odd-job man'.

10. A Parliamentary select committee has taken an increasing interest in the Inspectorate and since March this year have required quarterly figures from senior civil servants.

11. Changes in legislation:
    From June 19X3 the Government requires tendering for contract work on a five-yearly cycle. The Inspectorate will be little affected by this legislation since they currently invite competitive tenders on a regular basis.
12. Recent figures:

	19X2 estimate £000	19X1 £000	19X0 £000
Direct staff costs –			
Routine repairs	321	318	272
Contractors' charges –			
Emergency repairs	1,200	1,101	521
Contractors' charges –			
Routine repairs	1,600	1,702	127
Other expenses	55	56	206
	3,176	3,177	1,126
Apportioned overheads	390	374	401
Total expenditure	£3,566	£3,551	£1,527

13. Materiality and risk:
    Building maintenance is material to the Inspectorate and risky since the cost of building maintenance can be very high after a period of neglect. Consequently, the strategic plan allocated a substantial resource to this area. Detailed audit attention will depend on the preliminary findings and will be decided as the audit develops.
14. Source of figures:
    Figures used for analysis purposes will be provided by the client. Unless we have specific concerns about the accuracy of figures no further audit work is required.

Strategy
15. Detailed strategy and background information is given in the course material booklet, EZ 51.
16. Audit work is divided as follows:
    (a) Arrangements Review;
    (b) Performance Review.
17. Arrangements Review involves an evaluation of the structure of the Building Repairs Department and the controls within that department to ensure value for money.
18. Performance Review:
    This aspect of the audit makes a comparison between costs of planned and responsive (including emergency) maintenance. The ratios of

planned to responsive maintenance are compared to good practice bench-marks.

CONCLUDING POINTS

Detailed planning of audit assignments taking into account objectives, resources, materiality and the other aspects relevant to individual assignments is not a new process. Auditors have always addressed these matters. But it is important to realize that each stage needs to be fully documented following a recognized logical structure.

5 Controlling and recording the assignment

INTRODUCTION

This chapter starts by looking at the importance of strong control over the whole audit process. Methods of control are described followed by a discussion of the need to record assignments fully from start to finish. Practical methods of controlling and recording audit work are then given.

Audit work very often involves serious and objective criticism of other people's work. Auditors soon come to realize that much tact is required to avoid personal animosity arising. But no amount of tact will compensate for poor quality audit work. Informed and constructive criticism and intelligent checking by professional individuals is needed. Merely to point out faults may be seen as uninformed rudeness. Auditors that are good at their job are given credence by their clients, and the controlling and recording of the work is at the heart of such credence.

CREDENCE

Credence is an impression in the mind of the audited client. It represents a confidence in the auditor which has been earned either by reputation or direct experience of his or her audits. Checklist 5.1 lists the common failings which prevent the formation of credence.

It is inevitable that some of these negative attributes will be exhibited some of the time. But how does an auditor ensure that such lapses are at a minimum? Planning is one method, and Chapter 4 showed how complex audit areas, duplication of work and audit deadlines may be regulated by

Checklist 5.1 Audit shortcomings leading to reduced credence

- Unreliable opinions
- Superficial criticism/suggestions
- Avoidance of complex areas
- Duplications of work
- Slow response to client's queries
- Bending to client pressure
- Failure to meet deadlines
- Poorly trained and presented staff

the plan. In addition to planning, the **controlling** and **recording** of audit work greatly assists the formation of credence.

Rational, orderly and consistent work

The controlling and recording of audit work is based on the idea that all audit work should be:

(a) Rational
(b) Orderly
(c) Consistent

It is part of the approach to work shown by all professionals that they carry through rational ideas in an orderly and consistent manner until the object is achieved. Good judgement and flair assist the process but they are never substitutes.

Rationality

Traditionally audit work has been carried out with the emphasis on prevention of fraud and error. Significant elements of this approach were the physical presence of the auditor, and uncertainty about his methods. Within this framework rationality was **not** an important quality of the work.

In the past the auditor reported little. This gave him something approaching a mystic inscrutability. Now he is required to report explicitly on an increasing number of specific points, and in the last few years reporting in the public sector has changed dramatically, as we have already discussed.

Audit work approached in a rational manner has a hallmark: the audit evidence and conclusions can be clearly appreciated by those not involved in the work. The sources of the evidence used, the quantity and quality of the evidence, and the explanations for the chosen quality of evidence as well as the conclusions to be drawn, should all be presented clearly and articulately. The reader should be able to follow the work to a logical conclusion.

Rational audit opinion, criticism or suggestions are less likely to be flawed than those made using less rigorous haphazard methods. The work will be of a higher quality, but as importantly, opinions can be checked, not only by senior audit staff who review the work, but also should the opinions be called into question by the client. Both these benefits add greatly to audit credence.

A rational audit approach also helps the auditor to tackle complex issues. Work can be broken down into small, logical elements which can be grasped individually before overall conclusions are drawn. Again audit credence is enhanced.

All auditors come under direct pressure from time to time. If the work has been carried out in a rational manner it will be easier for an auditor to uphold his opinions in the face of pressure from a client unwilling to accept the audit report. The client will find it difficult to persuade the auditor to reconsider his conclusions.

Orderliness

Orderliness adds the benefits of tried and tested technique to rationality. It is the result of good staff training. Work is tackled and documented in a sensible order so that it will be done quickly and well and in such a manner that other staff can pick up on the work with the minimum of disturbance to the assignment.

Audit opinions produced as a result of ordered work are much less likely to be unreliable or superficial. Again complex audit areas can be tackled methodically and duplication of work will be unlikely. An ordered approach will take into account response times to client questions and will cater for deadlines. Staff will be seen to be well managed.

Consistency

Every auditor is weary of the complaint 'but that is not what you said last time'. Without a consistent approach audit opinions, criticisms and suggestions will not be seen as unbiased or considered by those they are directed at. Pressure from clients to change or modify audit suggestions or criticisms cannot be countered without a demonstrably consistent approach to work. Audit staff are likely to be seen to be controlled and well trained if they are consistent. Audit credence and auditor consistency always go hand in hand.

Consistency is the auditor's essential defence against both critical attacks on and concerted resistance to his opinion.

CONTROLLING AND RECORDING IN GENERAL

We have mentioned the importance of control to rationality, orderliness and consistency. We must now look at the nature of audit control in some detail.

Control is the direction of field staff by audit managers on a day-to-day basis, and the audit organization in the longer term:

(a) **In the short term** managers control their staff to ensure the audit plan is being properly carried out. If problems arise the manager is well able to replan quickly so that the assignment is not held up.

(b) **In the long term** controlling involves laying down audit procedures, and training staff in those procedures.

Control of assignments

Day-to-day control of an audit is the work, in essence, of administration. The assignment is methodically monitored from beginning to end to ensure that everything that should have been done has been done, and the correct conclusions have been drawn.

At the beginning of the work the audit manager has to make sure that the foundations of the audit are laid effectively so that latter stages of the work will not fail. This involves making sure the staff to be involved are capable of achieving the objectives of the work. The auditor will ensure that technically complex assignments or particularly sensitive ones are handled by more experienced personnel. Staff will require briefing and an audit plan will be needed as discussed in Chapter 4. The plan will require review so that both manager and staff know what the other expects. At this stage the field work can start with everyone secure in the knowledge that for the moment all is under control.

When the field work starts it is essential that it is fully recorded in the audit working papers. If work is not recorded it cannot be reviewed. If it cannot be reviewed it is not possible to be sure that all the necessary work has been done.

As the work continues the person in charge of the assignment will need to know how the audit is progressing. Imagine the chaos if at the end of the allotted time for the work, the field staff return to the audit manager to have the following conversation:

'As far as we can see the accounting system has completely broken down; we have not been able to undertake our audit work and it will require about three months' hard work by the client in conjunction with us to rectify the problems.'

'When did you realize things were so bad?' asks the manager.

'The chief accountant told us he had problems balancing the books on the second day we were there. That was about three weeks ago and we spent the rest of the time confirming that it was as bad as he said.'

An earlier stage in controlling such an audit has obviously failed and important developments had not been reported. If this happens in any audit additional resources are required extending the allotted time period, which delays the report and other audit work. Poor control of the audit has led to inefficiency, and credence will have been lost with the client.

Review

Review of work is a particularly important element of control. Many of the problems auditors face when discussing audit results and conclusions with their clients relate to ineffective review of the basic audit work.

Imagine the following situation. The field auditor has written in a report that authorization of invoices for payment is poor. The manager reviews the audit working papers. There is a list of invoices checked and a line of crosses signifying no authorization for payment. The working papers give no further information. On review the manager asks (in writing) how the client explains the lack of authorization. The field auditor, to clear the review point, asks the client the same question. He is told that financial regulations require invoice processing after the payment clerk has received invoices to which is attached the authorized order and signed delivery note. All invoices under £100 are dealt with using this method of certification so the more senior staff are left free for more important work. Had the manager not reviewed the work a clearly incorrect report would have been sent to the client.

There are a number of levels of review which are all important to proper control of the audit. Smaller audits require less review than more complex assignments. However, all audit work needs proper written review before opinions are released. No auditor is foolproof to the extent that he always picks up all the issues correctly all the time. Even very senior audit staff in charge of large audit organizations should have their work reviewed by colleagues or, if that is not possible, by more junior personnel. Review of work and conclusions drawn from the work, is an indispensable element of audit.

The various processes required to control an audit are set out in Checklist 5.2. This emphasizes the nature of control as a process of information feedback from junior to senior staff. The senior staff must know their

Checklist 5.2 For day-to-day control of assignments

---

1. Beginning of work:
   (a) Have the best available staff been assigned to the work? Do they have the necessary **training** and **experience** to do the work?
   (b) What is the essential information they must have before they can start work? Have they been adequately **briefed** for the assignment?
   (c) Has the necessary planning been done for the assignment? Will the **planned work** achieve the stated objectives?
2. While the audit is under way:
   (d) Are the field staff recording their work? Are **records** adequate to substantiate the work done, the reasons for that work and conclusions drawn?
   (e) Is the work of junior staff properly reviewed by more senior staff during the progress of the assignment? Is there an adequate record of **reviews** carried out?
   (f) Are senior field staff raising the more important audit findings with the manager as the work progresses? Is the manager being kept **informed**?
3. At the end of the assignment:
   (g) Have all the review points raised by senior field staff been satisfactorily dealt with? Is the field work **complete**?
   (h) Has the audit work been reviewed by the manager? Have all the audit work and conclusions been reviewed as a **totality**?
   (i) Has the final audit checklist of points to be covered been completed? Has the assignment been **completed**? Have all statutory or other **requirements** been complied with and has the **audit report** been correctly drafted?
4. Is the report in compliance with the law and other binding regulations?

---

junior staff, their client, the plan, the problems encountered, and the quality and extent of the work done. Only by exercising this type of control can high quality work be delivered to the client.

Recording

The recording of audit work has two distinct purposes. First, it is an essential part of control which makes review possible. Secondly, audit work is recorded to assist further work. Complex information can only be analysed if it is recorded either manually or on computer. Checklist 5.3 gives the tangible working benefits of recording work in detail. It can be seen that every aspect of the audit from planning to concluding is affected, and the quality of the work itself is enhanced.

When an auditor records his work how much detail should he include? There are two points to consider:

(a) The Audit Guideline Planning, Controlling and Recording states that:
   'Audit working papers should always be sufficiently complete and detailed to enable an experienced auditor with no previous connection

Checklist 5.3 Working benefits of fully recorded audit work

1. Complex accounting systems can be comprehended.
2. Internal controls can be fully evaluated so that the quantity of audit work can be reduced.
3. Cogent audit planning can be achieved.
4. Complex accounting entries can be followed.
5. VFM and other cost data can be compared.
6. Audit results can be systematically evaluated.
7. Previous work can be used to assist future assignments.

with the audit subsequently to ascertain from them what work was performed and to support the conclusions reached.'

(b) The minimum audit recording is required consistent with the above 'to provide an effective and economic service within an appropriate timescale'.

The Audit Guideline highlights an important requirement for audit records. It is not sufficient for the level of recording to be just adequate for the field auditor to negotiate problems as they arise. Rather the detail and quality of recording must be sufficient for both the field auditor and reviewing or other staff to comprehend the problems involved whilst the work was being carried out.

This requirement may appear unduly onerous. In fact that is certainly not the case. Most auditors are all too familiar with poor working papers from client staff:

The auditor has asked for the working papers supporting a figure under audit. The accountant responsible says that he probably has them somewhere. Later, when the auditor has returned to see whether they have been found, the conversation runs as follows:

'I was wondering whether you were able to find the working papers?'

'Oh! I've found some. I don't know if there were any others. It was rather a long time ago that I did it.'

'I suppose it must have been five months ago?'

'About then.'

'Can I see what you have got?'

A short pause ensues during which the auditor flicks through some scruffy pencil jottings done on the back of used photocopies. The auditor breaks the silence.

'I can't quite see how the workings tie in with the figure in the ledger.'

'Let me see. I can't quite remember. I think it must have been this figure off this sheet less this on here.'

There is another gap in the conversation. The auditor wonders whether to sit down. The accountant is feverishly punching figures into his calculator, repeatedly hitting the clear button. The auditor looks on and then says:

'Shall I come back in a few minutes so that you can work it out?'

The grateful accountant agrees. Half an hour later the accountant arrives at the auditor's office.

'I thought it was like that. I knew I had done an addlist, but it got lost. This figure at the bottom here is the gross total, but we need to adjust it for sales so I calculated an average sales figure here – the one I have circled in pencil. Another adjustment is needed for miscoding during the year. I went through the ledger and picked them up. They are on this sheet here. That's the total there, so I have to add – no, subtract them off the total. Can I borrow your calculator? I will show you.'

Every auditor has surely experienced this type of scene. If the accountant had left the employment of the audited body even more time would have been wasted.

The auditor is in a very similar position to the accountant in the scene above regarding his own working papers. If he, like the accountant above, produces rough workings that have not been cross-referenced in an incomplete and untidy file none of the benefits of properly recorded work given in Checklist 5.3 will arise. The auditor will not be able to follow the recorded detail of an accounting system so he will not fully understand it. If that happens the effect of internal controls will not be fully evaluated. If audit work is in the form of rough notes complex accounting entries cannot be followed, and data cannot be evaluated objectively either by the field auditor or a reviewer. High quality audit work cannot come from rough, incomplete working papers.

Consider a systems audit of, perhaps, purchases and payments. Such work should be carried out every year, and the working papers should normally include a flowchart and notes of the accounting system, a list of control objectives, a list of key controls and weaknesses, detail of the audit strategy, audit testing papers and conclusions drawn from the work done. Probably more than half of this work could be used on future assignments. The system notes, list of control objects and controls and weaknesses will all remain largely the same every time the work is done. If the documentation is of high quality on the first assignment, audit times on future assignments can be greatly reduced regardless of whether the staff member used on the original audit is employed. If the audit documentation is poor, review will be long and tedious. When important points arise from the work the reviewer will have to quiz the auditor who did the work face to face to be sure of the facts before including them in a report. If the work is well documented such uncertainties are far less likely to arise and valuable staff time is saved.

The work may contain details of important control account reconcilia-tions. These would be identified as one of the main internal controls in the audit systems documentation and they would be checked as part of the testing work. The checking work would tie the figures on the client's reconciliation back to prime records. If this were **not** clearly shown in the audit working papers, the reviewer or subsequent auditors would probably spend considerable periods of their time puzzling out the purpose and detail of the reconciliation. Again, valuable time would be lost.

For a medium-sized organization perhaps ten to fifteen days might be required to document, analyse and test a purchase and payments system. If this work is done well repeat assignments could be done with time alloca-tions of perhaps five to ten days. Review of high quality work would be included within the ten- to fifteen-day time allocation. For poorly docu-mented work at least a few extra days for review and answers of queries is likely. To produce high quality working papers perhaps an extra day of time will be used on the first assignment. This compares very favourably with time losses of perhaps four to six days on all subsequent work. The cost benefits of complete recording of work are therefore substantial.

CONTROLLING AND RECORDING IN ACTION

Audit could be recorded in a variety of ways. But in practice a finite number of generally accepted techniques are used to control and record the majority of audit work. To grasp the most important of these tech-niques it is necessary to see how they are applied in specific audit sit-uations. The attestation audit of the figures of one specific audit area illustrates much of the range, and for this reason the key aspects of such an audit will be looked at as summarized in Checklist 5.4. Specimen working papers are provided from p. 308. The reader may find it useful to look through these and consider their controlling and recording functions as he or she reads on.

Checklist 5.4 Controlling and recording techniques

---

1. The individual working schedule.
2. Lead schedules.
3. Use of the audit file and file dividers.
4. Working schedule referencing.
5. Cross-referencing of schedules.
6. Audit programmes.
7. Introductory information.
8. Test results and conclusions.
9. Review and review documentation.
10. Clearance of queries raised on review.

As we have already discussed, an audit will start with a detailed written plan. Since planning has been fully dealt with in Chapter 4 this stage of the audit will not be repeated here. We will assume that the figures for the period have been completed and are available to the auditor. He will need to document the accounting system (this is presumed to be his first year of audit) and he will carry out testing of both internal controls and detailed transactions. He will construct a **lead schedule** (see below) from the accounting records of the body and these he will ensure agree to the figures under audit. At the end of the work it will be clear to the reader of the audit file that each account figure had received a considered level of audit scrutiny. The detailed work and testing will be easily located.

The same recording and controlling methods can be used whenever a systems based approach is used, be it for internal or external audit purposes. Similarly, the use of lead schedules applies to all occasions where specific figures are under review.

Checklist 5.5 Essential information on individual working schedules

---

1. Information recorded at the start of work:
   (a) Name of client organization/department.
   (b) Year of audit (if applicable).
   (c) Date of preparation of schedule.
   (d) Initials of the person who prepared the schedule.
   (e) Heading relevant to the information on the schedule.
2. Information recorded during work:
   (a) A reference number specific to the schedule.
   (b) Evidence of review of the schedule.

The individual working schedule

The basic unit of audit documentation is the individual working paper or schedule. A working schedule can record any information or data relevant to the audit. However, all schedules should bear the information given in Checklist 5.5.

Wherever a new sheet of paper is used to record audit work, five pieces of information are recorded immediately as shown in the checklist. These items are required so that the schedule is given a specific identity. Should it become detached from the rest of the audit file this identity will remain allowing it to be recognized and returned to its correct place in the filing system.

As the audit work is pieced together by the field staff, schedules are ordered within the file. At this stage a reference number is given to each schedule. Later, during the review, the reviewer will initial the audit working papers as he reads them. Both referencing and review documentation are considered below.

Lead schedules

Audit paperwork has a structure which varies little with the type of work being carried out. This structure is hierarchical with documentation leading from summary schedules at the beginning to detailed information further in. Within any one section of attestation audit work the **lead schedule** is at the top of the hierarchy. Consequently it has a special importance.

A lead schedule will commonly summarize individual figures on which audit work has been carried out in such a way that they agree directly to the grant claim/published accounts/management accounts, on which an opinion has been requested. Case study 5.1 at the end of the chapter contains a typical lead schedule.

Use of the audit file

We have said that audit work has a hierarchical structure, and when planning was discussed we said that audit objectives were broken down into test objectives of which there could be many. Only by breaking the audit down into small elements could it be properly grasped. Audit documentation naturally follows this process of subdivision.

When auditing, say, a balance sheet the opinion is requested on the whole statement. However, audit work will be largely directed at the individual elements of the balance sheet such as fixed assets and creditors. When setting up the necessary documentation to control and record the audit a clear structure mirroring the form of the work itself is required.

Normally each element of the audit is given a reference. Fixed assets might be assigned the reference 'J' on every attestation audit. Creditors might be given 'H'. The papers for the audit of a balance sheet should all be kept in one file or series of files so that cross-referencing can take place. Consequently, the most effective method of controlling and recording the work is to use a ring binder file with an alphabetical set of file dividers or indices.

Some readers may feel that undue emphasis has been placed on the mechanics of the paperwork. This is, however, not the case. Audit documentation needs to be highly accessible both during the field work and during review. The use of ring files and alphabetical file dividers is a well tested form of access to information not dissimilar in mechanism to a telephone directory. The combination is of great assistance to efficient audit practice.

Case study 5.1 at the end of the chapter also contains a typical file index.

Working schedule referencing

Within each file section there will be detailed working papers or schedules backing up the lead schedule. The relationship between the lead schedule and the backing schedules is made clear by referencing all the schedules in order.

The lead schedule for, say, creditors will be referenced H1. The papers that follow will be referenced H2, H3, H4, . . . etc. Often a series of schedules will be linked; they may deal with one topic and follow on one to the next. These schedules should be referenced in such a way that their relationship is made clear. Each sheet will be headed with the information shown in Checklist 5.5 and the referencing might be H4.1, H4.2 and H4.3.

Generally, schedule references should be kept as simple as possible. Schedules are referenced to aid intelligent reading of the file and to assist this, referencing should be made to stand out by, say, highlighting in red. The use of referencing is further discussed below.

Cross-referencing of schedules

Two distinct aspects of audit work make cross-referencing of audit working schedules within and between sections important.

1. Audit work pieces together evidence from a number of sources to form conclusions.
2. Double-entry book-keeping ensures that all accounts figures will have opposite but matching book entries.

The simplest form of cross-referencing may involve referencing an index at the beginning of audit work to the work itself. For example:

Index	Reference
Introduction	A1
Systems documentation	B1
Audit programme	C1

Referencing is also used to link related information on an audit file. For example:

Our work on purchases and creditor payments also involved an evaluation of the new main accounting system control accounts – see B10.

Often it is useful to cross-reference in both directions. This is particularly the case when monetary amounts are the subject of the referencing. For example:

Schedule H10

Proof of a grant balance sheet creditor figure:

	£	
Grant payable to claimant 1 April Balance b/fwd	1,253,000	
Grant payable for the year	10,771,000	B6
Cash paid in the year	(10,012,000)	
Grants payable to claimants 31 March Balance c/fwd	£2,012,000	

Schedule B6

Summary of grant revenue a/c figures:

	£	
Grants payable at 75%	4,981,000	
Grants payable at 90%	4,545,000	
Grants payable at 95%	1,245,000	
	£10,771,000	H10

More examples of cross-referencing are shown in Case study 5.1 at the end of the chapter.

Audit test programmes

After the audit plan and systems recording and analysis it is necessary to set out detailed tests so that evidence can be obtained to support the opinions given.

It is always useful to produce an audit programme so that the audit file can clearly demonstrate that the testing considered necessary has in fact been carried out. The audit objectives to which the programme relates should be annotated on the first page. The programme takes the form of a list of instructions for tests. The reasons for each particular test are documented elsewhere either in the audit plan or the systems analysis and documentation.

A typical audit programme would probably start as follows:

Audit Objective: To ensure that all payments are for genuine claims.

Tests: Obtain a schedule itemizing all grants given in the year. Select 10 grants from the schedule and note the following:
(a) Name of claimant
(b) Date
(c) Amount
etc.

The audit programme schedule will have at least two columns, one to cross-reference to the test schedules, another used to initial completed work. In this way a reader of the file can see immediately where the records of audit testing are located. During the progress of the audit one can rapidly see from the initials how complete the work is without needing to look at the test schedules.

Further detailed examples of audit programmes are given in Chapter 6.

Summary information

We have described how an audit file will be divided up into sections and we have said how sections will commence with lead schedules setting out key figures. Working schedules will be referenced within the section and cross-referenced to the lead schedule and, where relevant, other sections. The audit programme will also be in the section and this will be referenced to the working papers. However, when audit work is read or reviewed, summary information is often used at the start of the file or individual sections to help the reader understand the nature of the work in the shortest possible space of time.

Summaries are usually quick to produce and they assist review by increasing the accessibility of work, reducing review time and increasing its quality. Summaries assist the field auditor because they draw together all that is important in a section of work. The field auditor proves to himself that he has covered the important points. Lastly, summaries assist future audits giving guidance on the nature of work that is required.

Test results and conclusions

Once the audit testing is complete and the audit programme has been signed off, it is time to form the conclusion on the work done. Account balances will be composed of a number of specific figures and a conclusion must be reached on the audit work on each of these figures. It is the sum of these conclusions that leads to the overall conclusion on the total account balance. Where a systems based approach has been taken, forming a conclusion will be more complex. The overall conclusion will still be required but the detailed conclusions will be more numerous.

Review and review documentation

Earlier in the chapter we stressed the importance of the review of all audit work. Once sections of work done by junior staff are complete, senior field staff should review them. At the end of the assignment managers should review all the work done. The reviewer's aim is to ensure that all the work

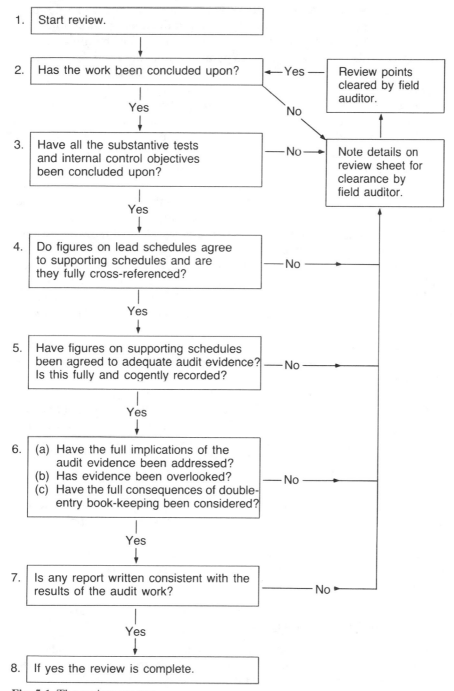

Fig. 5.1 The review process.

required has been done, and that the work done is of an acceptable standard. The manager will have already reviewed the audit plan and he may have reviewed the audit programmes used. In any event he must be well acquainted with both the audit strategy and the detailed testing required.

Having assimilated the above, the reviewer tackles the audit working papers. Figure 5.1 outlines the process involved.

Effective reviewers have two qualities. First, they make sure that documentation and figures are consistent with one another and totally complete. This quality is one of rigorousness. Secondly, reviewers need to think laterally and draw on experience of similar audit situations met in the past. A certain probing attitude to the work under review and the client is helpful. The full consequence of facts presented in the audit work need to be understood and, where appropriate, noted so that further action can be taken. Work may have been done on an accounting system where an on-line computer input is used, for example. The reviewer of the work will be on the look-out for evidence that these are genuine input controls to offset the potential weaknesses of on-line input. The effective reviewer will read the audit work to ensure that the field auditor has tackled such issues as computer access controls, access logs, data vet procedures, exception reports, use of input control totals and segregation of duties, etc.

Where accounts are under audit, reviewers will also have to consider the interests of those preparing the figures. Would a direct service organization be interested in showing a low or high profit for the year? Is its profit being 'saved' for the future as an insurance against possible lean years to come? Perhaps the DSO has tendered for a type of work it has never previously attempted – in this situation it may be interested in showing a better return on the work than was actually achieved. Reviewers should be aware of the background to events from reading minutes, meetings held and their past experience. They will use this knowledge to question the audit work and to draw up a list of additional points to be considered.

It should not be thought that reviews will necessitate a complete re-audit. Good field staff should have considered the important points in an audit and have documented them in the audit working papers. Review is not an alternative to staff training; it is a method of ensuring that important points have been addressed and that the audit work is of the highest quality.

Clearance of queries raised on review

Review schedules are often conveniently divided vertically into two halves. On the left, the reviewer notes his points. These are cross-referenced to the audit work where this is relevant so that the person clearing the points knows exactly what the reviewer is referring to and can find the relevant schedules immediately. The person clearing the review points has as his first aim the improvement of the audit work. The points raised in review give him specific guidance on how to achieve this. The second objective is to inform the reviewer that all his points have been addressed and dealt with.

When all review points have been cleared, the audit file will be returned to the reviewer. Written review ensures that the highest standards of work are achieved and maintained. This is done in such a way that costly discussion is kept to a minimum. Another major benefit is that the junior auditor obtains written criticism of all his work and a chance to reply. This is an important aspect of training.

Standing data

Much audit work can be reused on future assignments. To aid these future assignments, data usable in the longer term should be separately filed from data specific to the current audit.

The benefits of recording work thoroughly has been discussed and an example was given illustrating the uses to which well recorded documentation could be put in future years. But it is not only system notes and audit programmes which are required year after year. Audit working papers supporting a current year's audit work will be filed in a 'current' file. Standing data relevant to every repeat audit will be filed separately. Checklist 5.6 lists the contents typical of standing data, or 'permanent notes' files.

Checklist 5.6 Contents of standing data files

1. **Background information on the client.**
2. **Previous years' accounts and reports issued.**
3. **Important regulations affecting the client.** Copies of standing orders, desk instructions, important extracts from statutes and government departmental circulars should be kept.
4. **Personnel.** Details of key personnel within the client organization should be kept.
5. **Contracts.** Where a client has entered into major contracts copies should be kept on file, e.g. a local authority highways agency agreement.
6. **Fixed assets.** Where a client has substantial fixed assets, details of these should be kept and updated yearly.
7. **Audit programmes.** Audit programme master copies should be kept on file for reuse and amendment where appropriate.
8. **System notes.** System records and details of system internal controls and weaknesses should be kept.

Systems

Systems records should follow the same basic standards of documentation as all audit work. But care is needed if their full benefit is to be realized. The Auditor's Operational Standard states: 'The auditor should ascertain the enterprise's system of recording and processing transactions . . .' Both the Audit Guidelines on Accounting Systems and Planning, Controlling and Recording require that the auditor should record details of the systems relating to organizations under audit. It is the nature of accounting systems that they are often amended, but seldom radically changed. This infrequent change in systems means that once the auditor has obtained a record, he can usefully keep it for future years, hence the reason why system records are an integral part of any standing data file.

Recording a system

There are a wide number of ways of recording the details of a financial system. These can be summarized as:

(a) **Written narrative:** notes, internal control questionnaires, etc.
(b) **Pictorial flowcharts:** document flowcharts, block diagrams.

If great detail is required then a flowchart of some kind is essential. The system will probably have been designed using a flowchart and this technique is the best practice for both designing and recording systems.

In many audit situations only the important elements of a system need complete documentation. Time spent on system records is time not spent audit testing. However, if the systems record is too superficial, unnecessary or misdirected audit work may be done or important work may be omitted. The auditor must judge the level of recording required for present and possible future circumstances.

Generally the internal auditor will require a detailed system record. Departmental managers will expect the auditor to have a thorough understanding of their department's system, and any report given by the internal auditor will need to demonstrate this. External auditors will probably take a decision on the level of recording based on the materiality of the system's throughput in financial terms when compared to the organization as a whole. The level of detail required in documenting systems is discussed in Chapter 6.

It is normally necessary for all auditors to flowchart all the important systems in an organization under audit. Simple flowcharts, appended with brief notes, are particularly useful since they can reduce the details of a system to a few sheets of paper. This allows reviewers to comprehend quickly the essence of a system under audit without reading pages of dense narrative.

Since system records will be used over a period of years they must be flexible so that they can be easily updated with minor systems amendments. For this reason flowcharts and accompanying notes should be done in pencil. The pencil original is placed in the standing data file and photocopies are used for current audit files.

The professional accounting bodies offer extensive advice and training on flowcharting methods. Audit organizations should choose a method suited to their needs and stick to it.

SUMMARY

At the beginning of the chapter Checklist 5.1 gave a list of shortcomings common to a greater or lesser extent to all auditors. By discussing some relatively simple processes we have tried to demonstrate how the auditor's fallibility can be reduced, but it must be remembered that the techniques discussed are not particularly effective individually.

The checklists in the chapter summarize the important steps in controlling and recording assignments. These should be used as a framework for achieving efficient and effective audit work. When all the controlling and recording operations are used together in a unified approach the benefits outlined in this chapter will arise.

At the end of the book the specimen working papers provide examples of key recording documents which will help provide a structure for a unified approach.

The case study which follows illustrates the control and recording of an attestation audit of income in a typical public sector organization. This type of audit has been chosen as an example since a great variety of techniques can be illustrated concisely. The case study demonstrates most of the techniques dealt with in the chapter with the principal exceptions of review point clearance and standing data filing.

CASE STUDY 5.1 A PUBLIC BODY – ATTESTATION AUDIT OF INCOME

Schedule A0 shows the manager's review sheet for the audit. You will see that a wide range of useful points have been raised. The first relates to a lapse in internal audit procedures and is noted specifically as a training aid. Points 2 and 5 relate to audit efficiency and will assist future years' work. Points 3 and 4 relate to regularity as well as the value of specific assets of his client. Point 8 is the most important query raised. It appears that the accounts of this organization are mis-stated since no accrual appears to have been made for investment interest.

The reviewer has made some very useful observations on a good piece of audit work. The field auditor will now be able to answer these queries quickly and easily. Schedule A1 is the lead schedule. The reader can quickly see the items under audit and can locate the audit work using the cross-referencing. A2 summarizes the work done. You can see that by reading the schedule the reviewer is in no doubt as to the nature of the work. All the key points he would wish to know are simply set out. The most important is the conclusion.

A3 is the audit test programme. The level of detail shown here assists the field auditor, the reviewer and any subsequent auditors of the same figures. A4 and following, show the actual audit work carried out. Note how they give the reviewer **direct evidence** of the auditor's checking work. On A4 the exchequer grant due in the year is recorded with comparative figures. It has been ticked and expressly noted that it has been agreed to a notification letter from the government department. The field auditor has initialled the schedule, recorded the figure and stated the document he has vouched it to. The reviewer has cogent evidence that the right test has been carried out and carried out correctly.

A6 provides evidence for a chosen level of sampling which follows. This type of audit sampling is discussed in Chapter 8.

Schedule N1 shows the double-entry accounts for income – debtors. Income and debtors have been cross-referenced as appropriate. When auditing double-entry books it is important to consider both sides of a transaction to ensure that they are consistent and that errors have been avoided. In this case study it appears that the field auditor was not fully considering the book-keeping implications of his work. Chapter 7 discusses the importance of double-entry book-keeping in audit.

The simple layout of this audit work together with the cross-referencing and clearly described audit ticking make review straightforward and effective. The audit is well recorded and clearly controlled with the result that errors are avoided. The techniques shown are applicable to all the different types of audit work discussed in the book.

INCOME   A

Client: A Public Body		Year end: 31.12.89	Schedule No. A0
Subject: Income		Prepared by: STB	Reviewed by:
		Date: 21.5.89	Date:

REVIEW SHEET

Review point	Cross ref.	Point clearance	Initials
1. You have not concluded on your exchequer grant work.		A4	
2. Could you please put a copy of circular A10/Z on file.		A4	
3. Does the client have a policy on the type/ creditworthiness of institutions they will place investments with?		A5	
4. Is not this a management letter point? The 'Second Chance Building Society' does not sound a very safe haven for public funds.		A5	
5. We have relied rather too heavily on direct substantive testing of investment income. Next year we should use analytical review for more of our audit evidence. Please note on file for next year.		A6	
6. What is the average rate of interest paid in the year? Does it appear to be consistent with market rates?		A6	
7. From our testing it appears all investments were at a fixed rate of interest. Is this always the case or are variable rates also used?		A8	
8. Is there an accrual of investment income in the accounts? There does not appear to be accrual on the schedule of income received (A5). Nor is there a debtor on section N. Please clear this as soon as possible.		A5	
		N1	

Client: A Public Body	Year end: 31.3.89	Schedule No. A1
Subject: Income	Prepared by: ABS	Reviewed by: STB
	Date: 12.5.89	Date: 21.5.89

Summary of income – lead schedule

		1989 £	1988 £
Exchequer grant	A4	5,233,152 √	5,071,610
Investment income	A5	3,281,722 √	2,571,610
Sundry fees and charges	A9	3,077,791 √	2,999,023
		£11,592,665 β c	£10,642,243

√ = Agreed to ledger.
β = Agreed to accounts.
c = Cast agreed.

Client: A Public Body	Year end: 31.3.89	Schedule No. A2
Subject: Income	Prepared by: ABS Date: 12.5.89	Reviewed by: STB Date: 21.5.89

Introduction
Income is received from three sources the most important of which is exchequer grant. Investment income has increased recently due to higher interest rates and the continuing sale of surplus property. All amounts are invested short term in the money markets. Sundry fees and charges represent charges made to other public bodies for services provided under a small number of service contracts agreed every year.

Objective
That income is completely and accurately recorded in the accounts of the body.

Audit approach
Our audit approach is wholly substantive involving test checking of individual amounts to third party confirmations and documentation.

See Audit Programme for details.

Conclusion
Income is fairly stated.

A.B. Smith

Client: A Public Body	Year end: 31.3.89	Schedule No. A3
Subject: Income	Prepared by: ABS Date: 12.5.89	Reviewed by: STB Date: 21.5.89

Substantive Test Programme

Objective: That income is completely and accurately recorded in the accounts of the body.

	W.P. ref.	Initials
1. Obtain or compile a lead schedule showing income receivable by the body.	A1	ABS
2. Agree the lead schedule to the books of the body and ensure that the lead schedule agrees to the accounts under audit.	A1	ABS

Exchequer grant

	W.P. ref.	Initials
3. Obtain details of the exchequer grant due for the year from the notifications received from the government department.	A4	ABS
4. Ensure that the amount in the accounts for grant is the total due for the year rather than the cash received.	A4	ABS
5. Check that any debtor or creditor left on the grant account is correctly included in the accounts. Cross-reference to our debtor or creditor work.	A4	ABS

Investment income

	W.P. ref.	Initials
6. Obtain a schedule of investment income receivable in the year and agree this to the lead schedule.	A5	ABS
7. Obtain brokers' statements for each month of the year. Sampling will be made from these statements so as to test for understatement of income in the accounts.	A7	ABS
8. Calculate a monetary unit sample using the parameters laid out in the audit plan. Agree items sampled to the schedule of investment income and brokers' interest notifications.	A6 / A8	ABS / ABS

Client: A Public Body	Year end: 31.3.89	Schedule No. A4
Subject: Income	Prepared by: ABS Date: 12.5.89	Reviewed by: STB Date: 21.5.89

Exchequer grant

		1989 £	1988 £
B/fwd		507,161 ∧	497,103
Due in year	A1	5,233,152 √	5,071,610
Received in year		(5,216,998)	(5,061,552)
C/fwd		£523,315 α	£507,161
		c	c
		N1	

Payment details as set out in Circular A10/Z

Grant is paid in 10 equal instalments starting on 5 July each year. Consequently the last payment for the year is received after the year end.
    The 5 April payment has been agreed to the bank statement for the day.

∧ = Agreed to previous year's audit file.
√ = Agreed to notification.
α = Agreed to bank statement.
c = Cast agreed.

Client: A Public Body Subject: Income	Year end: 31.3.89 Prepared by: ABS Date: 12.5.89	Schedule No. A5 Reviewed by: STB Date: 21.5.89

Investment income received in the year

Date due	Investment	Amount £	Interest £
11.4.88	NatWest Bank	1,500,000	5,324.81
11.4.88	Newtown District Council	1,000,000	25,718.90
18.4.88	Hampshire Trust Company	5,000,000	201,232.88
24.4.88	Second Chance B.S.	2,500,000	10,743.01
•	•		
•	•		
•	•		
30.3.89	Abbey National B.S.	3,000,000	173,753.42
30.3.89	Lloyds Bank plc	1,000,000	130,222.60
			£3,077,790.74 c
			A1

c − Cast agreed.

Form MUS 1		Schedule No: Prepared by: ABS 12.5.89	
		Revised by: STB 21.5.89	
SAMPLE SIZE		Client/Dept: A Public Body	Ref: A6
Population	*Income*		
1. Testing materiality £	£75,000		
2. Population value £ A5	£3,077,791		
3. Reliability factor	2.3		
4. Sample size (2) × (3) (1)	94.39	The sample size is calculated at 95. However, since many interest figures are well over £32,607 in size the actual sample will probably be of about 30 items.	
5. Sample interval £ (2) (4)	32,607		

Note: Materiality and reliability factors are given in the audit plan.

| Client: A Public Body | Year end: 31.3.89 | Schedule No. A7 |
| Subject: Income | Prepared by: ABS Date: 12.5.89 | Reviewed by: STB Date: 21.5.89 |

Sampling from Brokers Statements
A Public Body uses 5 money market brokers for all its investments. Monthly statements of brokerage due are received from all 5 each month. They are all filed together for easy access by investment staff.

Method
Statements were arranged in alphabetical order of broker for each month and the monetary unit sample was taken manually using a calculator.

Results
No errors found.

Conclusion
Interest is fairly stated.

Client: A Public Body	Year end: 31.3.89	Schedule No. A8
Subject: Income	Prepared by: ABS Date: 12.5.89	Reviewed by: STB Date: 21.5.89

Test checking of investment income

Sampled from brokers' statements.

	Date	Name	Period (days)	Principal £	Rate	Agreed to sch. of income	Interest notific.	Interest correct
1.	18.4.88	Hampshire Trust	113	5,000,000	13%	√	√	√
2.	13.5.88	Abbey Nat.	101	4,000,000	12⅞%	√	√	√
	•	•						
	•	•						
	•	•						
28.	31.3.89	Abbey Nat.	151	3,000,000	14%	√	√	√
29.	31.3.89	Lloyds Bank	338	1,000,000	14%	√	√	√
					√	√	√	√
					×	—	—	—
					N/A	—	—	—
				Total		29	29	29

DEBTORS   N

Client: A Public Body	Year end: 31.3.89	Schedule No. N1
Subject: Debtor	Prepared by: ABS Date: 14.5.89	Reviewed by: STB Date: 21.5.89

Summary of debtors

		1989 £	*1988* £
Sundry debtors		972,573	851,973
Prepayments		157,890	207,154
Fees and charges receivable		175,987	301,362
Exchequer grant receivable	A4	523,315	507,161
		£1,829,765	£1,867,650

CONCLUDING POINTS

Most of the case studies in later chapters show the control and recording of audit work. The case study in this chapter shows such control and recording at a fairly basic level. However, the principles can be applied to all levels of work. The more complex the work the more important it is to have consistent recording and tight control over performance of work and review by senior staff. Standard documentation plays an important part in controlling the quality of audit. Examples of standard documentation are given in the appendix of working papers at the end of the book.

6 Gathering audit evidence – the systems based approach

INTRODUCTION

This chapter takes the reader through three distinct but related sections. That on audit evidence considers the need for, the nature of, and the methods of obtaining, audit evidence. Gathering audit evidence is at the heart of modern audit and this part of the chapter must be understood.

Internal controls are usually present in any organization and the ability to identify these controls is a prerequisite of systems based audit. The second section of the chapter covers this topic.

The section on the systems based approach takes up the rest of the chapter. An understanding of this approach is essential to achieve efficient and effective auditing. The approach discussed here provides a framework for undertaking the more refined techniques outlined in later chapters.

The examples within the chapter and the case studies which follow are chosen to illustrate typical stages of a systems based approach. Once the basic principles have been grasped they are applicable to virtually all audited bodies and a wide range of audit situations.

The chapter covers the central portion of the essential audit process. It discusses setting test objectives for systems based and non-systems based audit. Collecting test evidence is looked at with particular reference to the systems based approach. Lastly we consider test conclusions. Chapter 12 looks further at concluding on tests in the context of opinion forming.

AUDIT EVIDENCE

Need for audit evidence

'Gathering audit evidence' sounds deceptively easy, rather like gathering berries in a basket; first find the evidence then collect it all together. In practice things are more complicated. What is audit evidence, and why is it required?

Evidence is required to meet audit objectives. It can arise from almost any source and in many different forms. Here the advantages of a well planned audit come to the fore. The objectives of the audit and the consequent test objectives should furnish precise answers as to what evidence is required.

Audit objectives and test objectives

Broad objectives such as collecting 'evidence of sound internal controls', 'evidence of a suspected fraud', or 'evidence of good value for money' are high level objectives or audit objectives. A lower level objective might be 'that evidence exists of all payments being properly authorized'; this would be a test objective; it is narrower and helps fulfil one or more audit objectives. Ultimately, objectives and the evidence to satisfy these objectives are determined by the auditor's instructions (statutory or managerial) as was discussed in Chapter 2 (see Fig. 2.1). Auditors should always clarify objectives before testing.

As a general guide, the more relevant the evidence the easier it is to relate back to the objectives and instructions. This is a more effective and professional approach than that still sometimes practised by more 'traditional' auditors who, without setting high level objectives, merely check work in an effort to find past mistakes.

In a memorable case, almost equal time and manpower were given to auditing a miniscule personnel department with one full-time officer as to the housing department which employed over a hundred staff and was responsible for millions of pounds and the operation of highly complex systems. The original audit 'programmes' had been based on a list of heads of department in the front of the internal telephone directory.

The audits involved checking for errors similar to those found in past visits by vouching a large number of documents. The aim of such audits was basically 'to keep the staff on their toes, and to keep an eye out for fraud'. Even if resources had been more rationally allocated between departments much of the audit work would have been wasted. The staff spent weeks sifting through files and seizing on even the most trivial of inaccuracies. Without any high level audit objectives they were reduced to nitpicking with a consequent lowering of morale.

Table 6.1 gives some examples of high and low level objectives indicating the nature of the evidence required. Most of the questions and answers should have been raised during the preparation of an audit plan.

You will notice that some high level objectives are more usually associated with external auditors and others with internal auditors. This does not

Table 6.1 Audit evidence

High level audit objectives	Possible lower level test objectives	Possible sources of evidence[1]
Question: Evidence for what purpose? **Answer:** Evidence to satisfy:		
Such as:	Such as:	
To form an opinion on the accuracy of stock figures.	To assess the accuracy and reliability of stock-taking procedures (1 and 2). To evaluate stores purchases and issue systems (3 and 4).	1. Year-end stock certificates. 2. Audit attendance at stock-take. 3. System evaluation identifying controls and weaknesses followed by compliance testing of key controls. 4. Substantive testing of a sample of purchases and issues from requisition through to book-keeping.
To form an opinion on year-end cash figure in a set of accounts To form an opinion of security of cash income handling.	To assess the accuracy and reliability of accounting procedures (1, 2, 3 and 5). To evaluate the cash collection systems (3, 4 and 5)	1. Year-end bank reconciliations. 2. Year-end cash certificates for cash in hands of officers. 3. Bank statements and confirmations. 4. Systems evaluation and compliance testing controls. 5. Substantive testing of a sample of cash receipts.
To form an opinion and report to management on the reliability of the creditors system. To form an opinion on the accuracy of the year-end creditors figure	To ensure expenditure is adequately checked and controlled at each stage of the creditors system (1 and 2). To ensure only authorized expenditure is brought to account (3 and 5). To ensure all authorized expenditure is accounted for (4 and 5).	1. Document and evaluate controls and weaknesses in system. 2. Compliance test as required and determine the level of 3, 4 and 5 below. 3. Substantive checks from accounts to invoice and orders.[2] 4. Substantive checks from invoice to account.[2] 5. Analytically review current and prior years' figures and the figures for similar organizations.

1. Compliance and substantive tests referred to in the table are fully explained later in the chapter.
2. The need for these tests is discussed in Chapter 7.

prevent low level test objectives and evidence being of relevance to both auditors, though their relative priorities may differ. This accords with the basic theme outlined in Fig. 2.2.

When undertaking attestation audits, test objectives incorporate the following points:

(a) **Completeness** – to ensure all transactions that occurred were recorded, and that there is no understatement.
(b) **Occurrence** – to ensure that all recorded transactions did in fact occur, and that there is no overstatement.
(c) **Regularity** – to ensure all transactions are legal and properly auth-orized. This includes title to fixed assets.
(d) **Measurement** – to ensure all transactions are accurately calculated, measured or valued.
(e) **Disclosure** – to ensure all transactions are fairly classified and disclosed in the accounts.

Table 6.1 implies the need for a 'corporate' rather than a 'departmental' approach to audit. Most financial systems span at least two departments, and some span many departments. A 'departmental' approach along tradi-tional lines can only give a partial view of a large system. Thus records of cash collections or stores should be followed through all departments responsible. This is equally true for 'central' services such as creditors payments where different 'feeder' systems link into a common head-quarters system. Such a corporate approach will almost certainly reduce costs in the long term as auditors' efforts do not have to be repeated and common standards of recommendation can be more easily achieved. It is unlikely that evidence to meet audit objectives will be sufficient if it is not drawn from all parts of the relevant system.

The requirements of audit evidence

The Audit Practices Committee's Auditing Standard 'The Auditors' Operational Standard' states that: 'The Auditor should obtain relevant and reliable audit evidence sufficient to enable him to draw reasonable conclusions therefrom.' Three broad requirements are apparent from this statement, and it is on its ability to meet these requirements that the adequacy of audit evidence can be assessed. Audit evidence is required to be:

(a) Relevant,
(b) Reliable, and
(c) Sufficient.

The **relevance** of audit evidence depends upon its contribution to satisfying the audit objectives. The **reliability** of audit evidence depends upon its source. As a general rule, the hierarchy in Checklist 6.1 applies. Hard and fast rules are difficult to apply – apparently reliable evidence may turn out to be false or inaccurate at a later date. Finally, the **sufficiency** of audit evidence depends on the volume of testing required in the light of the materiality level chosen. The lower the materiality the larger the volume of testing. Sufficiency must also be considered in terms of the range of evidence from different sources. One source of evidence is seldom sufficient.

Checklist 6.1 Quality of evidence in descending order

1. **Sight of physical evidence**, e.g. verification of assets, title deeds, etc.
2. **Independent documentary evidence**, e.g. bank confirmations and statements, re-performance of checks and reconciliations by audit staff, vouching external invoices.
3. **In-house documentary evidence**, e.g. vouching of orders, analytical reviews, tests on internal controls (compliance testing).
4. **Independent oral evidence**, e.g. from customers, suppliers, etc.
5. **Statements by officers**, e.g. from interviewing key staff.

Two broad types of audit evidence

Checklist 6.1 illustrates that audit evidence can be of varying quality. Generally, the more direct, the better the quality of the evidence. Possession of deeds may prove ownership, though not value, of land for example, or counting stock may give evidence of purchases and stock balances. Such high quality **direct substantive evidence** is that which the auditor prefers. But unfortunately this quality of direct evidence is not always available.

This unavailability of direct evidence is not so much due to any inherent inaccessibility as to lack of audit resources. High quality direct evidence of the accuracy of accounts or the efficiency of a system costs much time and money to collect. For example, payments must be directly agreed to invoices, invoices to delivery advice notes, delivery advice note to orders, and for some items it may be necessary to view the asset purchased. Similarly, to substantiate the accuracy and completeness of rent debtors it may be necessary to substantiate debtor accounts and invoices raised and to agree till rolls and receipt books.

All this is very expensive and time-consuming work. One of the main advantages of the systems based approach is that it enables the auditor to use an indirect type of evidence – **compliance evidence**. Compliance evidence establishes the operational reliability of internal controls within a system which have been set up to control the processing of transactions such as those described above for payments and income. By relying on compliance evidence the amount of substantive evidence required can be reduced.

INTERNAL CONTROLS

Definition of internal control

The Auditing Guideline on Internal Controls defines an internal control as the 'individual component' of 'the whole system of controls financial and otherwise established by management in order to carry on the business of the enterprise in an orderly and efficient manner, ensure adherence to management policies, safeguard assets and secure as far as possible the completeness and accuracy of the records.' The definition is closely followed in CIPFA's Statement on Internal Control.

The auditor must isolate and examine those controls which contribute to his objectives. As the Guideline puts it: 'The auditor's objective in evaluating and testing internal controls is to determine the degree of reliance he may place on the information contained in the accounting records.'

Classification of internal control

Very broadly, controls fall into two categories:

(a) **Organizational** (often called general or environmental), and
(b) **Procedural** (often called application or specific).

Looking first at **procedural controls**, these can be conveniently classified into:

(a) **Physical** (Py) – designed to safeguard the custody of assets such as portable high value goods and cash. But note that they may be designed to limit access to these both directly, e.g. strongroom combinations, and via documents, e.g. plans of the location of high security areas.
(b) **Authorization** (Au) – designed to ensure that approval of transactions is undertaken by responsible and designated officials within regulatory limits, e.g. authorization of orders, invoices etc.
(c) **Accounting** (Ac) – usually these are arithmetical and recording functions. This will include such operations as checking of trial balances, checking invoice rates, reconciliation of cash accounts, and matching of documents such as orders with goods received notes.

Organizational controls are those that relate to the organization's working environment, in which procedural controls operate. These are more difficult to generalize but can be classified into:

(a) **Structural** (St) (note the Guideline calls these 'organizational') – involving a clear structure of responsibility and delegated authority. A structure plan or 'family-tree', for example, would identify items of reporting and delegated responsibility.

(b) **Segregation of duties** (Sg) – an important organizational control designed to avoid concentrating control in a single officer. Segregation can be set up at various stages of processing and recording. The following three functions are usually separated: custody of goods received, authorization of payment and the subsequent recording of payment in the accounts. Computerized systems should also, for example, separate system development (including programming) from operations.

(c) **Supervision** (Sp) – day-to-day arrangements for overseeing and checking transactions and security of assets. For example, supervision at opening of incoming post is an important control in most organizations.

(d) **Management** (M) – controls are very wide-ranging and include longer-term arrangements for overall supervision of staff, safeguarding of assets and review of financial and other arrangements. The provision of instructions, financial regulations and their updating, reviews and checks by internal audit, budgetary control, and monitoring of income and expenditure are all examples of possible management controls.

(e) **Personnel** (Pr) – controls inherent in formal recruitment procedures and minimum qualifications are often given less attention than other controls, but the reliability of personnel who operate other controls is a major factor in determining that these controls are themselves reliable.

Identification of internal controls

The examples of internal controls given in Table 6.2 have been chosen to show their most appropriate classification or combination of classifications according to the above types. In practice, two or three procedures can make up a control, often culminating in an authorization as written evidence that the control has taken place. This means that a single control may span two or even three of the above categories. Such 'hybrid' controls are not uncommon, for example where two or more authorizing signatures (Au) also represent a segregation of duties (Sg).

The examples outline some of the main controls needed to satisfy selected audit test objectives. As in Table 6.1 **the list is not exhaustive** and

Table 6.2 Examples of internal controls

Test objective	Possible system controls
Cash receipts system All cash receipts are promptly banked.	Daily bankings are recorded on paying-in slips date-stamped by bank. (Au) Bankings are made up and banked separately from cashiers'/cash collectors' duties. Paying-in slips are signed. Daily takings summaries are signed by cashiers and cash collectors. (Sp/Au) Till balances are checked, agreed and initialled by a chief cashier who does not undertake till duties. (Ac/Au/Sp) Late receipts and floats are locked in combination safe until next working day. (Py)
Capital contracts system Tenders are submitted on a fair and comparable basis.	Detailed and identical tender specifications are given simultaneously to all tendering firms. (Py/M) All firms are invited to attend all pre-tender site visits. (M/Py) All pre-tender enquiries and replies are documented and reviewed by a senior officer not involved in tendering. The senior officer certifies that standing orders have been complied with. (Sp/Au)
All submitted tenders are considered.	All tenders are opened in Committee and signed by those in attendance. (Au) All firms invited to tender are sent summary of rankings, non-receipts and late receipts. (M/Py)
Payroll system All additions, promotions and leavers are genuine, adequately authorized and timely.	A separation of duties exists between recruitment, promotion and termination undertaken by personnel department and payroll amendment by accounts staff. (Sp) All recruitments, promotions and terminations are amended on organization charts after approval by chief officer of the 'employing' branch and a senior personnel officer. (St/Sg) All recruitments, promotions and terminations are subject to: (a) agreed manpower budgets; (b) laid down qualifications; (c) laid down conditions of service. (M/Pr) All payroll amendments are calculated and signed by payroll officers on the basis of information provided by personnel and 'employing' branches. (Au/Sp)

Table 6.2 *Continued*

Test objective	Possible system controls

Payroll system *Continued*

<table>
<tr><td></td><td>Final signed authorization of payroll amendment is undertaken by a senior payroll officer not involved in calculating amendments
He has his own 'password' for computer input. (Au/Sp)
An annual staff in post (per personnel records) to payroll reconciliation – a 'ghost' check is undertaken by management. (M/Ac)</td></tr>
</table>

Sundry creditors expenditure system

Test objective	Possible system controls
Only required goods can be ordered.	All goods are requested on official orders requiring signatures of user/custodian and of head of branch. (Py/Au) All orders are made by central purchasing officer who agrees/negotiates the price and collates orders to ensure bulk discounts and avoid duplicate purchases. Purchasing officer countersigns order. (M/Au)
Only goods ordered can be paid for.	All invoices are agreed to orders and the invoices and orders are stamped 'Paid'. (Au)
All goods paid for were of satisfactory standard and cost.	Invoice signed by senior user or custodian to confirm adequacy and by purchasing officer to agree price. (Au/Sp)
All payments were for authorized invoices.	All invoices require final authorization by senior officer other than above, for example, head of branch to confirm all necessary procedures have been signed by responsible officials in whom he has complete confidence. Spot checks on supporting documentation are carried out and recorded by senior officer. (Au/M/St)

Benefit claims system

Test objective	Possible system controls
All claims correspond to laid down conditions of eligibility.	Claims are made on standard forms with a signed and dated declaration by claimant. (Au/Py) Countersignatures are requested from doctors, lawyers and social workers in laid down circumstances. (Au) Signed certificates of earnings or unemployment are received in all cases. (Au) Claim details are calculated and input checked and verified by separate officers who sign each application form after input to computer terminal. (Sp/Au)

you will have to isolate your own controls and test objectives in practice. Statements and publications by all the main professional bodies contain copious examples of internal controls, CIPFA's 'Internal Control Questionnaires' for example. It is unlikely that any one system will contain all possible relevant internal controls. In practice, the auditor will exercise his professional judgement when deciding if controls are relevant.

Common problems when identifying internal controls

Problems arising from complexity

Management will usually have a wide range of controls for purposes such as safeguarding assets, measuring and controlling workflows, and to ensure compliance with political and administrative directives. Some, if not most, of the controls will be internal controls of the type discussed above.

Difficulties can arise in distinguishing between genuine internal controls and similar procedures that are not internal controls. Difficulties also arise in choosing those controls that are 'key' financial controls from among all the controls of varying importance that may exist. In such difficulties the auditor must ask: 'How useful are the procedures in satisfying a test objective?' All key controls will help satisfy at least one test objective.

A source of possible confusion for the auditor, especially the external auditor, arises when procedures form a reliable internal control in one organization or branch, but when repeated in another do not form a control. Take stock records and stock-taking procedures, for example. These usually have the initials or stamp of some independent stockcheck, perhaps carried out to the highest standard, but often designed to meet different objectives.

All other things being equal, the initials or stamp left after stock records are agreed to stock will provide the auditor with much more confidence in the security of stock and accuracy of stock figures than the initials or stamp of a check against reorder level. Yet in both cases a 'stockcheck' may be carried out by independent officers, and both cases involve the counting of stock. Both leave similar documentary evidence behind and are often discussed in very similar ways by client staff.

Obviously the auditor must look beyond the mere signatures into the detailed mechanics of a control to determine its audit value. The auditor must always be certain of the purpose of the procedures that go to make up the control – 'How do these procedures satisfy the control test objective?' is the key question he must ask.

Problems arising from change

Not only can it be difficult to pick out important financial controls relevant for audit purposes but the nature of these controls is likely to change.

Changes in work practices, extra duties in response to new policies, changes in political leadership, or simply new management, all can have an effect on controls.

Changes brought about by new technology often risk weakening controls. Consider a new manager who sees an opportunity to decrease transaction processing times by introducing on-line computer updating to replace a manual system for benefit payments. Under a manual system, transactions from initial application, through payment calculation to actual payment and posting will most likely involve at least two and usually several officers, often including checks by supervisory staff. Miscalculation, fraud or mis-posting would normally require collusion to go unnoticed.

Control may be weakened under the on-line system in question if a single officer can handle all aspects of the transaction from start to finish. The manager must be aware of the control inherent in the manual separation of duties outlined above and must decide whether or not to institute compensatory controls. In this case, random checks by management of output to input, perhaps combined with 'reasonableness' checks written into the computer program might be considered. The auditor will need to assess his evaluation of internal controls in the light of each manager's decisions.

THE SYSTEMS BASED APPROACH

An overview

The systems based approach to audit is rather like modern architecture – easy to recognize but difficult to encompass in a single definition. The recent Exposure Draft on internal audit said:

> A system is a series of interrelated procedures composed of processes and controls designed to operate together to achieve a planned objective. Processes are those activities which aim to process data, transactions and operations through the system. Controls ensure that processes accord with the system's objectives. (Paragraph 71)

The Auditor's Operational Standard stresses the need to ascertain the system and evaluate the controls as two separate requirements, implying the former should always be undertaken but the latter may be dispensed with in some circumstances:

3. Accounting Systems: The auditor should ascertain the enterprise's system of recording and processing transactions and assess its adequacy as a basis for the preparation of financial statements.

5. Internal Controls: If the auditor wishes to place reliance on any internal controls, he should ascertain and evaluate those controls and perform compliance tests on their operation.

From the foregoing we can see that the systems based approach will include at least one of the following main stages:

(a) **It will record the structures and procedures making up the system** and, usually in conjunction with (b) below, assess their adequacy as a basis for the preparation of accounts or other financial information, such as budgets. Occasionally such basic work may reveal inadequacy and lack of internal control, indicating that (b) below may be a waste of time; (c) may then be tackled directly.

(b) **It will identify internal controls within the system**, procedural and organizational controls that enable the system to check and control its own behaviour including its reaction to both internal and external events. In this way the system can be, to varying degrees, self-checking. It may involve testing some or all of the controls identified to judge whether or not they function effectively – 'compliance' testing. It will identify and assess the consequences of the absence of or breakdown in the operation of internal controls.

(c) **It will use the results of compliance testing of internal controls to help determine the type and extent of further audit work.** This will include direct substantiation of the accuracy and validity of individual transactions, analytical reviews, predictive tests, inter-year comparisons and any other 'substantive' testing judged necessary.

Table 6.3 presents a chronological overview of the systems based approach. In normal circumstances the auditor will therefore undertake at least substantive testing and in most cases some level of compliance testing will be appropriate. This accords with Fig. 2.1 which highlights testing as the main feature of audit work. Occasionally the auditor may find himself unable to proceed beyond the system's evaluation and documentation stage. He may have pointed out the controls and weaknesses that appear to exist and have presented his initial documentation to management, either directly or summarized in a report or memorandum. Perhaps, because the management are confident in an apparently secure system or because they fear some criticism if tests reveal serious errors, they may refuse to sanction further work. In this situation the external auditor may be able to refuse to certify the accounts. But for the internal auditor this will be a time for testing his independence. If he cannot report his findings and concern to the very top of the organization his ability to circumvent the 'blocking' management and form a full professional opinion will be frustrated. Even in these rather extreme situations the auditor is duty bound

Table 6.3 The systems based audit – an overview

Stage 1 Initial evaluation and documentation

1. **Initial evaluation**. Define the extent of the system.
   Examine its role within the organization.
   Clarify audit objectives.
2. **Detailed documentation**. Record the system at the appropriate level, its structure, procedures and document flows.

Stage 2 Detailed assessment and compliance testing

3. **List test (control) objectives and identify internal controls** within the system that appear to satisfy one or more of these objectives.
4. **Assess internal controls** and weaknesses in the system. A clear assessment of the ability of an internal control to help satisfy an audit objective should be recorded. Any significant lack of control should be reported to management.
5. **Compliance and substantive test programmes** should be drawn up, or revised, on the basis of 4 above. Compliance testing should be undertaken to assess the operational reliability of internal controls as laid down in the Auditors' Operational Standard.
6. **Carry out compliance test programme**. The results of compliance testing should be used to update the detailed assessment and the level of substantive testing in the light of any deviations in internal control noticed during testing.

Stage 3 Substantive testing and concluding

7. **Substantive testing** should be undertaken in the light of the updated assessment and the auditor's professional judgement of the amount of direct evidence required to assess the validity, accuracy and completeness of transactions processed by the system.
8. **Conclude on the substantive testing**. The results of substantive testing should be reviewed and the ability of the system to produce reliable output figures should be concluded upon.
9. **Professional opinions** can now be formed on the security and effectiveness of the system and on the figures produced for accounts, budgets or other management information.
10. **Reporting** the results and opinions to management should take place, bearing in mind any points already raised at 4 above. If appropriate, the conclusions and opinions formed can be used in preparing an attestation certificate on the organization's annual accounts.

---

to form the best possible, albeit limited, opinion and to report this formally to management or, if sufficiently serious, the political members or appointees.

Initial evaluation and documentation

The **initial evaluation** should be a relatively brief procedure, but will normally be undertaken by experienced audit staff. At this stage the auditor is seeking to determine the overall appropriateness of the system for its role in the organization and the volumes and values of transactions processed. This would normally be mentioned in the audit plan. If a system purports to be one that processes invoices for payments, does it have the basic characteristics of a creditors payments system? Does it produce periodic totals and detailed breakdowns of each account? This initial evaluation should enable the auditor to judge the likely level of documentation required, and whether or not the system is appropriate as a basis for the preparation of accounts figures.

The **documentation stage** should be completed in whatever 'house style' the audit organization favours. Documenting controls and weaknesses can involve complex working papers. Documentation, particularly flowcharts, should as a general rule be sufficient for the auditor to perceive relevant procedures and identify the controls. A simple block diagram outlining key controls may be adequate. But when new staff come to take over the audit or the system changes rapidly, auditors can easily end up re-documenting the system or adding copious notes simply to familiarize themselves with document flows and procedures. The visiting auditor faced with the loss of a key control can find himself placing little or no reliance on a basically sound system, simply because he has insufficient documentation to identify compensating controls.

At the other extreme excessive documentation quickly becomes dated and misleading, or updating becomes a source of wasted time.

A balance between such extremes can often be struck by ensuring both internal controls and weaknesses are highlighted on flowcharts. Extensive areas devoid of either are likely to be irrelevant. Figure 6.1 illustrates a familiar flowcharting format with columns inserted to highlight controls 'C' and weaknesses 'W'. This format is particularly helpful when deciding whether procedures incorporate adequate controls and can compensate for identified weaknesses.

At Stage 2 in Table 6.3 the auditor will begin a **detailed assessment** of the system (assuming it is not completely inappropriate or obviously inadequate). By this stage, if not sooner, the auditor must have clarified his test objectives. Internal controls in the system should be chosen on the basis that they help satisfy these objectives. Table 6.1 gave examples of the line of reasoning to be followed from audit objective to test objective to internal control. It is possible for the auditor to follow this line of reasoning in either direction: having decided objectives he can seek out controls, or once he has identified a control he can ask what (if any) useful audit objective it serves.

Although the former direction is perhaps the most logical and should always be attempted, in practice it requires a high level of experience to identify all controls without working from both directions. This is

Client/Department

File Ref:

SYSTEM FLOWCHART

Title: Cash Income System

C = Control
KC = Key control
W = Weakness

Ref.	PROCEDURE		DOCUMENT FLOW	Comments and further notes

Cashing up at end of shift

⑧ Chief Cashier checks each cashier's takings to till roll, both parties sign a transfer control sheet (CD20)

CK

Sheet 2
CD20 → till roll
⑧

⑨ Cashier enters total on daily taking: summary (CD25) before posting to Head Office – copy retained.

Sheet 2
CD25
⑨

Banking the day's takings

⑬ Takings, carried in a pouch, are banked by single officers who follows a predictable route to the bank.

W

Sheet 4
Daily bankings

Sheet 4
Paying-in book

⑬

To sheet 6   To sheet 6

13 Weakness has been raised on two past occasions but management refuse to alter route or provide an escort. Report to go to Committee

Prepared AB	Revised CD	Revised	Revised

This sheet simply illustrates how a key control and a weakness might appear documented when part of a series of flowcharts of a major financial system.

particularly so if the auditor wishes to identify more than just a few key controls. It is sometimes the case that weaknesses identified in a system can be offset by 'compensating' controls. Before an auditor can decide whether the system as a whole has an adequate level of internal control he will need to identify a large number of controls before deciding which are ones upon which he wishes to place reliance. He will in any case normally wish to know whether he has found any significant weaknesses that exist. These considerations are often the source of practical difficulties in deciding the level of system documentation required for adequate evaluation.

It is on the basis of the documented controls and weaknesses that interim reports outlining any inherent weaknesses can even at this early stage be helpful to management. In fact management should be given every encouragement to view the auditor's evaluations and comment upon their accuracy. It is better for the auditor to learn of any mistakes or false impressions at this stage before starting detailed testing or writing off a control on which he may after all have been able to place reliance. Assuming the auditor's interim evaluations reveal an apparently adequate level of internal control the auditor should move quickly on to compliance testing, the first detailed stage of system testing (see Table 6.3). If even at this basic stage the internal controls in the system appear inadequate to achieve what he judges to be a worthwhile level of control then he should report his findings to management and move on to substantive testing.

Compliance testing

The basic idea underlying compliance testing is straightforward and outlined in Tables 6.1 and 6.3. A compliance test seeks to establish whether or not an internal control, already identified by the auditor, is working in practice throughout a given period. Examples are given in Fig. 6.1 column (3). The test is determined by the nature of the control and the auditor's judgement of how 'deeply' he needs to test the control procedures. In most cases, complete re-performance of the procedures will also amount to a 'substantive' test (see below, p. 127).

It is usual practice to draw up a 'programme' of compliance tests. Standard practice varies greatly between different organizations. At one extreme, tests can specify in great detail every action the auditor should perform, even quoting standard questions to obtain relevant documents. Such cases rarely tell the auditor why he is testing:

Stock Control No. 5 Stores
1. Take Audit Form 15 to Perform Stores Check 3.
2. Ask the Storekeeper for the keys for No. 5 storeroom.
3. Check room is locked before opening.

4. Open No. 5 storeroom.
5. Ask Storekeeper for his copy of form AB12.
6. Check each entry in column 5 of AB12 has been signed by Storekeeper.
7. Check each entry in column 7A has been signed by Purchasing Officer.
8. Check each code total for each item agrees to the total number for that coded item held on the shelf.
9. Note any discrepancies on Audit Form 15.
10. Lock storeroom No. 5 on completion of audit and return keys to Storekeeper.
11. File Audit Form 15 in File 22A33.

In this example the auditor could perform the tests without ever knowing what (if any) controls are being tested, and why it is necessary to test them.

At the other extreme compliance tests may be encountered that give the auditor little more than an objective without saying how it should be achieved:

Check that adequate stock checks are being carried out.

There is an understandable tendency for audit staff who are new to an audit to follow previous years' working papers. This is particularly true at either extreme illustrated above. In the first example the junior auditor is given the impression that a detailed number of precise steps must be followed and is likely to check his or her notes against those of the last auditor. In the second example a junior auditor is given far too little information and will probably follow every step taken by his or her predecessor. Neither case has much room for the auditor to spot irrelevant procedures, system changes or unsuspected errors, or to show initiative and an understanding of the purpose of the work.

In practice audit management must ensure that a programme meets the ability and needs of the audit staff. It should enable them to understand what controls must be tested, why they are performing the tests and how the controls in question can be tested. To reach such a balance of needs a programme must be sufficient for the auditor to understand:

(a) Why the test is required.
(b) What is being tested.
(c) How the test should be performed.
(d) What decisions or conclusions will need to be made from the findings.

It may be said that these points apply to any audit test, but in compliance tests these points need to be particularly clear because of the indirect nature of the evidence, otherwise it is very easy for the auditor to miss the point of the test. The points may be clarified as follows:

(a) **Why the test is required.** In compliance tests the purpose is always to obtain evidence of the operational reliability of the controls identified by the auditor.
(b) **What is being tested.** This follows from (a) – the control procedure is being tested, **not** the transactions being processed through the control procedure. Thus an error or 'deviation' in control over a £5 transaction is equally as serious as one over a £5,000 transaction from the viewpoint of compliance testing. If the system did not work for the £5 transaction the auditor has no evidence it will work for a £5,000 transaction being processed the same way.
(c) **How the test should be performed.** The relevant documents, locations, staff and procedures should be annotated on or cross-referenced to each test. This is particularly so for new staff who should be able to form an outline impression of people and events before starting the audit. A balance must be struck between the junior auditor arriving unprepared and unlikely to give an impression of professionalism and one filled with preconceived ideas. A senior auditor or manager must decide the level of appropriate detail.
(d) **Decisions or conclusions.** Whatever 'incidental' impressions are arrived at regarding, say, quality of staff and frequency of checking, the auditor's overriding objective is to form a conclusion on whether or not each chosen control was operating at the time or for the periods covered by the test.

Figure 6.2 takes the example of a contract audit. It lists the overall audit objectives that the system controls should satisfy and goes on to list key controls that might occur in practice. An auditor might well find that other controls operate within his organization; contract letting is often highly controlled and subject to very wide variations in circumstances between types of contract, different organizations and even different parts of the country. Nevertheless, for our purposes, the reader is asked to accept controls (a) to (m) and try relating the controls to objectives. The relationships given in the figure are the most likely, but in practice a key control may help satisfy more than one objective. (If, on reflection, the auditor considers the apparent control does not help satisfy an objective, then either the procedure does not after all constitute a worthwhile control or the auditor has not stated all his or her objectives.)

Procedures have been suggested for compliance testing some of the controls. You are invited to complete the list of tests and draw up a compliance test programme on the basis of your own organization. It is usually very helpful to have a single main document outlining the programme of compliance tests from which you can ascertain points (a) to (d) discussed above for each test to be undertaken. In most cases it is

Test objectives:

1. All contracts were necessary and adequately authorized.
2. All tenders were let on a fair and competitive basis (including compliance to standing orders).
3. All submitted tenders were equitably considered to arrive at the most suitable choice.
4. All contract work conformed to contract conditions (including variations and post-completion review).

Possible key controls:

Control	Related objective
(a) All contracts over £x must be approved by head of branch and the relevant Committee.	1
(b) All contracts over £2x are subject to a feasibility study before letting.	1
(c) Detailed and identical tender specifications are given to all tendering firms at the same time.	2
(d) All firms are invited to attend all pre-tender site visits.	2
(e) Tendering methods (e.g. open, select list, limited quotation, negotiation) are stipulated in standing orders for size of contract and any other prerequisite.	2
(f) A Chief Officer agrees/certifies that SOs have been complied with (or reason for deviation and Committee approval thereof).	2/1
(g) All tenders are opened by Committee and signed by those in attendance. If the lowest cost tender is not selected the reasons are fully documented.	3
(h) All firms invited to tender are sent list of tenders received, late receipts, nil returns.	3
(i) Each stage/variation of contract is certified by architect, surveyor or engineer as appropriate prior to any payment.	4
(j) All contracts over £x are subject to a laid down retention %.	4
(k) All site visits by certifying officers are recorded (date, location, those present, purpose and findings) in log/diary.	4
(l) All contract final accounts are subject to independent audit and certification.	4/1
(m) All contracts are subject to laid down post-completion performance review by senior officer who certifies an assessment sheet with gradings for key areas.	4

Possible compliance test:

Test	Related control	Related objective
A. Review Committee minutes and contract letting file to confirm:		
(i) Head of branch report	(a)	1
(ii) Committee approval	(a)	1
(iii) Feasibility study	(b)	1
(iv) Tender specs posted out to all firms on same date (date of letter)	(c)	2
(v) Invitations to site visits	(d)	2
(vi) Head of branch certificate of compliance.	(f)	2/1
B. Review SO's to confirm methods of tendering for size of contract.	(e)	2
C. Review tenders submitted and confirm signatures of Committee and lowest cost tender has been selected.	(g)	3

Fig. 6.2 Systems-based approach contract audit.

COMPLIANCE TEST PROGRAMME	Ref: I

System: Sundry Creditors Payments

Note: System evaluation and background information at File H should be read to confirm your understanding of the relevance of test procedures. Officers should be interviewed to confirm they understand the control element of their work.

Objective:
To discover whether or not the internal controls selected from our systems evaluation are operating effectively.

Prepared by: F.Irst

Undertaken by: S.Econd

Reviewed by: T.Hird

(1)	(2)	(3)	(4)	(5)	(6)
Control (test) objective (cross ref. to WPs if necessary)	Control procedures (cross ref. to File and WPs	Test ref.	Test procedure	Is the control operating? Y or N	Cross ref. to working papers
Only required goods are ordered	H.2.1	N/A	Select invoices as outlined on H.2.1 and check:		
	H.4.3	CT1	Only official orders used for each purchase.	Y	I 1.1
	H.4.3	CT2	All orders are signed and dated by line manager and any over £200 by Head of Branch.	Y	I 1.2
	H.4.3	CT3	All orders are countersigned by the Purchasing Officer.	Y	I 1.3
Only goods ordered are paid for	H.4.4	CT4	Select paid invoices as outlined on H.2.1 and check that corresponding orders stamped 'paid' are available to match each invoice.	Y	I 1.4
Goods paid for are satisfactory	H.4.4	CT5	For paid invoices selected check that senior custodian has signed to confirm adequacy and purchasing officer to confirm price acceptability.	Y	I 1.5
Only authorized invoices are paid	H.4.4	CT6	For paid invoices selected check that each is signed by Head of Branch.	Y	I 1.6

Conclusion:
The compliance testing objective has been satisfied. Internal controls are operating effectively.

Fig. 6.3 Compliance test programme format.

sufficient to cross-reference specific details of the control procedure if these are likely to clutter up the main programme. Figure 6.3 provides one possible format for a sundry creditors payments system.

In Fig. 6.3 the objective stated at the start of the programme and the control objectives listed in column (1) will satisfy requirement (a) why the auditor is testing. Column (2) should tell the auditor what he is testing, satisfying requirement (b), column (4) should explain how to perform the test, satisfying (c) and column (5) should satisfy requirement (d). The test procedures are based on the examples given in Table 6.2 for sundry creditors and are far from an exhaustive list.

The compliance test programme in Fig. 6.3 can become rather cluttered if a complex system with numerous controls is to be tested. Figure 6.8 later in the chapter illustrates a simpler format where each control is subject to a separate testing programme. This format is also useful where several controls and possible weaknesses relate to a single control objective.

Evaluating the results of compliance testing

The results of compliance testing will be used progressively to form three types of audit judgement:

(a) Whether or not the controls were operating satisfactorily throughout the period covered by the tests – usually up to a year.
(b) From (a) above it should be possible to decide how far each test objective has been satisfied.
(c) By considering (a) and (b) above for each test objective it will be possible for the auditor to build up an opinion of the level of operational control of the whole system. From this it can be decided how much audit assurance regarding the accuracy of the final output figures can be gained from the system controls and how much must be obtained from substantive evidence. This third judgement is crucial in deciding the number of transactions to be selected for detailed substantive testing, an aspect covered in detail in Chapter 8.

It will be apparent that in practice a significant element of professional judgement is called for in each of (a) to (c) above. For this reason evaluation of the results of compliance testing is usually undertaken by experienced audit staff and subjected to at least one 'peer' or management review.

Substantive testing

Substantive testing is always required if the auditor is to give more than very superficial opinions on the security of systems or any opinion on the accuracy of figures. Checklist 6.1 shows how the quality of substantive evidence is generally superior to that of compliance evidence. As described above, the auditor may **reduce** the level of substantive evidence required by taking into account compliance evidence of the satisfactory operation of controls. But it would be bordering on the irresponsible to ignore substantive evidence entirely. Compliance evidence is by nature indirect and can be several stages removed from the actual transaction event.

Substantive testing may be divided into two broad categories:

(a) **Direct substantive testing** (DST) where the accuracy, validity and completeness of transactions is substantiated;
(b) **Analytical review techniques** (AR) where trends and comparisons between balances and other related data such as output are compared over time or between locations.

Organizations may well use their own terms to describe the various tests. We will use these broad generic categories as they are becoming increasingly used throughout the public sector.

Direct substantive testing (DST)

Here the auditor seeks to verify the individual transaction selected for testing in respect of its completeness, occurrence, regularity and measurement. This is sometimes called a '100% DST' check.

The auditor will seek to confirm that the transaction (and thereby the total balance or population):

(a) has no missing parts, i.e. is completely recorded in the books and fairly disclosed in the accounts;
(b) has genuinely occurred and that any fixed assets and stock actually exist;
(c) is in accordance with the law and the regulations applying to the audited body;
(d) has been accurately calculated, valued or otherwise measured.

Consider routine purchases. The path followed is broadly to check:

(a) The expense recorded is supported by a valid invoice or other request such as a claim. This should be done to verify that the expense recorded is as requested by the supplier.
(b) The invoice to delivery or goods received note to confirm that the expense incurred was for goods satisfactorily received.
(c) The delivery or goods received note to authorized order to confirm that goods received were actually required by the organization.

In practice the auditor may need to test further, especially for high value or high risk items. He may need to see for himself the goods received, say vehicles or computer hardware, or the work done such as a consultant's report. Only experience will enable the auditor to decide that he is certain he has substantiated a transaction.

It is often convenient to carry out compliance and substantive testing together. This is particularly so when the auditor has decided on a level of substantive testing to give himself a chosen level of confidence in the accuracy of a figure and such a choice has involved some reliance on internal controls based on previous years' evaluations and compliance testing. If the auditor subsequently finds that internal controls are not as reliable as anticipated he may need to extend his substantive testing. In practice the degree of reliance on internal controls can prove crucial in determining the number of transactions to be substantively tested, and

---

SUBSTANTIVE TEST PROGRAMME

Client/Department:

System/audit area:

Monetary value £pa:

Objective:

Tick   1. To gain direct substantive evidence of the accuracy, fairness and
☐   regularity of the above figures.

Tick   2. To assess the impact of known weaknesses or failures in internal
☐   controls.

Cross ref.

Method of selection (tick box)   Judgemental selection   H.V.
Other
Statistical sample
Analytical review

IC/W ref.	ST ref.	Test	WP ref.	Initials and date

Fig. 6.4 Substantive test programme format.

often the cost of the audit. The mechanics of selecting the number of items to be tested in such situations are dealt with in Chapter 8.

As with compliance testing a single test programme should be drawn up for substantive testing (or a joint programme for both). This should enable the auditor to understand why, what and how he is testing and what conclusions he needs to form. One possible format is given in Fig. 6.4.

Particular problems arise when testing the completeness of income. In most public bodies income is received from some form of tax or through the provision of intangible services rather than from sales of goods. With the notable exception of property rates it is often difficult to obtain direct evidence of income owed to the body. The problems inherent in such evasion of tax and revenues are far too complex to explore in detail here. Nevertheless substantive testing from basic records such as details of vehicle ownership to motor tax or from registers of property and residents to rates and community charges can still be undertaken to confirm evasion is not material once the prime record has been compiled. Substantive testing from individual revenue generating events such as wage payments, residence, property or vehicle ownership to the prime records and registers can also be undertaken. Though it must be said that unless the auditor has specific reasons to question such prime records it is often difficult to select cost-effective samples as each revenue-generating event usually involves considerable time and money to check.

Analytical review (AR)

The sort of problems discussed above are good examples of those which lend themselves more readily to audit by analytical review than by direct substantive testing. Standard reviews involve comparing current out-turn figures for income or expenditure as coded in detail by the body to past out-turn figures to reveal any significant trends or sudden fluctuations to which the auditor can direct his attention. Statistical time-series and trend analysis can be taken to great detail, involving analysing the trend into components such as:

(a) long-term trend over several years;
(b) cyclical fluctuations within a year;
(c) short-term (often unpredictable) fluctuations on a daily or weekly basis.

These techniques, however, are more often used in forecasting output, demand and other key variables than in audit. The auditor can sometimes use forecasting techniques in a manner referred to as 'predictive' testing to estimate likely income figures and compare them to actual income. However, caution is required on two fronts:

(a) The auditor must be familiar with the required analytical techniques such as regression analysis. This should not be beyond qualified staff though advice should be sought from other experts if required.

(b) Much of the analysis required by the auditor should be already available to management as part of the budgetary and cost analysis information to support their decision-making. The auditor must be careful not to duplicate their effort.

More straightforward analytical review techniques are discussed in the section on physical relationships in Chapter 7.

Comparisons, especially cost comparisons, are often valid over different branches, out-stations or even different authorities. A good example of these are the 'profiles' provided to each local authority by the Audit Commission. Other examples include purchasing surveys, regular summaries of income at point of collection and the detailed breakdowns of bank reconciliations.

Analytical review provides only a general exploitation of financial relationships. The wider issues involved in such exploitation are discussed in detail in Chapter 7.

Concluding the audit and forming an overall professional opinion

At least one initial evaluation, and usually a more detailed assessment of the system based on its documentation and the results of compliance testing, will have been completed before substantive testing results are available. A number of interim evaluations are possible and it is not unusual to find testing results and conclusions reviewed and evaluated throughout an audit by various senior audit staff. Interim letters and memoranda may have been sent to and replies received from client management. But at some stage all evaluations and test results must be brought together and used to form a final professional opinion and, if applicable, a major report.

This stage of the system based audit should follow the basic procedures outlined later in Chapter 12. In an attestation audit this 'final' opinion forming stage of the audit of a major system will form one of several 'interim' opinion stages of the audit of a set of accounts. Each system will usually generate all or part of a main account balance.

The details of the final audit review and opinion forming will therefore be discussed in the final chapter, but at this stage it is important to appreciate the need to document the final systems review and opinion in detail. As with systems documentation in general the more compact and self-explanatory the better. Each audit organization will have its own 'house style' but it is often helpful to summarize each stage of the audit and

SYSTEM RELIABILITY AUDIT
Progress Sheet

Instructions:
Complete in pencil and
update as required.

File ref.	System M = Main system S = Sub-system	DOCUMENTATION				SYSTEM EVALUATION			TESTING		EVALUATION OF RESULTS		
		Narrative	Detailed flow chart	Key control chart	Examples of main docs.	Other, e.g. ICQ, depth test	IC and W identified	Compliance test prog.	Substantive test prog.	Testing (CT) (ST)	Extended testing (ST)	Memo report	Assurance H.M.L.N.*	Comments inits.

* For completion by audit management

IC Internal control
W Weakness
CT Compliance test
ST Substantive test
H High assurance
M Medium assurance
L Low assurance
N No assurance

Fig. 6.5 System position statement.

the final conclusions on a single sheet or computer spreadsheet. Figure 6.5 outlines one possible format which is particularly useful for internal auditors. Each main stage of the audit can be signed off and dated by the auditor in charge and the manager can review the results and evaluations as the work progresses. The manager can also review the relative progress of each system audit as the year progresses.

'Watchdogs' versus 'troubleshooters'

For major systems a 'watchdog' role will always be required by both internal and external auditors, pointing out weaknesses and recommending corrective action where these are serious, but the continuous and at times friction-generating, system amendment role is counter-productive. In practice the auditor can all too easily fall into the role of permanent 'troubleshooter'. Every time a system change is proposed he will be consulted, all his recommended changes are monitored and nurtured, and like young plants they start to grow. A signature becomes countersigned, more and more checks are proposed and on the basis of past precedents these become difficult to resist.

Such a scenario may lead to a well controlled system but:

(a) It is usually very time-consuming for both auditor and auditee.
(b) The auditor, ever more closely involved in the system controls, begins to lose his independence as he becomes involved in the design or redesign of the system rather than simply recommending controls.
(c) It is the role of management to manage. Once the auditor has recommended changes and warned of the dangers and costs that may be involved if his advice is not heeded, management must be allowed to get on with their role. Only in the most extreme circumstances of wilful neglect or when presented with evidence of fraud should the auditor go beyond a strong recommendation, or qualification of any certificate, to the courts if necessary.

It is usually far more cost-effective in practice for the auditor to form an opinion on the internal controls and weaknesses and, where this indicates a poor system, he should be prepared to gain sufficient substantive evidence of the transactions processed by the system to assess the accuracy, validity and completeness of the total output. If the effect turns out to be as bad as he thought likely he is then in a much stronger position to argue his case for improved controls. If the substantive tests indicate that few errors have actually occurred, his case is less defensible as the controls may be more difficult to justify in terms of cost-effectiveness, but at the very least he can rest assured that material errors have not yet arisen and there is time for management to be persuaded of the need for tighter controls.

SUMMARY

In this chapter we have considered the need for evidence, its nature and quality. We have described how evidence should meet objectives, and how it should be gathered. The actual role of the systems based approach has been outlined and discussed in detail. Particular attention has been paid to compliance and substantive testing and how the auditor should standardize his documentation and evaluation of each stage of the audit.

The case studies which follow illustrate how systems based audits might progress. Case study 6.1 is set in a standard transaction processing environment and illustrates the main stages and possible documentation of an audit along the lines of Table 6.3. It is a fairly complicated case, and it is assumed the reader fully understands the chapter. Case study 6.2 is very short and illustrates a likely response to a completely unacceptable level of internal control discovered by an external auditor. The scenario is easy to understand but the implications require some thought. What action would you, the reader, recommend?

CASE STUDY 6.1 THE PATE OFFICE OF EMERGENCY TRAINING – SYSTEMS BASED AUDIT

The Pate Office of Emergency Training (POET) has recently been established. It provides emergency training courses for the police, fire, ambulance, mountain rescue, medical and armed services. It employs a headquarters staff of sixty and twenty more at three special training sites.

A central purchasing system is in operation covering all sites. The newly appointed Internal Auditor has decided to commence his evaluations of the main financial systems with the purchases system. Purchases are estimated to amount to £5,000,000 by the year end.

Stage 1 Initial evaluation and documentation

He has set his audit objectives – to form an opinion on the reliability of the purchases and creditor payments system. The primary objectives are as follows:

(a) Internal controls in the purchases and creditor payments system operate effectively.
(b) Financial records of purchases are complete and accurate.

There are as yet no internal financial regulations though *Government Accounting* has been adopted as a temporary model. POET has only been in existence for two months and the Auditor has little background

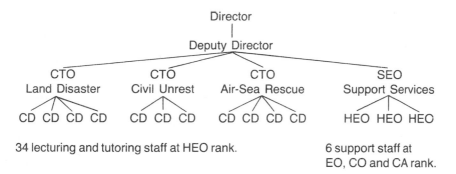

Fig. 6.6 Organizational structure of POET.

information available. A general 'family tree' is one of the few useful documents available, and is reproduced in Fig. 6.6.

By interviewing officers and planning document flows the Auditor notes the following information and begins drawing up the flowchart reproduced in Fig. 6.7. Note, points (a) to (j) following would be written out in addition to the flowchart, but are provided for the benefit of the reader.

(a) All orders are placed on triplicate official order form AF20; any telephone emergency orders are followed by an AF20 confirmation the same day. Orders are completed and signed by any requesting officer at CO level or above. Any order over £100 is countersigned by SEO or above. Bottom copy order is retained by the requisitioning officer, top two copies are sent to the Central Purchasing Officer (CPO).

(b) Each CD is in charge of a spending budget per course. Savings on one course can be vired to another.

(c) An EO working to HEO support services acts as the CPO. He forwards the top copy order to the supplier and retains the remaining copy.

(d) All purchases over £1,000 require three written estimates. Any purchases over £5,000 (mostly computer hardware) are subject to open tendering procedures including sealed bids. There are very few of the latter type and the Auditor decides he will substantiate each one individually.

Client/Department

File Ref:

SYSTEM FLOWCHART Title Purchases

C = Control
KC = Key control   W = Weakness

Ref.	PROCEDURE	C	W	DOCUMENT FLOW — Requesting Officer	C.P.O.	Stores/ site	Supplier	Accounts	Comments and further notes
1.	Triplicate official order AF20 made out and *signed*–countersigned if over £100.	KC							
2.	CPO splits AF20 top copy to supplier–order entered onto log. Undercopies held on temporary file.	C							
3.	On delivery to store/site delivery note *signed* by driver and storeman (or GRN made out and signed).	C							
4.	CPO *marks* order (copy 3) to record delivery.	C							
5.	Requesting officer *signs* order after checking quality and quantity of goods.	C							
6.	CPO attaches authorization slip AF22 to invoice.								
7.	CPO signs 'goods received' and 'prices acceptable' boxes after comparison of AF20s to invoice.	KC							
8.	Requesting officer signs and dates 'quantity correct' and condition satisfactory' boxes on AF22.	KC							

Prepared AB   Revised   Revised   Revised   Revised

Client/Department

File Ref:

SYSTEM FLOWCHART Title Purchases

C = Control
KC = Key control

W = Weakness

DOCUMENT FLOW

Ref.	PROCEDURE	C	W	Requesting Officer	Course Direction or SEO—5p5vs	Accounts—Crs.	Comments and further notes
9.	CD or SEO support services review invoice and slip for reasonableness of transaction and signatures evidencing prior stages of control. If satisfied he *signs* to authorize payment.	KC		AF22 / INV	9	From 1 (b)	
10.	CD/SEO marks off against budget and inserts budget code on AF22.	C			10	AF20s	
11.	CD/SEO stamps AF22 'Passed for Payment dated .../.../...'. AF22 and invoice are passed to Accounts Creditors for Payment.	C			11		
12.	Accounts clerk matches invoice to copy AF20s of order and checks arithmetic and coding before *signing* AF22 to confirm the match. Invoice is then processed through the creditors payments system. (Note this joint control procedure for both Purchases and Creditors systems.)		W			12	Weakness refers to the possibility that AF22 may become detached, perhaps deliberately, and find its way onto another invoice.

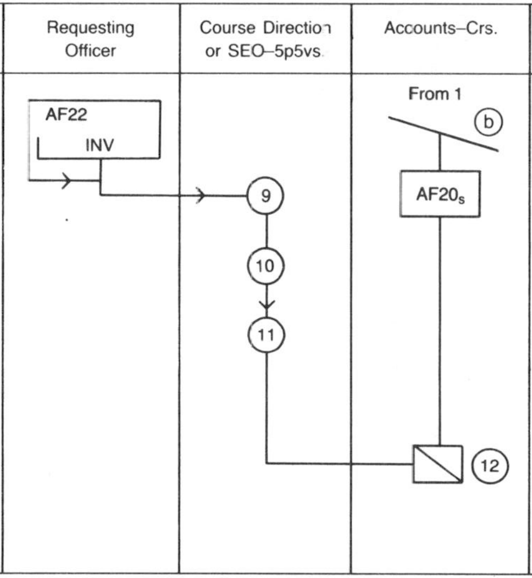

Prepared Revised Revised Revised Revised
AB

Fig. 6.7 System flowchart/POET.

(e) All HQ goods are received into a central stores; most special site goods are delivered direct to site. Normally a top copy of a delivery note is signed by the delivery driver and the storeman or site official to confirm delivery details. If not, a special goods received note is made out and signed by both parties.

(f) The CPO matches up all orders and deliveries. He also marks off all deliveries on his copy 2 orders and forwards these to Accounts, creditors payments section. The officer requesting the order, after being told of the delivery by the CPO, is required to check the satisfactory quantity and quality of the goods, and initials the CPO's copy 3 of the order.

(g) All invoices are marked for attention of the CPO, who agrees the details to his copy 3. This applies to combined invoice/delivery notes also.

(h) The CPO staples an authorization slip, AF22, and initials and dates the 'goods received' and 'prices acceptable' boxes on the slip. He forwards the invoice plus slip to the requesting officer who initials and dates the 'quantity correct' and 'condition satisfactory' boxes.

(i) The invoices are forwarded to the relevant CD or SEO support services, who checks that all the relevant stages are evidenced by correct signatures or initials of the appropriate officers and marks off the amount against the relevant budget. The CD or SEO enters the budget code onto the AF22 before stamping it 'Passed for Payment' and the date.

(j) Stamped documents are passed to Accounts (Creditors Section) for matching to copy 2 of orders and further processing through the creditors payments system.

Stage 2 Detailed assessment and compliance testing

As a result of the work in Stage 1, the auditor is now able to formulate his internal control objectives as follows:

Control objectives:
  (a) only genuinely required and authorized goods can be ordered;
  (b) only goods ordered can be accepted into stores or onto site;
  (c) only invoices for goods received and of satisfactory amount, condition and price can be passed for payment.

With these objectives in mind the Auditor identifies the controls in the system that help satisfy them and notes any system weaknesses (see, for example, Fig. 6.8 with regard to control objective (a) above). He records his work on the flowchart reproduced in Fig. 6.7.

From this work it can be noted that two weaknesses occur in the system:

Client/Department: POET File ref: Subject: Purchases system	Year end: Prepared by: Date:	Schedule No: Reviewed by: Date:

CONTROL OBJECTIVE ANALYSIS SHEET

Control objective:
Only genuinely required and authorized goods can be ordered.

Controls:	**Test procedures**
1. Triplicate official order AF20 is made out for every purchase. 2. All orders are signed by authorized personnel. Orders over £100 are countersigned by a second authorized signatory. (See H.8.) **Weaknesses:** 1. General lack of budgetary control. Budget holders need to give approval before commitment. (See H.9.1.)	Select *x* individual purchases from the expenditure tabulation. Trace these to copies of AF20 orders. Ensure AF20 has been signed and, where appropriate, countersigned to authorize the purchases by an authorized CO or above. (See audit programme at H.12.2.)

Conclusion:

Fig. 6.8 Audit documentation/POET.

(a) The authorization slip rather than the invoice is stamped 'Passed for Payment'. Although this is attached to the invoice it could easily become detached and the invoice paid twice. It is generally safer to stamp the invoice 'Passed for Payment'. Some organizations prefer to stamp a 'grid' on the reverse of each invoice rather than use a slip.

(b) The budget holders are not notified of payment until the organization is effectively committed to paying for the services or goods. Although this does not directly affect the security of the individual transaction it weakens management control. It would seem appropriate for each CD to be notified of each order prior to purchase.

At this early stage the Auditor does not intend to form an opinion on the completeness, accuracy and validity of a period's purchases and so no DST is proposed until the year-end. A compliance test programme is, however,

COMPLIANCE TEST PROGRAMME	Schedule No: H.12.2
Client/Department: POET	File Ref:
System: Purchases system	Prepared by
	Date:

Objective:

To discover whether or not the Internal Controls identified by our systems evaluation are operating effectively and can be relied upon when forming an audit opinion.

Note: System evaluation should be read before starting tests.

Control objective	Control (Fig. 6.7)	CT ref.	Test	WP ref.	Is the control working? Y/N	Initial and Date
(a)	1	CT$_1$	*Goods purchased* For a selection of purchases trace back to copies of AF20s. Ensure these have been authorized and if over £100 countersigned at appropriate level (CO and above).	H.17	Y	AB 20/1/X0
(b)	4	CT$_2$	For a selection of deliveries check that order AF20 has been marked off.	H.17	Y	AB 20/1/X0
(c)	6	CT$_3$	For a selection of purchases trace back to AF22 to verify that CPO signs correct boxes	H.18	Y	AB 20/1/X0
	7	CT$_4$	and that requesting officer signs correct boxes.	H.18	Y	AB 20/1/X0

Fig. 6.9 Audit documentation/POET.

drawn up by the Auditor along the lines of Fig. 6.3 (see Fig. 6.9) to test the operational reliability of the controls identified. The results of compliance testing will be taken into account in deciding upon the level of DST to be undertaken on the yearly out-turn figures.

At the year-end the Auditor has assembled the results of his compliance testing at several times throughout the year. The system weaknesses raised after his evaluation have been corrected by management and, to date, only two minor cases of deviations in internal control have been revealed, all of which appear to be isolated lapses of no significance. The Auditor's key working papers are shown in Figs 6.10 to 6.15.

On the basis of these results the auditor decides that he is justified in placing reliance on the internal controls in the system. He discusses his results with management and it is generally agreed that a system of this soundness should ensure that no material error is likely to arise.

Client/Department: POET File ref: H Subject: Purchases system	Year end: Prepared by: AB Date: 12.1.X1	Schedule No: H.14 Reviewed by: Date:

WORKING PAPER   Summary of results of compliance testing

Work undertaken:
   Working papers H.10 to H.25 refer. Lead schedule is at H.12. The Audit Programme at H.12.2.3 was undertaken on the dates noted at H.12.4 to give coverage throughout the year.

Findings:
   All controls appear to have been operating adequately throughout the year. Two minor deviations are noted at H.14.7, caused by an injury at work, that could only affect 14 transactions over a period of 1 day worth £210.47 in total.

Conclusions:
   A high level of audit assurance can be obtained from the internal controls over purchases.

Recommendation:
   Reliance on internal control be used to reduce our reliability factor by 1/3 for substantive testing.

2

Fig. 6.10 Audit documentation/POET.

Client/Department: POET File ref: H	Year end:	Schedule No: H.8
Subject: Purchases system	Prepared by: AB	Reviewed by:
	Date: 12.1.X1	Date:

P* ref.	C** ref.	Key control summary for: Purchases System
1	(a)	Authorization of triplicate official order.
8	(b)	Authorization of invoice by CD or SEO.
11	(c)	Matching of passed for payment invoices to orders by independent clerk in Accounts.
	(d)	Reliable level of separation of duties between custody, authorization of payment and book-keeping.

Fig. 6.11 Audit documentation/POET.

* Flowchart procedure reference, ** Control reference.

Client/Department: POET File ref: H	Year end:	Schedule No: H.8
Subject: Purchases system	Prepared by: AB	Reviewed by:
	Date: 12.1.X1	Date:

P* ref.	C** ref.	Summary of weakness and risk in: Purchases System
10	(a)	'Passed for Payment' stamp applied to AF22, rather than the invoice.
	(b)	General need for budget holders to be informed of expenditure before commitment to enhance overall management control.

Fig. 6.12 Audit documentation/POET.

* Flowchart procedure reference, ** Control reference.

Stage 3 Substantive testing and concluding

Both parties, management and audit, agree that they will be content to be 95% confident that errors do not amount to more than £50,000. To date, errors totalling £2.47 (overpayment) and £4.72 (underpayment) have been notified by suppliers.

SUBSTANTIVE TEST PROGRAMME	Schedule No.: H.13
System/audit area: Creditors/Purchases	File ref:
Monetary Value £pa:	Prepared by
Objective:	Date: 15.1.X0

Tick 1. To gain direct substantive evidence of accuracy, fairness and
☐✓   regularity of the above figures.

Tick 2. To assess the impact of known weaknesses or failures in internal
☐✓   controls.

Cross ref.

Method of selection (tick box) Judgemental selection H.V
                                                    Other
                                     Statistical sample
                                     Analytical review ☐✓

IC/W ref.	ST ref.	Test	WP ref.	Initials and date
N/A	ST1	For items selected according to our MUS sample of payments trace:	WP H.29.	AB 4.1.X1
	(a)	Back to supporting invoices for payee, amount (including rates and discounts) date and authorization. Check that the nature of the item is reasonable and does not appear *ultra vires*.		
N/A	(b)	Back to supporting orders to confirm agreement to invoices and review authorization and reasonableness of order.	WP H.29.	AB 4.1.X1

Fig. 6.13 Audit documentation/POET.

The auditor has now reached agreement on a sufficient number of variables to choose a statistical sample of payments to test substantively his (and management's) confidence in the system and estimate a monetary value of errors. From this he can judge the system's financial effectiveness. Chapter 8 discusses the procedures involved in obtaining and evaluating statistical samples.

Client/Department: POET File ref: H Subject: Purchases system	Year end: Prepared by: AB Date: 18.1.X1	Schedule No: H.18 Reviewed by: Date:

WORKING PAPER   Summary of results of substantive testing

Work undertaken:
> Working papers H.4 to H.9 and H.30 refer. Lead schedule is at H.5.
> The Audit Programme at H.6 was undertaken on the dates noted at
> H.12.4 for a monetary sample of transactions from throughout the year.

Findings:
> One overpayment error of £4.17 was discovered, which upon
> extrapolation gave a final upper error limit of £3,700. This is well within
> the materiality level chosen of £50,000. See WPs H.27 to 29.

Conclusion:
> The system appears to be operating effectively.

Recommendation:
> Next year's testing should take account of analytical review of
> comparative figures from this year.

2

Fig. 6.14 Audit documentation/POET.

Summary

This example has illustrated a quite common type of system and some of
the more likely internal controls. It represents a predictable situation in
which internal auditors can be expected to perform evaluations of new
systems.

CASE STUDY 6.2 HOW-BOTTOMY DISTRICT HEALTH AUTHORITY – INADEQUATE INTERNAL CONTROL

How-Bottomy District Health Authority employ 3,000 staff full time and
900 part time. A weekly payroll is produced each Thursday for weekly paid
staff and a monthly payroll is produced on the last working day of each
month.

POET (19×0–19×1)
SYSTEM RELIABILITY AUDIT
Progress Sheet

Schedule No: H.12.1
File ref:
Sheet: 1

File ref.	System M = Main system S = Sub-system	DOCUMENTATION					SYSTEM EVALUATION			TESTING		EVALUATION OF RESULTS		
		Narrative	Detailed flowchart	Key control chart	Examples of main docs.	Other, e.g. ICQ, depth test	IC and W identified	Compliance test prog.	Substantive test prog.	Testing (CT) (ST)	Extended testing (ST)	Memo report	Assurance H.M.L.N.	Comments inits.
	M PURCHASES	10/1/X0	13/1/X0	14/1/X0	10/1/X0		15/1/X0	10/1/X0	15/1/X0	20/1/X0 3/3/X0 3/8/X0 12/9/X0 20/12/X0	4–11/1/X1	14/1/X0 16/1/X1	H H H H H	AB AB AB Two miror deviations see WPH21 AB
	M CREDITORS	1/2/X0	8/2/X0		9.2.X0	11.3.X0	12.3.X0	12.3.X0	12.3.X0	17.3.X0 18.8.X0 21.11.X0 2.2.X1	19.7.X0	11.4.X1	H H M H	AB AB AB AB
	PAYROLL	4.5.X0	5.6.X0	5.6.X0	5.6.X0		6.6.X0	7.6.X0	7.6.X0	11.5.X0 9.11.X0	3.4.X1 12.12.X0	11.4.X1 14.12.X0	L L	AB Moneta y Errors WPL14 AB

IC Internal control
W Weakness

CT Compliance test
ST Substantive test

H High assurance
M Medium assurance

L Low assurance
N No assurance

Fig. 6.15 System position statement/POET.

The external auditor wishes to form an opinion on an account figure of £20,000,000 salaries and £5,000,000 wages. His examination of the system leads him to the following conclusions.

Stage 1 Initial evaluation

Although a regular and systematic set of procedures is followed by experienced staff, the following weaknesses in controls are immediately evident:

(a) Inadequate separation of duties between Personnel (including recruitment) and payroll amendment duties. The possibility of 'ghost' employees cannot be ruled out.

(b) Most of the weekly and some of the monthly staff work unsocial hours. The controls over the authorizing and checking of timesheets are inadequate. Some examples of unsigned timesheets have come to light during compliance testing by internal audit and the matter is under discussion with management.

(c) Controls over payroll amendment forms for starters, promotions and leavers are generally weak. Forms are not pre-numbered and are held in an unlockable cupboard from which almost any member of staff could obtain copies and forward to computer section.

(d) Computer input section are not aware of an authorized signatory list for authorizing amendment forms (even though such a list exists). One case has recently come to light of an unauthorized amendment being input.

(e) Wage packets are not signed for by employees who are paid in cash. A list is ticked, and uncollected packets are held in the cashier's safe.

Various other weaknesses in internal control were suspected by the auditor but by this point he had decided that he could place no reliance on the internal controls in the system.

Stage 3 Substantive testing

His interim letter to management points out weaknesses and his conclusion stresses that in order to form an opinion on the figures he will have to undertake extensive direct substantive testing of the year's payroll. He proposes to select a monetary unit sample (this procedure is explained in Chapter 8). He also mentions that if the management are not prepared to sanction this extra audit work he will have to consider qualifying his certificate of the accounts.

Summary

This brief example serves to illustrate a likely course of action in cases of serious lack of internal controls.

CONCLUDING POINTS

The logical nature of the systems based approach must be fully appreciated. It is always very risky to 'skimp' a stage. Just because the system controls appear to be operating does not mean that the auditor can forget about substantive testing. No auditor should rely too heavily upon unsubstantiated compliance evidence.

The auditor should always view his testing, compliance or substantive, as part of a wider audit and should judge the evidence produced in the light of his test and audit objectives.

Chapter 8 discusses statistical sampling techniques which are ideally suited to optimizing the efficiency of both compliance and substantive testing.

7 Exploiting financial relationships

INTRODUCTION

This chapter discusses how an auditor can pick the most efficient way of collecting audit evidence. First we look at how double-entry book-keeping systems can be used to cut audit testing substantially. We then go on to look at other relationships, some of them of an arithmetic nature, others more physical, which can often assist the auditor. Within the chapter analytical review techniques are also considered.

The chapter illustrates the techniques needed to exploit financial relationships both within the text and in the case studies at the end.

DIRECTIONAL TESTING

Given a set of figures that purport to represent information accurately the auditor has to check for both over- and understatement. As an example, assume that a list of revenue account expenses needs auditing. For the auditor to be confident that the list is correct he must be sure that two possibilities have not occurred:

(a) That some expenses that ought to be in the list are missing – check for understatement (the completeness of the list).
(b) That incorrect expenses have been included – check for overstatement (the genuine occurrence of items).

If the figures are the product of a double-entry book-keeping system that the auditor intends to examine in full then he can limit his audit testing of any one balance to **either** overstatement **or** understatement. If, however, the expense list has been produced from a single-entry receipts and payments accounting system such as those employed by many central government departments the auditor will have to check directly for **both** over- and understatement.

How is it, then, that the auditor of a system of double-entry books can reduce his testing by half? Remarkably few auditors are aware of the enormous labour-saving benefits of using **directional testing** as an integral part of their work. But the 'secret' of directional testing is no other than that double-entry books normally balance.

Once understood, directional testing is quite straightforward, although picking up the idea to begin with can present a few problems. The best way to explain it is by using an example illustrated with 'T' accounts. We will consider the small set of books below:

	Trial balance	
	Dr	Cr
	£	£
Income		200
Purchases (revenue)	100	
Debtors	160	
Creditors		60
	£260	£260

In this example debit accounts contain debit entries only and credit accounts only credit entries.

Let us say – as is normally done – that we will test all credits, in this case income and creditors for understatement and all debits for overstatement. First, it is necessary to explain exactly what over- and understatement mean in terms of testing methods:

(a) **Overstatement (or occurrence).** Overstatement occurs when a figure or a list of figures includes items additional to the correctly stated figures. In terms of testing this means that the list will be checked to supporting information to ensure that recorded transactions did, in fact, occur.

(b) **Understatement (or completeness).** Understatement occurs when a list of figures is incomplete. To ascertain this a complete population must be checked back to the list to ensure that this list has not missed figures.

These two checking ideas can be shown diagrammatically as in Fig. 7.1.

Let us assume we are checking revenue purchases. Since they are a debit we have said we will check these only for overstatement. We start, then, by selecting items from the purchase account and check them to supporting information – individual invoices. In testing like this, we are checking that there is an invoice and supporting documentation for all the entries in the purchases account, that is that the purchases account is not overstated by postings for which there is no proper evidence.

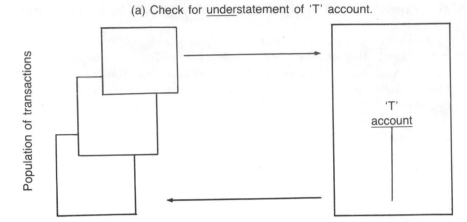

(a) Check for <u>under</u>statement of 'T' account.

(b) Check for <u>over</u>statement of 'T' account.

Fig. 7.1 Checking for overstatement and understatement.

At the same time, audit work is being carried out on balance sheet creditors. These will only be checked for understatement. This involves checking a sample of suppliers' statements or invoices to the creditors list (NB: **not** the list to the statements). The crucial aspect here is that when testing from the auditor's best estimate of a complete population, in this case a file of all known suppliers' statements, the accounts are not seen to be deficient. An invoice for use in checking for understatement must demonstrably be part of a complete population of purchases, whereas an invoice used for checking for overstatement is merely used to support an item in the list. Checking for understatement may seem a difficult task, but if for each invoice there were, say, a goods received note pre-numbered and part of a complete series, this would normally be sufficient to conclude that sampling was from a 'complete population'.

Similar work to that carried out on creditors and purchases is also carried out on debtors and income. Suppose that at the end of all this work the errors shown below were found. The journals for rectifying these errors are shown alongside so that the book-keeping effect can be clearly seen.

Errors   **Rectifying journal entries**

Purchases account

		Dr	Cr
		£	£
(a) Purchases included a figure of £10 believed to be a debtor misposted.	(a) Dr Debtors	10	
	Cr Purchases		10
	Being a misposting rectified.		

	Dr £	Cr £

(b) Purchases includes three invoices totalling £3 which should have been recorded in the new period.

(b) Dr Creditors   3
Cr Purchases   3
Being a cut-off error rectified.

Creditors account
(c) Creditors omit two invoices totalling £2 which were for goods received in old year.

(c) Dr Purchases   2
Cr Creditors   2
Being a cut-off error rectified.

Debtors account
(d) Debtors include a purchase misposted in error of £1.

(d) Dr Purchases   1
Cr Debtors   1
Being a misposting rectified.

Income account
(e) Income is understated due to a misposting of £5 to the creditors account.

(e) Dr Creditors   5
Cr Income   5
Being a misposting rectified.

Dr		Purchases A/c		Cr
	£			£
B/d	100	Journal (a)		10
Journal (c)	2	Journal (b)		3
Journal (d)	1	C/d		90
	£103			£103

Dr		Creditors A/c		Cr
	£			£
Journal (b)	3	B/d		60
Journal (e)	5	Journal (c)		2
C/d	54			
	£62			£62

Dr		Debtors A/c		Cr
	£			£
B/d	160	Journal (d)		1
Journal (a)	10	C/d		169
	£170			£170

Dr		Income A/c		Cr
	£			£
C/d	205	B/d		200
		Journal (e)		5
	£205			£205

It can be seen that by single one-way auditing, the four accounts listed have been audited for both over- and understatement.

General rules

The general rules we can draw from this are as follows:

(a) **A debit a/c**
   (i) Overstatement – picked up directly by audit testing that account, e.g. error (a).
   (ii) Understatement – found either as an overstatement of another debit account, e.g. error (d), or as the understatement of a creditor account, e.g. error (c).

(b) **A credit a/c**
   (i) Understatement – picked up directly by audit testing of that account, e.g. error (c).
   (ii) Overstatement – found either as an overstatement of the corresponding debit account for that double-entry, e.g. error (b), or as the understatement of another credit account from which the figure was omitted, e.g. error (e).

Overall situation

The completeness of directional testing can be shown in a matrix. Figure 7.2 displays the relationship between the primary testing, that is the direct testing of debit accounts for overstatement and the direct testing of credits for understatement, and the secondary results of those tests. In our example errors (d) and (b) for debit accounts and (b) and (e) for credit accounts are the secondary test results of the basic primary tests for overstatement on debits and understatement on credits.

Put more briefly, the matrix demonstrates that a test for overstatement on an asset or expense account simultaneously gives evidence on other asset and expense accounts regarding understatement and liability and income accounts concerning overstatement.

When the logic of directional testing is fully explained for all possible

Account polarity	Original directional test	Secondary testing result of original directional test			
		B/S A/cs		Revenue A/cs	
		Dr	Cr	Dr	Cr
Debit (assets and expenses)	Overstatement (+)	−	+	−	+
Credit (liabilities and income)	Understatement (−)	−	+	−	+

Fig. 7.2 Relationship between overstatement and understatement.

error types, some complexity may be perceived. However, the five basic errors found in our simple example were not difficult for any auditor to spot with due care. Neither were the journal entries required to rectify the errors unduly complex. Once the validity of the principle of directional testing has been absorbed, its application is not complicated.

PRACTICAL APPLICATION OF DIRECTIONAL TESTING

Having demonstrated the principles of this important labour-saving technique, we now need to present a few working rules. Normally credits are tested for understatement and debits for overstatement. There is no theoretical reason why testing cannot be carried out in the opposite direction. All accounts are relatively easily tested for overstatement, but some figures are very difficult to test for understatement. It is this which determines the polarity used.

The main point is that all audit staff must be working with a common directionality since failure to achieve this undermines the whole basis of the work. In most cases the norm of testing credits for understatement and debits for overstatement should be observed.

Accounts containing both debits and credits

Many accounts contain a mixture of both debit and credit entries. In most situations the number of one type will far out-number those of the other.

For instance, a purchase account may contain a few credit notes adjusting the original figures.

In situations where accounts contain a material number of such adjustments, the auditor must treat these adjustments as a separate population and test them under the correct directionality. Thus in the case of material amounts of credit notes in a revenue purchase account credit notes would be tested for understatement starting from a complete population of such credit notes.

Journals are a major source of adjustments and may require separate auditing for both over- and understatement. However, many ledger accounts subject to large journal adjustments are audited not as many separate accounting transactions but as one balance. For instance, fixed assets and stock accounts represent a finite number of physical items adding up to a single figure. If the balance as a whole is checked for overstatement by test checks on the 'physical' items of which it is composed, then the diverse accounting entries responsible for the balance will not require separate audit treatment. In this way, much work on journals is avoided.

Understatement

Checking for understatement is a major problem for all auditors. It is always difficult to know whether the set of books subject to audit is complete. Under creative accounting schemes, for instance, capital assets and their financing may be candidates for deliberate omission from accounts so that issues concerning government capital controls are not raised.

When using a directional testing approach, full consideration should be given to matters of understatement. Normally this will require the design of effective audit strategies for income, balance sheet creditors and loans (i.e. credit accounts). Auditors should **not** reject a directional testing approach if audit of understatement appears difficult. Audit of understatement is always as problematic whatever audit system is used. The validity of the directional testing approach rests primarily on the nature of double-entry book-keeping. Failure to find missing income or creditors will not affect this.

When a number of separate accounts are prepared by one accounts department there is always the possibility that transactions will be recorded in the wrong set of books. For example, purchase invoices relating to the Housing Revenue Account of a local authority may be recorded in error in the General Fund books.

If an HRA and GF are under simultaneous audit, then an omission in one fund should be simply found as an overstatement in the other. If, however, audit work is limited perhaps to the HRA alone, then audit problems may arise. Understatement of income is unlikely to be a special difficulty since the income prime records, such as produced by a housing rent system, should be complete. It is when auditing expenses that a difficulty may arise. How can the auditor be sure that housing expenses are complete? When incompleteness appears to be a problem, the auditor normally looks for a corresponding complete population to start testing from. In this case he would in any event agree supplier statements or, if not available, invoices to accounts in the books to ensure that entries have not been omitted. Using directional testing this is exactly the test undertaken since balance sheet creditors will in any case be tested for understatement by agreement of supplier statements or invoices to the accounts. If the auditor is further concerned with respect to understatement of purchases then he may consider it wise to test check more supplier statements back through the year.

Summary

Directional testing is an essential element of modern audit practice. The bases upon which it relies for completeness are those which are fundamental to double-entry book-keeping and hence all book-keeping systems of more than minimal complexity.

OTHER FINANCIAL RELATIONSHIPS

There are many financial relationships which can be used by auditors. Some depend directly on the nature of the service being provided by the organization under audit, while others, such as directional testing, are more accounts based and may be applied in most situations.

Financial relationships can be divided into two types, accounts based relationships and physical relationships.

The accounts based relationships

These relationships, which include directional testing, are based on the arithmetical nature of the accounts. The major audit tool derived from the use of these types of relationship, and which can be applied to nearly every audit, is the non-testing of cash receipts and payments. In audit work on revenue accounts – and in part capital accounts – the use of this financial relationship can halve the amount of work to be done. Together with directional testing these two audit techniques are of great use to the auditor.

Non-testing of cash receipts and payments

When work is done on revenue accounts, many auditors feel it is wise to check the cash receipts and payments transactions that relate to purchases and income. This particularly applies to large creditor supply payments. Such testing may not be an economical use of audit time and usually can be omitted totally when work is being carried out on purchases and income.

Consider the following trial balance and revenue accounts, perhaps relating to a museum shop. (A trading situation has been taken to illustrate the whole range of techniques available.)

Trial balance

	Dr £	Cr £
Income		100
Purchases	50	
Opening stock (Revenue A/c)		Nil
Opening stock (B/S)	Nil	
Closing stock (Revenue A/c)		10
Closing stock (B/S)	10	
Creditors		20
Debtors	70	
	£130	£130

Revenue account

	£	£
Income		100
Cost of sales:		
Purchases	50	
Stock movement	(10)	(40)
		£60
Surplus		

Balance sheet

	£
Debtors	70
Stock	10
	80
	(20)
Creditors	
	£60
Surplus for year	£60

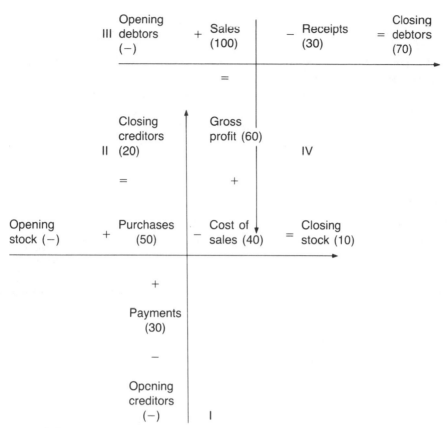

Fig. 7.3 Revenue/cash/balance sheet relationships.

These figures may be shown in diagrammatical form as in Fig. 7.3. When audit work is carried out on an account, the opening balance sheet figures may well have been audited the previous year. This will mean that opening creditors, debtors and stock are all figures in which the auditor already has confidence. By auditing the closing balance sheet, closing creditors, debtors and stock will be taken care of. For revenue account purposes, purchases and sales will be checked and that is the total work necessary.

(a) In the creditors' cycle (I) three out of four elements have been checked. Simple arithmetic ensures that further work on payment would be pure duplication.
(b) In the stock cycle (II) cost of sales needs no checking following the same logic as above.
(c) In the sales cycle (III) no work need be done on receipts if the other three figures have the auditor's confidence.

(d) Lastly, in the trading account relationship (IV) normally no figures are directly checked as sales and cost of sales are covered in (II) and (III).

Of course this audit scenario is only one possible way of auditing these figures. It may well be the case that gross mark-up is always 150% of cost, as in this example. In this case, the cost of sales figure could be checked by work on sales and gross profit margins. In this position little work need be done on either purchases or payments in the creditors' cycle. In some situations this may be a very efficient way of quickly auditing figures that at first sight may appear daunting.

Summary

In normal circumstances, the auditor will find that audit of the cash transactions, payments and receipts, are duplications of audit effort. In the wider concept of audit planning, the auditor should consider whether the nature of the figures subject to audit is such that the relationships inherent in all accounting systems can be used to advantage to eliminate much tedious and costly work.

At all events in the creditor, debtor, trading and stock cycles, the audit of one element within each cycle should normally be omitted.

PHYSICAL RELATIONSHIPS

Many figures in accounts represent physical activities. Usually there are relationships associated with these activities which the auditor can beneficially use in his work.

It is important to differentiate at this point between physical relationships for use by the auditor as part of his systems and transactions testing and those which may provide scope for analytical review techniques. In the former case, we are concerned with an exact relationship, for instance the contract disposal cost per tonne of rubbish for a local authority, and the number of tonnes collected and disposed of. The relationship here is exact, perhaps £5 per tonne and 50,000 tonnes disposed of.

Analytical review is concerned with less exact, but still potent, relationships, for example average wages, average staff numbers and personnel costs in revenue accounts. In their less exact form many of the physical relationships discussed in the chapter can be used to give substantive audit evidence by way of analytical review. (See also Chapter 6 on gathering audit evidence.)

The essence of physical relationships is that they are totally specific to the body subject to audit. Unlike directional testing and the other accounts based relationship discussed already, physical relationships cannot be automatically applied. Careful consideration of the nature of the undertaking and the audit objective are required. This analysis of the audit problem can be particularly satisfying if at the outcome a powerful and efficient method of auditing is devised.

On the majority of audits undertaken, it will become apparent that much traditional audit work can be cut to a bare minimum by relying on physical relationships. Income from squash court rentals, for instance, will depend on the number of bookings achieved during the year. Brief calculations using the booking sheets, given a standard charge per hour, will provide a precise figure for total income. This type of work can be extended to most of the income from a sports hall. The satisfaction gained in reducing perhaps days of traditionally based audit work to a few hours of interesting research and calculation can be immense.

The more common signs to look for when considering the possibility of the use of physical relationships can be listed.

(a) **Contractual relationships.** Wherever there is a contract in operation which is dependent on physical quantities that can be checked, there is a physical relationship that may be of audit use. Examples include refuse disposal, distribution costs and architect's fees.

(b) **Government grants.** The body under audit may be in receipt of grants based on physical criteria. A good example of these are the central government grants received by local authorities. These are generally calculated using formulae based on criteria such as numbers and ages of population. Using these figures the auditor can usually agree a substantial income figure.

(c) **Taxes and rates.** Some taxes and business rates are based on physical criteria. In the case of business rates, this is property. It is often a simple matter for the auditor to check rate or tax income by reference to the 'physical' data. In the case of rates, rateable values can be obtained directly and independently from the district valuer prior to checking rate income.

(d) **Overheads.** Overheads may be allocated on physical criteria, perhaps staff numbers. The auditor can easily check these figures.

(e) **Processing and treatment works.** Where either products or waste are chemically treated there is great scope for the use of physical relationships within the audit. Examples include the treatment of waste and refuse by urban authorities with a disposal problem and water treatment by water companies.

The important points to look for are fixed ratios. By using the ratio to predict, or more formally, to provide additional cogent audit evidence on accounts figures, very substantial time savings are possible.

Summary

Some physical relationships are so straightforward that the auditor may not normally categorize his work in this way; this possibly applies to the audit of overhead allocations. At other times the auditor will have to plan his use of these techniques thoroughly and carefully before work starts. In public sector audit work, it is indeed seldom that physical relations are not profitably employed by the auditor.

OVERALL SUMMARY

This chapter has dealt with some of the most important aspects of efficient audit techniques. These use relationships implicit in accounting systems or in the organization under audit to reduce work loads and improve efficiency.

Every modern audit should be able to rely heavily on directional testing where there are double-entry books. Cash receipt and payment transactions should seldom be tested. Accounting relationships should always be borne in mind and used to exploit the situation to the auditor's advantage. Physical relationships should always be used as audit tools for rate levies and government grants, as well as in many other specific situations, as mentioned above.

For many auditors the ideas dealt with in the chapter should be highly relevant. They are explicitly designed to remove drudgery and replace it with a fast, efficient, reasoned approach.

Case study 7.1 which follows relates to a local authority lottery audit. This example sets out to show the basic principles of directional testing in a straightforward audit situation. Examples of likely working papers are included. Working paper headings are omitted for conciseness.

Case study 7.2 again relates to a local authority but this time the situation is more complex. The emphasis is on the directional testing approach but with illustrations of other financial and physical relationships. Some explanation of the nature of the balances audited is given but some simplifying assumptions have been made to help highlight the techniques.

CASE STUDY 7.1 A LOCAL AUTHORITY LOTTERY AUDIT

This example uses two accounting relationships (directional testing and non-testing of cash payments and receipts) and one physical relationship.

Background

This is the first year of the lottery at Minacre District Council. The following figures are in the books of the authority as a whole and are the subject of the audit.

	Dr £	Cr £
Sales of tickets		10,000
Cash	9,000	
Purchases	1,500	
Creditors (B/S)		500
	£10,500	£10,500

The following information relates to the lottery:

(a) Each lottery ticket has a prenumbered counterfoil. This is retained after the sale of a ticket. Counterfoils are bound in small booklets which are stored in numerical order.

(b) Purchases recorded in the account relate to ticket purchases only. All other costs are borne by the Recreation Committee. A Council minute has been seen confirming this point.

(c) At the year-end there is no stock of unused tickets.

(d) All prizes were donated by eminent local people.

Objective: To ensure that the figures in the accounts properly represent the running of the lottery during the year.

Audit approach

(a) **Income (£10,000 credit).** Using the principle of directional testing, sales will be tested for understatement only. No work will be done on cash receipts.

The booklets of counterfoils will be test-checked to ensure complete continuity of numbering. Using this as a complete population of tickets sold, the value of tickets sold will be agreed in total to the sales account in the ledger. By using this physical relationship between the number of counterfoils and income, much detailed substantive testing is avoided.

(b) **Cash (£9,000 debit).** Cash, as always, is checked by re-performance of the period-end bank reconciliation.

(c) **Purchase (£1,500 debit).** Audit work will check for overstatement only. Cash transactions completing individual purchases will not be audited. Individual purchases will be test-checked to purchase invoices.

(d) **Creditors (£500).** Audit work will check for understatement only.

Ticket supplier statements for the period-end will be agreed or reconciled to the accounts.

Working papers

Income
Complete Population

The first and last booklets used in the year were found and agreed to details on purchase invoices – see purchases work.

First booklet No. 572000 $\sqrt{}$
Last booklet No. 591999 $\sqrt{}$

Five batches of ten booklets of counterfoils were checked for completeness.

573200–573250 $\wedge$
574350–574400 $\wedge$
574500–584550 $\wedge$
589950–590000 $\wedge$

No errors were found.

Conclusion:

Boxes of counterfoil booklets are a complete population of tickets sold.

J. Smith

$\wedge$ = Agreed to booklets. $\sqrt{}$ = Details agreed to purchase invoices.

Income
Accuracy of Income Acount

Income per a/c	£10,000
Sale price of ticket	50p
No. sold (572000–591999)	20,000
50p × 20,000 = £10,000.	$\wedge$

Conclusion:

Income is fairly stated.

J. Smith

$\wedge$ = Calculation agreed.

Cash
Reperformance of bank reconciliation

	£	
Balance per bank statement/letter	9,250	V
Unpresented cheques	(500)	β
Unbanked cash	250	α
	£9,000	$\sqrt{}$

Conclusion:

Cash is fairly stated.

J. Smith

∨ = Agreed to bank letter.
√ = Agreed to accounts.
β = Agreed to cash book and bank statement as cleared post year-end.
α = Counted physically at year-end and agreed.

Purchases

A sample of invoices selected from the purchase account were agreed to purchase invoices.

Date	Amount	Supplier	Agreed to invoices
4.4.86	£100	J. Bloggs	√
6.6.86	£50	B. Brown	√
10.10.86	£90	J. Bloggs	√
4.12.86	£40	B. Brown	√
10.1.87	£40	B. Brown	√

Conclusion:

Purchases are not overstated.

J. Smith

Creditors

Period-end supplier statement balances for the two ticket suppliers.

	£	
J. Bloggs	300	∧
B. Brown	200	∧
	£500	√
		c

Conclusion:

Creditors are fairly stated.

J. Smith

∧ = Agreed from statement to accounts.
√ = Agreed to accounts.
c = Cast agreed.

Statement of Audit Opinion

To be completed by Senior Auditor in charge of work:

(a) Have terms of the audit instructions been complied with?	√	P.R.
(b) Have satisfactory conclusions been drawn on all audit work?	√	P.R.
(c) Has all audit work been properly reviewed by senior staff?	√	P.R.
(d) Have all audit review points been satisfactorily answered by those carrying out the work?	√	P.R.

Audit Opinion

To the Chief Executive

In my opinion the lottery accounts as contained within the books of account of the authority as a whole on 31 March 1987 properly represent the running of the lottery during the year end of its position at the year-end.

P. Robinson
24.4.87

CASE STUDY 7.2 PLANNING MEMORANDUM FOR EXTERNAL AUDIT OF A SIMPLIFIED LOCAL AUTHORITY

This example shows a planning memorandum such as described in Chapter 4 on planning for a simplified local authority with no housing duties, subject to external audit. The memorandum lays particular stress on directional testing and accounts based relationships.

The object of the audit work is to be able to give an opinion on the 'fair presentation' of the position of the authority at the balance sheet date and during the year up to that date as shown in the authority's statement of accounts prepared under local authority account and audit regulations.

Planning Memorandum for Brighoughton-in-the Marsh District Council year-end 31 March 199X

Contents   *Notes*
(1) Background
(2) Client contacts
(3) Audit staffing

(4) Agenda

(5) Matters occurring during the year.

(6) Recent figures

(7) Materiality

(8) Detailed audit approach

⎫
⎬
⎭ Details of 2, 3, 4, 5 and 7 omitted in this example.

(1) Background

Brighoughton-in-the-Marsh District Council is a relatively small, basically rural, district. The offices have been recently centralized in Brighoughton in a new purpose-built block. In previous years the Finance Department was in the small village of Batbury somewhat removed from the other council functions. This office has yet to be sold.

(6) Recent figures

Consolidated Balance Sheet

	199X £000		199X £000
Revenue balances	15,100	Capital outlay	35,000
Specific funds	1,600	Capital discharged	(16,200)
	16,700		18,800
		Deferred charges	8,500
Short-term creditors	460	Short-term debtors	470
Loans	11,810	Other debtors	1,100
		Cash	100
	£28,970		£28,970

Revenue Account

	199X £000	199X £000
Net Committee expenditure		4,500
Less: Rates	1,050	
Community charge	1,150	
Central Government grant	3,190	6,110
Net contribution to funds		£(1,610)

(8) Detailed audit approach

Balance sheet accounts

(a) Capital outlay

The majority of fixed assets are council leisure centres, offices and industrial units. There are no council houses.

Audit testing is for overstatement. Our work will concentrate on sub-stantive testing vouching additions. However, some physical testing of assets from the property register will be done. This will give additional audit evidence on brought forward asset figures and help in ensuring complete alienation of assets disposed of. Care will be taken to ensure that the new centralized office building has been properly accounted for and that there has not been a breach of government capital controls. No material disposals are expected.

Understatement of fixed assets is primarily covered by work on revenue expense accounts. No fixed asset purchases will be traced for evidence of payment.

(b) Capital discharged
This figure represents internal movements. The balance of capital outlay less capital discharged is the value of fixed assets financed by loan at the balance sheet date. The yearly movement of capital discharged is taken to revenue accounts and represents the repayment of debt. The accounting double entries for insertion into the books are as follows:

Dr   Revenue A/cs (Debt charges)   X
Cr   Capital outlay (Capital discharged)   X

being internal capital repaid on assets during the year.

Since capital discharged is a credit in the balance sheet and a debit in the revenue accounts, it is directly audited for both over- and understatement. Movements in the year will be tied in with the loans pool figures and capital outlay movements. Care will be taken to ensure that fixed asset disposals are correctly reflected in all relevant accounts. Loans pool repayment calculations will be test-checked for numerical accuracy and reviewed to ensure that reasonable repayment rates consistent with statutory guidelines have been complied with.

(c) Deferred charges
The majority of deferred charges at this authority relate to historic building grants. Again, we test for overstatement, since deferred charges are assets. Our audit work concentrates on movements in the year. We will substan-tively test debits from the account in the authority's books to properly authorized supporting documentation. Our work will include limited phy-sical checking of properties to ensure that improvement work was indeed carried out. Our major source of evidence on understatement comes from work on other asset/expense accounts. No testing is necessary on the actual payment of grant monies.

(d) Government and local authority debtors and creditors
These sums, in the main, represent the residues on grant accounts with

the county and central government. In accounting terms they can be represented as follows:

Highways Claim

Brought forward:	£		£
Residue unpaid at the end of last year	X		
Amount claimed and due in year	X	Amount received from the county in the year	X
Carried forward:			X
Over-payment due to the county	X	Adjustment for previous years	
	£X		£X

The amounts claimed for the year will be audited for understatement as part of our income work – see (k) (iii) below.

In some cases it is possible to verify the year-end balance with the authority or government department concerned. In these situations no work will be done on the cash transactions that took place. However, where direct verification is not possible the cash figures will be checked to remittance slips to ensure that the year-end balance is correct.

(e) Other debtors

Brighoughton District Council has had a problem in the collection of its rates and community charge for a number of years now. About a third of debtors are as a result of this problem. Other debtors relate to sundry income and staff car loans.

This year we propose to audit rate and community charge debts for overstatement by direct postal circularization of a sample of the debtors concerned. The same method will be used to audit staff car loans. Sundry debtors will be substantively tested for overstatement to supporting records. The assistance of internal audit may be useful in this area. Understatement of debtors is in part covered by the process of circularization but work on the understatement of income gives strong audit assurance on understatement of debtors.

(f) Cash

As normal, audit work will be by circularization of all banks used by the authority and full re-performance of the year-end bank reconciliations.

The cash systems of Brighoughton District Council are a little antiquated making the reconciliation process complex. Special care will therefore be taken in this audit area.

(g) Loans
Despite the magnitude of these figures, audit work is reasonably straight-forward. The vast majority of borrowing is from the Public Works Loans Board from whom we receive independent balance confirmation.

Audit work concentrates on understatement for liabilities so the remainder of loans are audited by agreeing balances outstanding on money market brokers' statements, for all those used recently, to the accounts. The unlikely occurrence of overstatement would be picked up on the balance confirmation from the Loans Board, and more generally by work on overstatement of cash or investments.

(h) Short-term creditors
Creditors are composed of a number of important figures of about equal size.

(i) *Supplier creditors*. This figure is audited for understatement substantively by checking from files of supplier statements or paid after-date invoices to accounts figures.
(ii) *Loan interest accrued*. Loans Board statements are agreed to the accounts figure, effectively checking for understatement.
(iii) *Salaries accrued*. This figure is tied in with our revenue account work.
(iv) *Provisions and contingencies*. These figures are audited for both over- and understatement in conjunction with the revenue accounts, by discussion with authority officials, checking with the authority's documentation and agreement to council minutes. Particular care should be taken if there are any 'reserved creditors', figures for estimates of expenditure incurred in the year but not billed. Often these figures are unrealistically high in an attempt to utilize fully expenditure allocations for the year. As part of the audit of the debit in the revenue account these figures should be carefully audited for overstatement. (NB: Reserved creditors are not the same as contingency reserve movements authorized by council minutes.)

Overstatement of creditors is covered by the routine overstatement testing of revenue expenses and asset accounts. No additional testing is needed on most creditors.

(i) Revenue reserves
Reserve figures will be audited to ensure that movements are consistent with revenue account surpluses and deficiencies.

(j) Funds
Funds are amounts of money 'saved' for specific uses. Fund assets are normally cash invested internally with the loans fund reducing overall borrowing. Our audit work concentrates on the movements in the year on fund balances and seeks to tie these movements in with the relevant

council minute authorizing the moves. Routine movements such as on the repairs and renewals fund will be reviewed for reasonability and test-checked to the various receiving and contributing revenue accounts.

Revenue accounts

(k) Income
As with most district authorities income at this authority is an area which, in the main, can be quickly and efficiently audited using the physical relationships on which the income is based.

(i) *Business rates*. These are audited substantively for understatement by recalculation of the sums due from the information given on the government valuer's valuation report for the area. Voids and write-offs should be checked for overstatement (as debits to the revenue account) if material. No audit work is required on cash receipts since the debtor will have been audited as part of our balance sheet work.

(ii) *Government grant*. The grant is based on a formula which uses a number of physical characteristics within the district, such as population. The grant income figure in the accounts should be checked by recalculating the grant due and checking the figures used in the formula to government statistics.

(iii) *Grant income netted off committee expenditure*. The audit of grant income for final accounts purposes is marginally problematic in that grants receivable are often based on expenditure authorized by the authority itself. For the purpose of this audit no detailed authorization work will be carried out. Our work on income understatement will, therefore, be based on agreement of grant documentation from paying authorities to the accounts, followed by a searching review of grant income and allowable expenditure to ensure that gross authorizational errors are absent. This work then ties in with our work on grant claim debtors and creditors – see (d) above.

(iv) *Sundry income netted off committee expenditure*. This form of income is from a variety of sources such as car parking charges and rental of town halls. Depending on the size of the figures this year, review of the income in each category should be sufficient. If this should prove inadequate, substantive testing of some major income areas for understatement will be required. Such testing may involve such work as testing from hall booking sheets to income figures in the accounts.

(l) Expenditure
Expenditure divides into five areas all of which will be tested for over-statement. Expenditure is a debit in the revenue account. Some very major sources of expenditure – debt charges and loan interest – may be audited reasonably quickly in conjunction with our loans work. Other expenses require more detailed checking.

(i)   *Supplier payments.* Our testing involves substantive work from the books of account to invoices. Emphasis will be placed on the applicability of coding of expenses to the correct account areas. The extent to which we will be able to rely on compliance work in this area will depend on the strength of controls present. However, with the recent worries about fraud in this department we should pin little hope on internal controls allowing us to reducing our substantive work.

(ii) *Payroll.* Staff costs are one of the major expenses an authority has to bear. Our work is based on checking for overstatement, so audit work will concentrate on testing the accounts to the payrolls and the payrolls to personnel records and time sheets. Analytical review of staff costs and pay rises will provide useful additional evidence.

(iii) *Loan interest.* Major interest payments will be test-checked from the books of account to Loan Board statements.

(iv) *Debt charges.* This work will be carried out as a part of the work on capital discharged – see (b) above.

(v)   *Payments made to funds.* Again, this work is done in conjunction with our balance sheet fund work – see (j) above.

(m) Conclusion

The audit approach is similar to that used at last year's visit. Few problems were encountered that year although it became apparent during the work that much audit evidence was available from physical relationships. Accordingly this year the audit strategy has incorporated much more physical relationship work, particularly on income. The directional testing approach is highly suited to the client and has always fitted naturally into our audit.

CONCLUDING POINTS

At first sight the case studies may have appeared a little simplistic, but it is the principles rather than the situations that count. Many auditors use some form of directional testing on an *ad hoc* and unplanned basis depending largely upon their experience. In fact this technique combined with statistical sampling can be a valuable aid to reduce the time spent examining sample transactions.

A recurring theme throughout this book is that techniques should not be considered in isolation from each other, or from the audit objectives. The second example mentioned other techniques and areas of testing to illustrate the wider audit situation. To exploit successfully financial relationships the auditor must consider relationships throughout the organization and at each stage of its activities.

8 Audit selection and sampling

INTRODUCTION

This chapter is about selecting the items to be tested. The auditor may wish to obtain audit evidence regarding the accuracy and fairness of stated figures and the operation of internal controls, or simply to investigate suspicious balances. In most cases the number of transactions and documents involved will be more than he can hope to examine completely, and so he must decide which ones to select for detailed testing. We begin by distinguishing sampling from simple selection. We then outline some of the basic statistical concepts and questions that the auditor will need to consider. The amount of statistical theory has been kept to the bare minimum which the authors feel will be required by auditors when making decisions on selecting and sampling items to test.

The sampling technique generally of greatest audit value, monetary unit sampling, is considered in detail. We examine specific problems, such as defining errors, obtaining audit assurance, choosing a 'reliability' factor and the detailed extraction of samples. Methods of evaluating errors are discussed. The reader is alerted to some of the problems of extrapolating errors found to wider populations. The text is rounded off with a summary displayed in Fig. 8.2 and Checklist 8.2, and a short conclusion.

Four case studies follow to provide practical examples. The first three take the reader through attribute and monetary unit sampling; the fourth, in contrast, illustrates a non-statistical approach often used by auditors, and highlights the need for such an approach to be supplemented by statistical sampling.

The difference between 'selection' and 'sampling'

The term 'selection' can be used to cover any extraction of items from a large population. Judgemental selections of, for example, high value, high risk or frequently recurring items will often be made. It is only when the auditor intends to select **representative** items typical of all items in the population, and from this selection to draw a conclusion about the larger population, that audit 'sampling' is undertaken. Thus generally speaking:

(a) **Selection** is usually reserved for judgemental and haphazard extractions, the former directed at particular classes of items not typical of the larger population;
(b) **Sampling** is usually undertaken on a statistical or systematic basis, and the items are extracted randomly or at fixed intervals.

Basic objectives, populations and errors

The auditor must first be clear about his reasons for selecting or sampling. He must have clearly stated audit objectives and understand the ways in which those objectives may be satisfied. Having decided that sampling or selection is required he must be able to obtain the relevant population from which to select a sample.

Audit objectives that require selection or sampling, such as forming an opinion on an accounts figure or on the operation of key controls, usually involve estimating the value or the rate of occurrence of errors in a population. Errors must be clearly defined in terms of the audit objectives otherwise any estimations may be misleading.

The selection or sample is usually subjected to substantive testing or compliance testing. The former would normally be undertaken on a population of monetary transactions, while the latter would normally be undertaken on a population of documents the monetary value of which would be of secondary, if any, importance.

The choice and definition of a population and errors are therefore dependent on the auditor's objectives. Objectives that require substantive testing for over/underpayments on the one hand, and the objectives of compliance testing on the other, are likely to lead to different definitions of population and of errors. Errors are discussed in more detail later in the text.

Planning

An audit plan requires a reasonably detailed understanding of the characteristics of the population. For example, it may be possible to test all high value items and only a small sample of the remainder. This would normally give more efficient and reliable results than would a similar sized 'unstratified' sample. The more knowledge about the population and the constituent transactions or other items to be tested, the greater the ability to select the most appropriate sample in terms of risk and cost. The reader is referred to the issues raised in Chapter 4 on planning the audit assignment. For planning sampling and selection some important basic questions are summarized below:

(a) Can the population be conveniently stratified?
(b) Can any unusual items be identified? Payments of unusual size or nature, for example.
(c) Is a very high level of risk associated with particular groups of trans-actions? This could be due to recently uncovered frauds, for example.
(d) For statistical sampling, can the basic conditions outlined on pp. 174–5 be satisfied?

SELECTION AND SAMPLING METHODS

The auditor has three broad choices of method: haphazard, judgemental and statistical. These are summarized in Checklist 8.1.

Checklist 8.1 Selection and sampling methods

Haphazard	*Judgemental*	*Statistical*
1. Generally a biased method of selection (e.g. picking the 'easy' transactions).	Generally biased selection but usually deliberately so.	Deliberately seeks to avoid bias.
2. Takes no account of risk, materiality, etc.	Takes into account considerations of risk, materiality, past events, etc., in a **qualitative** manner.	Takes into account risk and materiality usually in a **quantitative** manner.
3. Usually quick and inexpensive to perform.	Speed and expense vary, depending upon initial judgements.	Speed and expense depend on sample size and accessibility.
4. Sample results cannot be extrapolated to population. Risk of errors in balance not known.	Sample results cannot be extrapolated to the population.	Sample results can be extrapolated and used to make statements about the population. Risk of error in balance stated in measurable terms, e.g. X% confident that errors are no more than £Y.
5. No precision.*	No precision.*	Precision* defined in measurable terms.

*The concept of 'precision' is explained on pp. 177 and 179.

Most of this chapter is about statistical sampling, nevertheless both haphazard and judgemental selections are used (and sometimes misused) by auditors. **Haphazard** selection has relatively few practical uses. Perhaps it is most useful when selections are made to clarify systems procedures when documenting a system. This is particularly so when the auditor is approaching a new client or department.

Judgemental selections have a long history of audit use. They are frequently the basic tool of fraud and irregularity investigations. Auditors will usually be able to exercise judgement to isolate individual transactions or groups with common faults. These are often called 'key items' and are usually examined completely. Examples of key items might include payments over a certain value, charges made by a contractor subsequently found to be dishonest, or the first few returns from a new branch. In short, judgemental selections are usually made from areas of known risk or weakness.

The auditor is, however, normally required to form an opinion on the probability of errors in a population when few, if any, key items are known. In this situation **statistical** sampling is particularly useful. It enables the auditor to apply the laws of statistical probability to estimating the errors in the population from those found in his sample. This perhaps is the main attraction for the external auditor; his opinion on accounts figures is, in most cases, a matter of probability and the statistical laws of probability often provide him with a powerful tool. For the internal auditor, too, statistical techniques can greatly assist both in compliance testing internal controls and in assessing the effectiveness of a system in terms of the estimated value of errors occurring over a given period.

STATISTICAL SAMPLING CONDITIONS

Statistical sampling cannot be undertaken unless certain basic conditions apply:

(a) The 'population' or balance in most audit situations must contain a large number of items. Statistical 'laws' of probability can only be practically applied to large numbers.

How 'large' is large? This will vary in different circumstances but it is unusual to find auditors using statistical techniques on populations of less than a hundred, and in most cases populations are measured in thousands.

(b) The items within the population must be homogeneous. It is often difficult to achieve complete homogeneity, but for audit purposes it is usually sufficient to ensure that the transactions are of the same nature and have been produced by the same system in which all have been subject to the same procedures and controls. A transaction 'stream' with two or more 'branches' – salaries and wages perhaps – is not likely to be a single homogeneous population. In such cases two or more separate populations will be available for sampling.

(c) Each individual item in the population will need to be identifiable, measurable and not of wildly divergent size. The first two are obvious practical conditions and will be considered further in the examples that follow. Exceptionally large transactions will need to be isolated prior to sampling. Stratification is generally cost-efficient and will help ensure each stratum is homogeneous.

(d) Each individual item must have an equal chance or probability of being selected in the sample. This means that each item must be randomly selected. Without this very important condition being satisfied, the sample may be biased and therefore unrepresentative of the population from which it is drawn. From an auditor's perspective, accusations of bias are generally worth avoiding.

If bias is avoided by selecting a random sample, then relatively little extra work will be required to evaluate the results statistically.

So far we have dealt with general considerations and conditions when choosing a sample. Now we must consider some more specific steps.

THE POPULATION CHARACTERISTIC

The population 'characteristic' is the property we wish to investigate. This could be, say, the average value of transactions or the percentage of errors in a population. Sampling is usually classified into two broad types according to the characteristic to be investigated. These types are known as **attribute** sampling and **variable** sampling. Most audit samples are attribute samples and the attribute being investigated is usually that of 'errors'. Thus an attribute is an 'either/or' characteristic; a transaction is either correct or in error, however small the error. Variable sampling is used to investigate population measures. The **average** and the **standard deviation** are the two most common measures looked at.

MONETARY UNIT SAMPLING (MUS)

Introduction

This sampling technique provides an efficient and often revolutionary approach to audit. A Dutch accountant Van Heerden first used this technique in the late 1950s. In 1962, Haskins and Sells, with the aid of Yale Professor Frederick Stephens, developed MUS techniques in the USA. Since the 1960s, the use of various MUS schemes has spread, and MUS is now used by many large British accountancy firms and the National Audit Office.

MUS was initially developed for use by external auditors, though the technique may be very useful in situations faced by internal auditors. This is particularly true when the auditor wishes to demonstrate that his conclusions are rational and based upon systematic work and objective interpretation of results.

As with other sampling schemes, the objective is to estimate the population error after measuring the error found in a sample. Unlike many other sampling schemes it is not necessary to calculate the standard deviation. Neither is it necessary to know the total number of transactions making up the population.

The basic requirements are knowledge of the monetary value of the population, and the choice of the confidence level and monetary precision required. The £ units in the population are usually taken as the basic sampling items and the confidence level chosen is translated into a **reliability factor**. This technique is normally used as part of direct substantive testing of value transactions. When the sample plan is designed to identify monetary errors, whether alone or as part of a combined compliance and substantive test sample, then a monetary unit sample is usually applicable.

An error rate of, say, 2% discovered using ordinary attribute sampling is difficult to translate into money value. If up to 2% of sales invoices totalling £1 million may be in error this could account for any monetary value depending on which invoices make up the 2%. But, using MUS, if we discovered that up to 2% of £1 units may be in error this would represent £20,000. This **upper error limit**, as it is called in MUS, is normally expressed as so many £s rather than as a percentage. The great advantage of being able to draw monetary conclusions from sampling is that these can be used much more readily to help form an opinion of the balance or set of accounts being audited. We must now move on to consider errors in more detail.

Errors

The first reaction of many auditors to the question 'What constitutes an error?' is to start reeling off a long list of possible mistakes and misdemeanours. An experienced auditor can usually quote a very long list indeed, exemplifying all manner of incompetence and dishonesty. This is valuable knowledge, but needs to be considered selectively to be useful in statistical sampling.

Defining an 'error' for purposes of sampling will depend upon the objectives of the sample test. For example, 'completeness' is violated if a transaction was not recorded and an error of understatement occurs. Conversely, 'occurrence' is violated if a recorded transaction did not in fact occur causing an error of overstatement.

Compliance test errors are normally uncovered during systems testing, being errors in the operation of internal controls. They need to be defined in terms of actions or situations, e.g. failure to check an invoice to its order before passing for payment, whether or not the invoice amount is correct. Substantive errors, on the other hand, can be extrapolated from the results of the monetary unit sample to estimate the total likely monetary errors in the population.

Compliance errors can be used to assess the reliability of internal controls, often an important objective in its own right for internal audit. Compliance errors, it will be recalled from Chapter 6, are a major determinant of the extent of substantive testing.

Errors, therefore, are generally defined in terms of the audit objectives of the test for which the sample is being chosen. A single item selected may be tested for various substantive or compliance objectives, and although separate samples are often chosen for compliance tests and substantive tests, multi-purpose samples are frequently appropriate. Table 8.1 lists examples of errors highlighting the nature of substantive and compliance errors.

Assurance

Statistical assurance is usually considered in terms of the 'risk' and 'precision'. **Risk** in the context of attribute and monetary unit sampling is the likelihood of errors occurring and remaining undetected. It is usually thought of as being the complement of 'confidence'. Thus if we are 90% confident of a population characteristic such as an error rate, we accept that there is a 10% risk of being proved wrong.

The assessment of risk, together with the need to define an error, are among the main advantages of statistical sampling. They force the auditor to make measured judgements, and to form an audit opinion in quantifiable terms. The auditor must use his judgement to decide in advance what he means by an 'error' and what sort of evidence he is searching for. He must then use his judgement to decide in advance of testing what level of assurance he requires from his sample which in most sampling – including monetary unit sampling – amounts to making two quantifiable decisions:

(a) First, about what level of confidence is required and thus what level of risk is acceptable. This determines how confident he will be that the sample is representative of the population.

Table 8.1 Examples of errors

All errors result in over/understatements of the accounts or compliance deviations including regularity errors, but the causes vary. The following examples may help to sharpen the reader's perception of errors.

Example 1: Test objective – all goods received were properly ordered

Goods invoiced were not supported by written orders. On enquiry, the auditor finds that an urgent order was made by telephone, but not followed by a prompt official order. This is a compliance error; the control violated was the use of official signed and dated orders.

Example 2: Test objective – the balance under audit is fairly stated

Invoice for £500 paid for by £560. This is a substantive error of measurement resulting in an overstatement.

Example 3: Test objective – balance under audit is fairly stated

An invoice for £20 was paid twice. This is a substantive error of 'occurrence' resulting in overstatement. (A possible compliance error such as failing to cancel the invoice might affect the objective of proper payment procedure.)

Example 4: Test objective – balance under audit is fairly stated

An invoice for £800 sent to a local sports association for field hire was recorded as £500 on a schedule of year-end debtors. This is a substantive error of 'completeness' causing understatement of the balance.

Example 5: Test objectives – (a) the balance is fairly stated; (b) adequate controls apply to payments procedure

A receipt of £400 for use of a hall has been miscoded and has ended up being credited to the Housing Revenue Account income instead of the General Fund. Fund.

1. A substantive error in disclosure will occur in the final revenue accounts concerned. The HRA will be overstated and the GF understated.
2. A compliance error will also be likely to have occurred if the coding was one of the items being checked during the processing of receipts.

Example 6: Test objectives – (a) the balance is fairly stated; (b) adequate controls apply

£6,000 has been spent to support a local group called Landscape Improvements. Enquiries reveal that Landscape Improvements is not an eligible local voluntary organization as the officers and members thought, but is a private company called Landscape Improvements Ltd. This involves an error of regularity. A variety of compliance errors are likely to have occurred in this transaction and the possibility of fraud exists.

(b) Secondly, about how precisely he wishes to measure the sampling characteristic. A 'precision range' usually expressed as a percentage or 'monetary precision' expressed in £s determines how certain he is that the error proportion, or value, in the sample applies to the population.

The two decisions are usually taken together, so that an auditor may decide for substantive testing that he wants to be 95% confident the value of errors are no more than £1,000. This means he accepts a 5% risk that errors are more than £1,000, £1,000 being his monetary precision. For compliance testing he may wish to be, say, 90% confident that a control lapses no more than 2% of the times it is operated. These decisions are further discussed as the text progresses and are illustrated in the case studies at the end of the chapter.

Sample size and obtaining a reliability factor

Before we go on to illustrate sampling and discuss how to evaluate the sample results, it is necessary to consider how to calculate sample sizes. We first obtain the 'reliability factor' or 'confidence related factor'. Confidence levels, risks and reliability factors are interdependent:

If a 95% confidence level is required, i.e. 5% risk, the reliability factor = 3
If a 97% confidence level is required, i.e. 3% risk, the reliability factor = 3.5
If a 75% confidence level is required, i.e. 25% risk, the reliability factor = 1.4
If a 63% confidence level is required, i.e. 37% risk, the reliability factor = 1.0

and so on.

Several tables of reliability factors are available, such as those in Table 8.2 which are derived from the cumulative Poisson distribution. It will be seen from Table 8.2 that the reliability factor increases as more sample errors are anticipated, for any given confidence level. This means that a

Table 8.2 Reliability factors*

Sample anticipated error frequency	Chosen confidence level (%)					
	50	*75*	*85*	*90*	*95*	*99*
0	0.69	1.39	1.90	2.31	3.00	4.61
1	1.68	2.69	3.38	3.89	4.75	6.64
2	2.68	3.92	4.73	5.33	6.30	8.41
3	3.67	5.11	6.02	6.69	7.76	10.05
4	4.67	6.28	7.27	8.00	9.16	11.61
5	5.67	7.42	8.50	9.28	10.52	13.11

*This table has been computed from cumulative Poisson probabilities.

sample calculated using the reliability factor gets larger as the number of errors anticipated increases. The table is therefore only useful provided relatively few errors are expected. If large numbers of errors are expected then other sampling methods, usually variable sampling, are more likely to be appropriate.

An important use of the reliability factor is to enable relatively straight-forward accumulation and allocation of the risk levels associated with audit assurance from the three main sources of audit evidence:

(a) Internal controls;
(b) Analytical review;
(c) Substantive tests (sometimes further subdivided between 'other substantive tests' and 'this substantive test').

We may, for example, anticipate no sample errors and require a 95% confidence level with a reliability factor of 3. We might judge internal controls to be operated effectively and analytical review to be adequately performed with satisfactory results. We may decide to allocate our reliability as follows:

		Reliability factor	
Internal controls	= 1	Associated risk	= 37%
Analytical review	= 1	Associated risk	= 37%
Substantive tests	= 1	Associated risk	= 37%
Total	= 3	Associated risk	= 5% (0.37 × 0.37 × 0.37)

Alternatively, if we felt that both the internal controls and analytical review could not be relied upon then the entire reliability factor of 3 would need to be allocated to substantive testing. This would increase the corresponding sample size (see formula below).

Once the reliability factor has been determined, it can be used to calculate sample size by the formulae:

$$\text{Monetary unit sample size} = \frac{\text{Population value} \times \text{Reliability factor}}{\text{Precision in £s}}$$

$$\text{Sample size for compliance testing alone} = \frac{\text{Reliability factor}}{\text{Precision as a \%}}$$

In practice there will be wider judgemental considerations to be taken into account, for example the practicality of testing a sample of the size calculated. The significance of errors both in monetary and political terms will need to be considered in determining materiality. The estimated risk of errors and the degree of reliance placed upon the test will both help determine the level of confidence and consequent reliability factor. These considerations are easier to recognize and take into account as familiarity with the audited organization increases. Over time the auditor should rapidly be able to refine his initial judgements.

During the first year of an audit the auditor's judgements are likely to be based on far less information and experience than for established clients. It is wise therefore to allow a margin for extra time and to take limited assurance from the system. Determination of confidence levels and resultant reliability factors as well as expected errors are, initially, as much an art as a science. Various writers have suggested confidence levels and reliability factors to be associated with different standards of internal control (see Bibliography). Broadly speaking Fig. 8.1 summarizes the 'equation' of audit confidence.

The auditor must decide the percentage of confidence that can be placed on completely reliable internal controls. In Fig. 8.1 this has been taken as 50%. Some level of substantive testing is always required. The diagram shows how an auditor can split his reliance between compliance testing and direct substantive sampling according to the quality of the internal controls. Assume he requires a combined confidence level of 95% – a reliability factor of 3.00. He judges internal controls to be 'good'. A reasonable audit strategy might then involve an allocation of reliability factors as

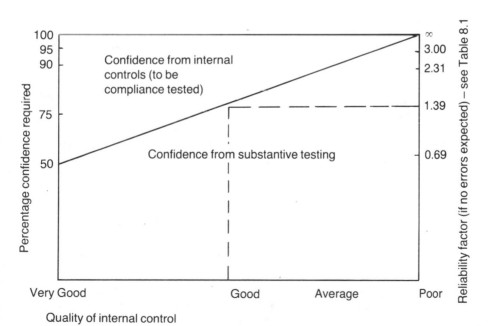

Fig. 8.1 Split of audit confidence between compliance and substantive testing.

1.39 to substantive test sampling and 1.61 to the system, as illustrated by the dotted line on the figure.

Sample extraction

Once the sample size has been calculated the **sampling interval** is obtained by dividing the population by the sample size. For monetary unit samples this gives a value in £s: say, £10,000,000/20 = £500,000. Every 500,000th £1 would thus be a 'hit point' and the transaction of which it forms a part would be extracted and tested. A random start should be chosen to commence extraction, in this case between 1 and 499,999 pounds. This is interval sampling with a random start.

In theory a small disadvantage is that the interval may correspond to a pattern within the population and so the representative property of a random sample could be lost. Using monetary unit sampling this is not usually a serious risk as each transaction contains a different number of pounds. If the auditor thinks distinct patterns exist and is concerned that interval sampling may not be random even with a random start, then the sampling intervals can be thought of as 'cells' and a random point chosen from each cell. Cell selection is usually equally convenient if the sample is extracted by computer interrogation.

Nil balances

It is worth noting that if a population contains a substantial number of nil balances these should be extracted from the population and tested separately. Nil balances are missed out when working through the population to extract the sample.

Negative items, e.g. credit notes in an invoice listing, also have no chance of selection, and may reduce the chance of concurrent positive items being selected. It is usual to treat such negative items as positive for sampling purposes, or like nil balances, to treat them as a separate population.

Evaluating the results

Haphazard and judgemental selections are usually open to many more interpretations than statistical sampling, and thus objective evaluation by the auditor is normally more difficult. The auditor may 'feel' that if most of his selection of, say, vouchers, were incorrect, then so would be most of the population; or that having found no errors among the types of transactions in which he normally expects to find some, then the whole account is likely to be correct, or at least free of material error. In neither case can he say precisely how confident he is of his conclusion, and in such cases the auditor can usually form conclusions only about particular transactions or small common groupings. This may give assurance that a particular type of error or a fraud has not occurred among particular transactions or at particular times and places, which is useful when testing 'key' items or undertaking special investigations. But additional sampling or other substantive testing would normally be required for an audit opinion on a set of accounts. These points are raised in Case study 8.4.

In attribute sampling (illustrated in Case Study 8.1) the results either fall within the parameters set when choosing the sample size or they do not. If they do then the auditor can say that he is X% confident that no more than Y errors, usually compliance deviations, have occurred in the population; if not, then he can say that he is X% confident that the error rate is unacceptable.

When using monetary sampling the evaluation of results is usually taken a stage further than for normal attribute sampling. The auditor, as for attribute sampling, chooses the sampling parameters and judges the level of errors he can expect; he will need to estimate both the expected value of the sample errors as well as their frequency. Usually no sample errors are expected, but if frequent errors were expected then the auditor would most likely consider variable sampling or non-sampling methods. The actual sample errors are compared to the anticipated errors and as soon as more errors than expected are discovered he must 'widen' his basic precision.

Precision gap widening, as it is called, is undertaken to take account of the fact that the auditor must make a less precise statement of the value of the population errors once more errors than he expected have been found in the sample. The basic precision chosen by the auditor plus the precision gap widening resulting from sample errors are usually summed to give the **upper error limit**. The upper limit can then be compared to the materiality level of the account under audit. If it is less than materiality the auditor can usually conclude that, within his chosen parameters of confidence and precision, a material error has not occurred. If it is more then he must increase his sample size, or carry out other audit work, or both. It is also open to him to revise his chosen parameters, which may lead an external auditor to qualify his opinion, though normally this would be a last resort. These stages, which often require considered audit judgement, are more fully explained in the case studies.

SUMMARY

Figure 8.2 and Checklist 8.2 summarize some of the decision stages involved in the principles of selection and sampling discussed so far.

When to use:

(a) Haphazard selection   – for 'walkthrough' tests.
(b) Judgemental selection   – for testing 'key' items in known problem/ risk areas following one's 'audit nose'.

(c) Statistical sampling   – to help form an audit opinion on the figures and on the operation of internal controls.

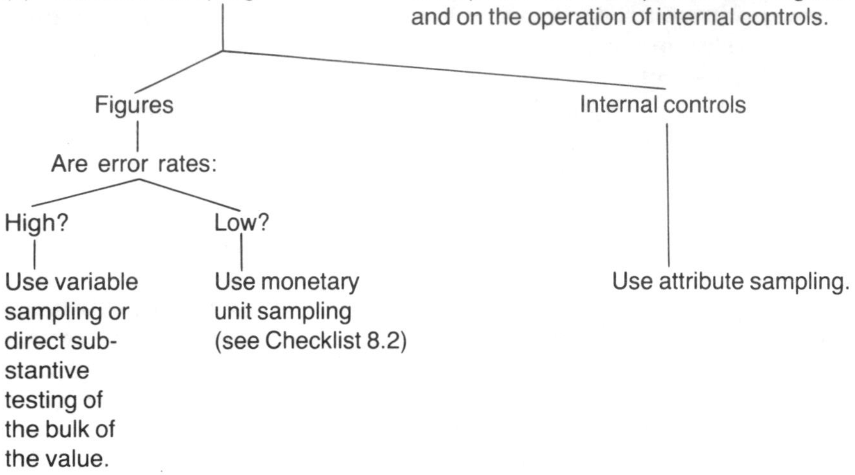

Figures   Internal controls

Are error rates:

High?   Low?

Use variable sampling or direct sub- stantive testing of the bulk of the value.   Use monetary unit sampling (see Checklist 8.2)   Use attribute sampling.

Fig. 8.2 Key decision stages in selection and sampling.

Selection and sampling are techniques at the heart of the essential audit process – see Fig. 2.1. The auditor must test to obtain his compliance and substantive evidence. He cannot test every transaction or event so he must sample or select items. Whatever opinion he forms, there will always be a probability of it being the wrong one. It therefore makes sense to use the statistical laws of probability wherever practical and cost-effective, and undertake statistical sampling.

Statistical sampling and judgemental selection should not be seen as mutually exclusive alternatives. It is the authors' view that both are mutually supportive in a well planned audit, or indeed when investigating unexpected situations.

Now that we have stated certain of the basic statistical principles and techniques, we provide some detailed examples involving choosing and evaluating samples and selections.

(a) Case study 8.1 briefly introduces attribute sampling as applied to compliance testing.
(b) Case study 8.2 introduces monetary sampling, illustrating how initial judgements affect sample size and the acceptability of the final result.
(c) Case study 8.3 goes on to examine monetary unit sampling in relation to the wider audit plan and the evidence needed to form an opinion. It considers the evaluation of errors in some detail.

Checklist 8.2 Key decision stages in monetary unit sampling

1. Consider the nature of the population and error types in the light of audit objectives.
2. Choose confidence levels and precision limits with regard to audit planning and the materiality level.
3. Convert the confidence level to reliability factor for the number of anticipated errors – refer to tables.
4. If appropriate, allocate reliability factor between sampling test and other sources of audit evidence.
5. Extract known key and high value items.
6. Determine sample size – by formula.
7. Determine sampling interval (or cell size) – divide the population by the sample size.
8. Select a random start between 0 and the sampling interval, then add through population sampling a transaction at each £1 'hit point'. Most populations can be conveniently sampled using a computer interrogation program.
9. Evaluate errors undertaking any precision gap widening as required.
10. Compare upper error limit to materiality and form conclusion.

(d) Case study 8.4 illustrates a judgemental approach, showing how selection decisions often take place in stages and that judgemental selections are often the most convenient response to sudden and unexpected discoveries such as frauds. It concludes that judgemental selection needs to be supplemented by statistical sampling if a reliable audit opinion is to be formed.

CASE STUDY 8.1 ATTRIBUTE SAMPLING

Introduction

Careless District Council have a main store depot housing a wide range of goods, mostly for the housing and highways direct labour organizations.

Systems evaluations by internal audit have identified as a 'key' control the matching of orders to supplies delivery notes. This confirms that goods received were indeed ordered. The control is evidenced by the stores clerk stamping 'Received' on the order, or crossing through and initialling partially received orders in red.

Sampling parameters

In order to compliance test this key control the Chief Internal Auditor has decided a sample of documents will be checked. His sampling parameters are:

(a) He wishes to be 90% confident that no more than 4% of the population are actually in compliance error.
(b) No compliance errors are anticipated in a sample.

This is an example where attribute sampling is appropriate. Attribute sampling is well suited to compliance testing generally: the items tested are either subject or not effectively subject to the control – a 'Yes/No' situation.

Sample size

From the reliability factor (see Table 8.1) we can calculate the required sample size using the formula on p. 180:

$$\text{Sample size} = \frac{\text{Reliability factor}}{\text{Precision \%}}$$

The reliability factor for zero errors at 90% confidence level is 2.31. Thus sample size is:

$$\frac{2.31}{0.04} = 57.75, \text{ say } 58$$

Sample extraction

The auditor sees that all delivery notes are attached to pre-numbered computer input punching headers and filed in this order. Orders are filed separately in order number, and can be matched to delivery notes, allowing for approximately four weeks' delivery time lag.

The auditor's testing objective is to check that a control operates over goods received. Therefore to ensure he has a complete population of cancelled orders he needs to sample from the delivery notes. Each time he selects a note he will check to see the corresponding order has been marked or stamped. (Conversely, if he had wanted to test that orders marked 'Received' were indeed received he would sample from the orders and check to the delivery notes.) The notes for the past year from which he wants to select his sample are numbered X7/1 to X7/24742. Using random number tables he selects 58 five-figure numbers between 00001 and 24742. On average each selection and cross-check takes two minutes, so he allows himself two hours.

Results

After compliance testing his sample, he summarizes the results as follows:

Population size 24,742
Sample size 58
Errors Nil

Evaluation of results:
The auditor can be 90% confident that *no more* than 4% of items in the population are in error.

Conclusion

From this result the Chief Internal Auditor may decide to inform the head of the stores department that he considers internal control over goods received to be within agreed tolerances.

Further considerations

If one or more errors had been uncovered, then given that this sample was calculated on the basis of no expected errors, the auditor would be forced to conclude that he cannot be 90% confident that no more than 4% of population items are in error. In which case he would, having reported his concern to senior management, be forced to accept either a lower level of confidence in the system or undertake further audit work.

If, say, two sample errors **had** been anticipated, then to be 90% confident that the population error rate was no more than 4%, a sample size of 113 (5.33/0.04) would have been required. The reliability factor of 5.33 is that required at 90% confidence level (see Table 8.2) when up to two sample errors are anticipated. The greater the number of errors, the larger the sample required to maintain a given confidence level and precision.

CASE STUDY 8.2 MONETARY UNIT SAMPLING – A SIMPLE EXAMPLE

Introduction

An auditor wishes to audit a Sundry Debtors balance of, say, £200,000. His main audit objective is occurrence, that is testing for overstatement, as part of a wider audit approach involving directional testing (see Chapter 7). Errors are recorded as monetary differences between book, or recorded, value and audited value. Overall materiality has been set at £8,000. Audit planning and preliminary work on the accounts reveal a relatively poor level of internal control, and has led the auditor to choose a reliability factor for substantive testing of 3.0 (see Table 8.1). He wishes to be 95% confident that errors in the population do not exceed his materiality. He takes his precision, or testing materiality, as the £8,000.

Let us also assume that two high value items of £68,000 and £2,800 (both higher than the sampling interval) are withdrawn for separate testing.

Sample size

Sample size is calculated as on p. 180:

$$\frac{\text{Population value} \times \text{Reliability factor}}{\text{Precision}}$$

In this case:

$$\frac{(200,000 - (68,000 + 2,800)) \times 3}{8,000} = 48.45$$

Assume that interval sampling with a random start is to be employed. The sampling interval will be:

$$\frac{\text{Population value}}{\text{Sample size}}$$

In this case:

$$\frac{£129,200}{48.45} = 2,667$$

Sample every 2,667th pound.

Sample extraction

After a random start between 1 and 2,667, every 2,667th £ unit will be extracted from the population, and the transaction of which it is a part will be tested. If the population balance had not been known with reasonable accuracy then the sampling interval will be calculated as:

$$\frac{\text{Precision}}{\text{Reliability factor}} = \frac{£8,000}{3} = £2,667$$

Finding every 2,667th £ by working manually through the population can be time consuming, though the reduction in sample size from using MUS will partially offset this. If the balance needs to be cast, as is often the case, or if sub-totals are already listed, this will reduce the extra effort involved. Samples can often be conveniently extracted from computerized records using modern interrogation software, with the added advantage of dividing the population into 'cells' of sampling interval width and extracting a unit randomly from within each cell. Such cell-sampling adds a little extra safeguard against a 'hidden pattern' in the population, but is rather tedious if undertaken manually.

Results

For the sample of 49 used in this example let us assume that manual interval extraction was carried out. The results were as follows:

High value items:	Book value £	Audit value £	Error +/−£
	68,000	68,000	−
	2,800	2,780	+20
Total high value error			£+20

Representative sample:			
Items	Book value £	Audit value £	Error +/−£
1	140.73	140.73	−
2	720.41	720.41	−
3	42.21	42.21	−
etc.			
12	241.28	131.28	+110.00
etc.			
38	405.00	401.25	+3.75
etc.			
49	1,598.58	1,598.58	−
	£38,148.27		£+113.75

Apart from such monetary errors, which are often the result of arithmetical errors and miscodings, compliance deviations and errors not affecting the balance might also be uncovered. Although these may be ignored for the purpose of any extrapolation, they should be considered on their own merits and reported to the appropriate level of management.

Let us now move on to consider possible extrapolations of the monetary errors that affect the account balance being audited. It may be sufficient to opt for a non-statistical extrapolation, perhaps when a formal published opinion is not being given on, say, a trading account of a works department. In the absence of any contrary evidence the auditor is likely to assume that the population error is of approximately the same proportion as the sample error, depending on how representative the sample really is. In this case:

$$\frac{\text{Sample error}}{\text{Sample value}} \times \text{Population} = \text{Estimated population error}$$

$$\frac{113.75}{38,148.27} \times 129,200 = £385.25$$

Note: The high value items have been taken out of the population for extrapolation purposes.

Conclusion

In this example the known errors of £20 + £113.75 plus a proportionate extrapolation of, say, between £300 and £400 compare very favourably with the materiality level of £8,000. Consequently, the auditor is likely to conclude that he can accept the balance after minor adjustments of £133.75 and £20 for the known error.

Further considerations

This is, however, a relatively simple, some might say over-simple, extrapolation. The reliability factor 3.0 applies when no errors are expected. As soon as an error is found – and in the above sample there were two – the auditor can no longer say he is 95% confident that population errors do not exceed his precision level (£8,000). He must decide to reject the balance, accept less stringent confidence levels and/or precision, or undertake further audit. In practice the auditor will usually set his basic precision (testing materiality) lower than the overall materiality for the account under audit and so would not face the aforementioned decision until several errors had arisen. This situation is examined further in the next case study.

CASE STUDY 8.3 MONETARY UNIT SAMPLING – THE JOINT ARDSHIRE RECLAMATION AND DEVELOPMENT SCHEME

Introduction

This case study envisages the attestation or certification audit of a joint development between various local authorities, the National Reclamation Office (NRO) and the private sector company Land Developments plc. The development is called the Joint Ardshire Reclamation and Development Scheme, or JARDS for short.

JARDS was set up in response to pressures for development land in Ardshire. The NRO purchases or rents land left derelict after mining and manufacturing shut-downs, to be reclaimed and redeveloped either by itself or, as in this case, jointly. After planning permission has been obtained the land is brought up to a standard suitable for new housing or light industrial uses. In this particular case Ardshire County Council, Northern and Western District Councils and Land Developments plc have each agreed to provide a quarter of the cost for the reclamation of a major site, the Big Flat Tip, recently purchased by the NRO.

In accordance with its sponsoring organizations' stipulations JARDS has compiled the following financial report at the end of its first year. The auditors have been asked to give a 'fair presentation' certificate.

The Chief Auditor in charge of the audit has drawn up a detailed audit plan, along the lines of Chapter 4, extracts from which follow.

JARDS 19X0 – Extracts from Planning Memorandum

6. **Recent figures:**

JARDS Balance Sheet at
31 March 19X0

	£000	£000	£000
Fixed assets:			
Land at Big Flat Tip		2,000	
Plant and machinery		3,000	
Net current assets:			
Stock	500		
Debtors	30		
Cash	60		
Creditors	(10)	580	£5,580
Financed by:			
NRO capital outlay		4,800	
ACC working capital		200	
NDC working capital		200	
WDC working capital		200	
LDs working capital		200	
Working deficit for year		(20)	£5,580

JARDS Income and Expenditure Account
for year ended 31 March 19X0

	£000	£000
Income from sale of reclaimed ores		2,370
Expenses:		
Wages	400	
Planning and other fees	40	
Supplies	1,920	
Maintenance	30	2,390
Operating deficit		£(20)

No depreciation or debt charges are entered in JARDS' books.

7. **Materiality:** £50,000 – this is set at 2% of turnover and accounts for 0.9% of the balance sheet value.
8. **Audit approach:** Summarized extracts of the strategy for each balance are given below:

Balance	£000	Approach
Land	2,000	Undertake direct verification by examination of deeds and letters. Review valuations.
Plant and machinery	3,000	Examine asset register. Complete check of items over £50,000. Payments are subject to the purchases system – see below. Use MUS for direct substantive testing of items below £50,000. Some analytical review possible.
Stocks	500	Review system – it is known to be poor. Direct substantive testing, using MUS, is required. Year-end stock certificate is thought unreliable.
Debtors	30	Carry out review and test as necessary.
Creditors	10	Carry out review and test as necessary.
Cash	60	Obtain bank confirmations. Re-perform bank reconciliation at B/S date.
Funding of working capital	800	Obtain written confirmations and tie in with audit of £4,800K NRO funding under fixed assets.
Income	2,370	Only four quarterly payments are received from a single contract purchaser. Examine contract and test each transaction completely.
Wages	400	Review system. Perform substantive tests using MUS.
Fees	40	Review and test as necessary.
Supplies	1,920	Evaluate system – internal controls are thought to be reliable; compliance test as necessary on items of MUS extracted for substantive tests.

Balance	£000	Approach
Maintenance	30	Fixed annual contract sum paid half-yearly. Examine both payments completely.

A discussion of the details behind the extracts is not relevant here. Assume that the Chief Auditor has consulted his staff and the Chief Financial Officer of JARDS and that a full audit planning file exists.

Samples required

The extracts show that MUS samples of Plant and Machinery, Wages, Stock and Supplies are required. MUS can usually be applied to other balances such as Creditors, but this particular case study has, to avoid repetition, been deliberately limited.

Plant and Machinery payments, numbering approximately 8,000, are mostly for amounts from £2,000 to £20,000. Items over £50,000 (materiality) account for £970,000 of the £3,000,000 balance.

Wages consist of 3,120 payments to up to fifty weekly-paid staff and 48 payments to four monthly-paid executive officers. All of the weekly-paid staff involve standard, overtime and bonus rates, and various statutory and voluntary deductions, calculated manually by one executive officer. The EOs salaries are fairly simple to check as they are full-time Civil Servants (on secondment) and salary is standard for their grade, paid by NRO, and recharged to JARDS. The weekly-paid staff are locally recruited and in total were paid £320,000.

The **supplies** expenditure, £1,920,000, consists of a very large number, approximately 50,000 payments, varying in value from under £1 up to £10,000. Most of the items are for equipment, tools, protective clothing, explosives and food (free meals are provided while on duty). Explosives are invoiced quarterly by the supplier and all four can be checked completely. For the current year, they amounted to £610,000.

Stocks consist of approximately 10,000 items mostly less than £100 in value.

Systems reliance

The Chief Auditor on reviewing the systems evaluations prepared by his staff and internal auditors decides that little or no reliance can be placed upon the wages system, as almost all duties are concentrated in the hands of the one executive officer. This point has been raised with senior officers at NRO and the local authorities, but to date no further steps have been taken. The same is true of stocks; the system of stock control is poor and stocktakes are thought to be unreliable. A new storekeeper has recently been appointed and improvements are expected. He considers, however, that considerable reliance can be placed on the purchases system. Good internal controls exist and initial testing – carried out by Ardshire Internal Audit staff – indicate they are operated satisfactorily. Both revenue purchases of supplies and capital purchases of plant and machinery are subject to this system.

Reliability factors

The Chief Auditor decides that he wishes to be 95% confident that no material error exists in the Account. This entails a reliability factor of 3.00 (see Table 8.1), provided no errors are expected. The Chief Auditor cannot allocate part of this reliability factor to internal controls in the case of wages or of stocks and decides not to allocate any part of it to analytical review as there are no prior-year figures.

For supplies purchases, however, he decides to allocate the reliability factor 2 to the substantive testing and 1 to the systems (see p. 180 for an explanation of the allocation of reliability factors). A reliability factor of 1 is rather cautious for a good system, but he decides to err on the side of caution during the first year of audit. Similarly no reliance will be taken from the analytical review of purchases at this early stage.

For plant and machinery the total reliability factor of 3 can also be split. The Chief Auditor decides that, as for purchases, a factor of 1 can be allocated to the system, and a further factor of 1 can be allocated to analytical review. Although no prior-years' figures are available, NRO records show that expenditure on plant and machinery for this type of work is closely related to the volume of waste reclaimed and the tonnage of ore sold. This leaves only a factor of 1 to be allocated to sampling.

Sample size

The Chief Auditor is now in a position to determine his sample size (from this point onwards the audit working papers are presented in a standard form) – see Form MUS 1.

Sample extraction

In this case the Chief Auditor decides to undertake interval sampling with a random start. Purchases transactions will be extracted starting at a point between the first and up to the 25,192nd £ and every 25,192nd £ thereafter. Similarly every 16,923rd £ for stocks, every 49,512th £ for plant and every 16,842nd £ for wages will be extracted. Each hit point pulls out a trans-

Form MUS 1			Schedule No: Prepared by: A.B. 1.9.X6	
			Reviewed by:	
SAMPLE SIZE			Client/Dept: JARDS	Ref: JOB A.1
Population	Purchases	Wages	Stock	Plant/Mcy
1. Testing materiality £	50,000	50,000	50,000	50,000
2. Population value £	* 1,310,000	* 320,000	* 440,000	* 2,030,000
3. Reliability factor	2	3	3	1
4. Sample size $\underline{(2) \times (3)}$ (1)	52.4 say 52	19.2 say 19	26.4 say 26	40.6 say 41
5. Sample interval £ $\underline{(2)}$ (4)	25,192	16,842	16,923	49,512
Notes:	* £1,920,000 less 4 invoices for explosives totalling £610,000	* £400,000 less EO salaries totalling £80,000 to be examined separately	* £500,000 less 'key' items valued at £60,000 to be examined separately due to high risk of theft	* £3,000,000 less high value items over £50,000 totalling £970,000 to be examined separately

action voucher to be tested. In this case some high value items (i.e. greater than the sampling interval) have been extracted at the start of the exercise. If any still remain they will be hit at least once and can be analysed as they occur. Some 'key' items have also been extracted for detailed examination.

Results I

No errors were found in high value or in key items, and as expected, no errors were found in the samples. Therefore the Chief Auditor could say he was 90% confident that the total value of errors in each of the balances is less than £50,000. He would be completely confident that the high value and key items contained no errors, and his conclusion would state this separately. As a general rule it is less likely to lead to confusion if the conclusions of each sample and each judgemental selection are stated separately in the working papers.

Further considerations

All the above is fairly straightforward; however, when errors **are** found the situation becomes more complicated. If compliance errors are found and a significant degree of reliance has been placed on the system, then the auditor will need to consider increasing the confidence level and consequent reliability factor and re-sampling. It is normally assumed that significant reliance will not be placed on the system unless the auditor is already very hopeful, probably from previous compliance testing, that it is indeed sound. The need for adjustments resulting from compliance errors is therefore unlikely to arise; monetary errors are more likely. Some attempt has already been made by the Chief Auditor to judge the expected sample error frequency. He initially decided no errors were expected. If frequent errors, say 6 or more in this type of sample, are **expected**, then the auditor would be well advised to reconsider his approach to the audit. Extensive direct substantive testing, perhaps by the client organization or department, would normally be required.

Let us assume that two errors of overstatement, one of understatement and one high value error were discovered in purchases. As explained in Case study 8.2, if we stick strictly to our assumption that no errors are expected then any sample error will lead us to a negative conclusion.

Precision gap widening

In effect any error decreases, i.e. widens, the precision beyond the tolerable error, so that the auditor cannot form a statistical conclusion that a material error is acceptably unlikely. Most audit organizations employ varying methods to create a 'gap' between overall materiality and basic precision. The sample size will of course increase as precision decreases.

In this case study (see Fig. 8.3 below) it is assumed that the Chief Auditor decides to set his basic precision after estimating a 'most likely' or 'anticipated' error on the basis of similar sized accounts. An estimate of the precision gap widening (see below) would also be made by the Chief Auditor, usually on the basis of the ratio of previous years' anticipated error/precision gap widening. In this case no previous years' results are

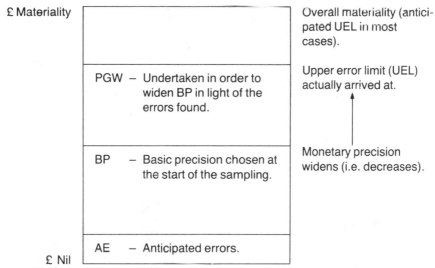

£ Materiality — Overall materiality (anticipated UEL in most cases).

PGW — Undertaken in order to widen BP in light of the errors found. — Upper error limit (UEL) actually arrived at.

BP — Basic precision chosen at the start of the sampling. — Monetary precision widens (i.e. decreases).

AE — Anticipated errors.

£ Nil

Precision gap widening (PGW) is measured as one less than the difference between reliability factors at a given confidence level for each increasing error, ie:

PGW Factor = (b) − (a) − 1

where (a) is reliability factor for x errors; (b) is reliability factor for $x + 1$ errors; as set out in Table 8.1. For example, at 95% confidence level for zero anticipated error frequency in sample, the first error would require a PGW factor of (4.75 − 3.00) − 1 = 0.75

Fig. 8.3 Materiality and precision widening.

available, but assume his experience of audits of similar organizations to JARDS suggests precision gap widening should be about half the anticipated error (see Form MUS 2).

The actual upper error limit (UEL) eventually calculated from the results of testing should be as close as practical to the overall materiality level without exceeding it. This is because, if at the end of the testing the UEL is far below overall materiality, the sample chosen was probably too large. If the actual UEL is above materiality then resampling or other more detailed examination may be needed.

The Chief Auditor initially decided to place some reliance upon the controls in the system. Given that he now expects errors, is he still justified in placing the same degree of reliance upon the system? This is a matter of audit judgement. Given the relatively low anticipated error he might well be inclined to maintain his confidence in the system's internal controls, especially as such confidence is based on satisfactory compliance testing,

Form MUS 2		Schedule No: Prepared by: A.B. 2.2.X0
		Reviewed by:
SAMPLE PRECISION AND ESTIMATED ADJUSTMENTS		Client/Dept: Ref: JARDS JOB A.1

Account/overall materiality:	£50,000
Basic precision:	£49,250
Anticipated adjustments: 　　1. Anticipated Error (AE) 　　　　Estimated PGW	 £500 £250
Upper error limited anticipated:	£50,000

Notes:
1. A.E. for JARDS is based upon our figures for actual errors found in similar
   organizations. PGW has tended to be around 50% of AE in similar audits.
2. These figures will need to be revised in the light of actual results.
3. Anticipated UEL has been set at materiality.

and the reliability factor of 1 assigned to the system was considered low in
the first place – see revised Form MUS 1A.

Results II

The results of the sample audit are set out on Forms MUS 3 to 6. In this
case study the recent draft guidelines of the Auditing Practices Committee
have been taken into account in extrapolating the results. This form of
evaluation has been successfully adopted by external auditors for some
years. Each error is projected over its sampling interval in proportion or
'tainting' to its book value. Errors are then ranked in tainting order and
a PGW adjustment, as described on p. 197, is applied to each error in
descending order.

Forms MUS 3 and 5 have been designed to evaluate overstatements
separately from understatements. Understatements are sometimes given a
lower weighting than overstatements and a separate set of PGW factors
used in their evaluation; in this case study both are considered of equal
value. Some auditors decide not to net off over- and understatements at

Form MUS 1A		Schedule No: Prepared by:	AB 2.2.X0	
		Reviewed by:		
SAMPLE SIZE		Client/Dept: JARDS	Ref: JOB A1	
Population	Purchases			
1. Testing materiality £	49,250			
2. Population value £	1,310,000			
3. Reliability factor	2			
4. Sample size (2) × (3) ——— (1)	53.2 say 53			
5. Sample interval £ (2) —— (4)	24,717			

all, as this may give a misleading impression of accuracy, especially if the nct projected error is nil on Form MUS 6.

No extrapolation is needed for the results of testing the high value and key itcms. These judgemental selections are examined completely (see Form MUS 4) and taken into account in evaluating the total error on Form MUS 6.

From Form MUS 6 we can see that the known and projected most likely errors total £161.19 and that the upper error limit is just less than materiality of £50,000. On this evidence the Chief Auditor would be likely to accept the purchases figure, though known errors totalling £106.41 would be deducted. In practice MUS is relatively intolerant of errors due to the effects of tainting and precision gap widening; in this example the PGW greatly exceeded the actual and projected sample errors.

Form MUS 3				Schedule No: Prepared by: AB 2.2.X0			
				Reviewed by:			
ERROR PROJECTIONS (Book value less than sampling interval – SI)				Client/Dept: JARDS		Ref: JOB A1	

	Book value	Audit value	Error	Tainting error/BV	Rank T	Projectd error (SI × T%)	Cross ref.
Overstatement errors:	£	£	£	%	%	£	
1.	471.11	471.00	0.11+	0.02%	2nd	(24717) (.0002) = 4.94+	P1
2.	21.30	20.00	1.30+	6.1%	1st	(24717) (.061) = 1508.55+	P3
Understatement errors:							
1.	17.00	18.00	1.0−	5.9%	1st	(24717) (.059) = 1458.30−	P2

Net value of errors	0.41+	Net projected error	55.19+

Form MUS 4			Schedule No: Prepared by: AB 2.2.X0	
			Reviewed by:	
ERRORS–HIGH VALUE AND KEY ITEMS			Client/Dept: JARDS	Ref: JOB A1

Book value	Audit value	Difference	Cross ref.
£ 2736.48 6124.00	£ 2730.48 6024.00	£ 6.00+ 100.00+	All item examined 100%
	Net total errors	106.00+	

Form MUS 5		Schedule No:	AB 2.2.80
		Prepared by:	
		Reviewed by:	
SAMPLE PRECISION AND PRECISION GAP WIDENING		Client/Dept: JARDS	Ref: JOB A1

Basic Precision		£4,925		
	PGW Factor*	Tainting	Sampling interval	PGW**
Overstatements:		%		£
1.30	0.75	6.10	24,717	1,470.04
0.11	0.55	0.02	24,717	0.30
Understatements:				
1.00	0.75	5.90	24,717	1,093.73
Net total PGW				376.61

* Calculated as per formula given with Fig. 8.3.
** PGW is the product of over/understatements, PGW factor, tainting % and sampling
interval.

Form MUS 6		Schedule No:	AB 2.2.80
		Prepared by:	
		Reviewed by:	
TOTAL ERRORS AND PRECISION		Client/Dept: JARDS	Ref: JOB A1

	£
1. Most likely error (net) (Forms MUS 3 and MUS 4)	55.19
	106.00
	161.19
2. Basic precision (Form MUS 2)	49,250.00
3. Precision gap widening (Form MUS 5)	367.61
4. Upper error limit	49,778.80

Notes:
      UEL is less than overall materiality
                i.e.   50,000.00
                     49,778.80
                     221.20

Conclusion:
      No evidence of material error at given statistical parameters.

Conclusion

The Chief Auditor may conclude that the most likely net error is £161.19, and that he is 95% confident that total errors in the balance do not exceed the £50,000 materiality level. The precise phrasing of the conclusion will vary in the light of each organization's 'house style'. In all cases the common advantage from using MUS is the ability to form such a conclusion in measurable terms using techniques that take advantage of the auditor's traditional objectives and values.

Checklist 8.3 summarizes some of the main considerations the auditor should bear in mind when choosing monetary unit sampling.

Checklist 8.3 Some general considerations in applying monetary unit sampling

When deciding whether or not to apply monetary unit sampling the following considerations should be borne in mind:
1. Sample sizes are generally small. Sizes will increase if increasing numbers of errors are anticipated, but in this situation further work would in any case be normally required.
2. The auditor is provided with a framework that helps him plan his work well in advance. It is necessary to define critical elements, such as errors, and to keep his understanding of the accounts and systems up to date. Both the informed client and the auditor are in a relatively strong position to justify the quality of audit work.
3. This technique is easier to use than most sampling schemes in an audit context, particularly as it lends itself to computerized systems.
4. The sample is stratified during selection, all items over the sampling interval size being automatically selected, and the higher value items remaining have a greater chance of being selected as they contain more £1 units. The probability of selection is proportionate to size.
5. Items of nil value will not be selected and must be dealt with separately if significant.
6. Understatement errors, which reduce the size of the transaction, are less likely to be selected than overstatement errors.
7. Monetary unit sampling tends to be relatively intolerant of errors increasing the risks of rejecting an otherwise acceptable sample. Sometimes auditors may consider this built-in prudent bias an advantage.

CASE STUDY 8.4 JUDGEMENTAL SELECTION

This example is taken from the Internal Audit Section of Southern District Council.

Introduction

During the past year, two serious cases of fraud have come to light. Both involve Sports Centre staff. The first case involved gross overclaiming of expenses (£3,000 in one year) by the Assistant Manager for which he was prosecuted, fined and dismissed from his post.

The second case involved a clerk forging the signature of an assistant finance officer, certifying that an annual squash court insurance premium of £10,000 was due to the Racquet Insurance Co. In fact no such policy or company existed, and the address to which the cheque was sent was a recently vacated office for which the clerk's wife, a cleaner, had a set of keys. One month later the fraud was discovered by monitoring expenditure against budget. By this time, the cheque had been cashed and the dishonest couple were nowhere to be found. Investigations into this fraud revealed that scant regard was being paid to the financial regulations. When invoices were processed all cheques over £5,000 should have been countersigned by the Treasurer.

The Treasurer has come under criticism from the Finance and Policy Committee. They want to know by next meeting what 'tests for frauds' have been undertaken at the Centre. The Treasurer has in turn passed the matter on to the Chief Auditor (see Internal Memorandum).

INTERNAL MEMORANDUM SOUTHERN DISTRICT COUNCIL	
DATE 6.4.X0	DATE
FROM Treasurer	FROM
TO Chief Internal Auditor	TO
SUBJECT Frauds at Sports Centre	
As we discussed, I would like you to include a special exercise in the audit timetable to check payments for frauds or serious errors. Check any areas you consider risky. Can you please tackle expenditure by the end of next week and report to me in time for my meeting with members.	

Table 8.3 Expenditure

L.50	Sports Centre	Actual 19X4/X5 £	Estimate 19X5/X6 £	Revised estimate 19X5/X6 £	Estimate 19X6/X7 £
50.1	Salaries and wages	301,000	309,500	312,800	310,000
50.2	Other employee expenses	24,050	24,000	31,000	31,000
50.3	Buildings, repairs and equipment	7,251	7,600	7,500	7,100
50.4	Heat, light, cleaning	20,140	20,200	20,460	20,500
50.5	Furniture, fittings	306	300	240	240
50.6	Rates	11,000	11,250	11,250	11,560
50.7	Materials, equipment, fuels, clothing	23,605	23,900	26,500	26,000
50.8	Printing, stationery, general office expenses	5,007	5,000	5,300	5,200
50.9	Travelling and subsistence	15,100	20,000	20,000	20,000
50.10	Insurance	11,100	11,500	21,500	11,500
50.11	Emergency purchases fund	200	200	200	200
50.12	Contribution to disabled sports fund	120	120	120	120
50.13	Central establishment charges	2,400	2,800	2,900	2,900
50.14	Special items	912	900	900	1,000
		£421,191	£437,270	£460,670	£447,320

Basic data

Table 8.3 is taken from the Arts and Recreation Committee estimate.

The internal audit staff were able to obtain a breakdown of some of the amalgamated code items as follows:

		Revised estimate 19X5/X6 £
50.14	Special items:	
	Display cases	196
	Case lights	59
	Trampolines	300
	Sports trip	145
	Publicity	200
		£900

50.8 Printing, stationery, general
office expenses:

Printing	600
Stationery	300
Telephone	3,600
Postage	500
Advertising	300
	£5,300

50.2 Other employee expenses:

National insurance	20,400
Superannuation	10,200
Training	300
Miscellaneous	100
	£31,000

Initial judgemental selection

Although the Chief Internal Auditor now has twenty-five expenditure budget areas (14 main codes three of which are further broken down as above), it is unlikely that he will consider them all to be 'risky' areas, and so he must make a judgemental selection from these twenty-five. Random sampling of these areas, even if the number were much greater than twenty-five, could not take account of 'riskiness'.

Codes 50.9 (travel and subsistence) and 50.10 (insurance) are known areas of fraud. Some codes, such as other employee's expenses, have increased sharply compared to their original estimates, and suggest investigation on this account. Other codes such as 50.7 (materials) are inherently risky in most organizations and require tight controls to avoid the possibility of misappropriation.

Apart from the figures above, the Chief Internal Auditor will probably have access to the results of previous audit work, and the knowledge of the auditors concerned. Salaries and wages, 50.1, is likely to be chosen due to its size. Individual weekly or monthly payments are unlikely to be material compared to the whole figure, but the misapplication of a condition of service or the presence of a payroll 'ghost' could be material.

For the sake of our case study let us assume that the Chief Internal Auditor has chosen the following selection of 'risky' areas.

		Revised estimate 19X5/X6 £
50.1	Salaries and wages	312,800
50.2	Other employee expenses	
	NI	20,400
	Superannuation	10,200
50.4	Heat, light and cleaning	20,460
50.7	Materials, equipment, etc.	26,500
50.9	Travel and subsistence	20,000
50.10	Insurance	21,500
		£431,860

These areas amount to 94% of the total for Revised estimates for the Sports Centre for 19X5/X6. The expenditure is classified mainly for budgetary purposes. Let us assume that the classifications above are useful and meaningful and that the Chief Internal Auditor's judgemental selection is sound.

Further selection and stratification

A decision must now be made on a second stage of selection. Random sampling is sometimes chosen as the second stage, but in our example the Chief Internal Auditor is likely to make some further judgements.

He might decide to stratify the population into payments of £5,000 and above and those below. In fact, there are not likely to be a large number of payments over £5,000 given the nature of the expenditure involved. Let us assume that, apart from the insurance fraud already uncovered, there are only six such payments and it is practical for each to be checked in detail as follows:

		£
50.4	Electricity 1st quarter	8,200
50.4	Electricity 4th quarter	5,100
50.6	Rates (not included in table as not considered 'risky')	11,250
50.7	Timber consignment	5,000
50.10	Insurance – buildings	6,140
50.10	Insurance – fire/theft	5,400
		£41,090

By checking the last two items **Insurance** (50.10) is eliminated from further sampling.

Salaries and wages are often examined by random sampling sometimes combined with analytical review. The Chief Internal Auditor is concerned to ensure that no major misapplication of conditions of service and no 'ghosts' have occurred. He decides to 'stratify' this area according to types of employee and work done so that examples of special allowances, overtime and other different payments are all sampled:

	No. of employees		£	% Overtime
	Full-time	*Part-time*		
Managerial	2		28,800	
Technical	4		36,000	3
Administration	3	3	38,000	3
Security	1		8,500	29
Attendants:				
Grade 1	16	2	100,600	6
Grade 2	3	40	100,900	
	29	45	£312,800	

Overtime takes up various proportions of salaries and wages as annotated above. Special allowances apply only to the four technical officers and one of the typists classed under Administration, and account for £4,000 of the above figures.

Assume that **Salaries and wages** (including overtime) is evenly distributed throughout the year (approximately £26,000 per month) and the Chief Internal Auditor decides he will allow a pay slip chosen randomly from every employee to be checked to ensure it is valid and accurate.

The rise in **Other employee expenses** (50.2) was, on further investigation, found to be due to an upgraded pension scheme, and so the Chief Internal Auditor considered this area was now no longer one of significant risk.

Discussions with the clerk who processed the **Travelling and subsistence** payments (50.9) showed that the vast majority went to five staff. It was discovered that these five were the only officers with over £1,000 paid, and accounted for £15,900 in 19X5/X6 to date. The Chief Internal Auditor decides to allow checks of 50% of the claims of the five officers (20 claims) – mostly mileage allowances.

Heat, light and cleaning (50.4) and **Materials etc.** (50.7) are very varied payments. But they are often subject to a single payment system, involving authorization of an order or contract, checks of receipt of goods or services, and authorization of invoices for payment. A final check of payment to authorized invoices is also usually made.

No obvious systems weaknesses have come to light in recent audits. The internal audit officer responsible for a recent examination estimates that each payment would take about half an hour on average to agree substantively to invoice, goods received, order, and any other relevant documents. The Chief Internal Auditor instructs that 16 payments, chosen randomly, be checked.

We can now summarize the Chief Internal Auditor's decisions in stages:

(a) **First stage.** A judgemental selection of risky areas.
(b) **Second stage.** Judgemental stratification between payments of £5,000 and above and the remainder.
(c) **Third stage.** Judgemental decisions of selection sizes, and method of selection. Items are selected either judgementally, e.g. the five officers from Travelling and subsistence payments, or randomly, for example the wages slips.

In practice, many populations are sampled in stages and stratified into 'layers' of similar sized transactions, and it is possible to use one's judgement repeatedly taking samples randomly or judgementally at different stages. In this particular example, the Chief Internal Auditor used his knowledge of the population to 'narrow the field' until finally he was forced to decide upon the merits of different classes and even individual transactions in the light of practical manpower and time constraints. (It is of course such constraints that make selections necessary in the first place.)

Results

A week later, shortly before the meeting with members, the Chief Internal Auditor has the results of the audit before him. He summarizes these as follows:

SALARIES AND WAGES

19X5/X6	Population value	£312,800

19X5/X6	Population number of transactions:	
	Monthly	120
	Weekly full-time	1,006
	Weekly part-time	1,324
		2,450

Sample size – 74, one per employee.
Sample value – £14,920.

Errors:

1. An overpayment of £4.80, part of a special allowance of £39.80 paid to Technical Officer, A. Blower. This appears to be no more than a one-off clerical error of addition taken from untidy timecard.

2. One full-time attendant grade 2, who has been in post for two months, has yet to receive his official letter of appointment. The appointment has been checked by the auditor and found to be genuine. This is a deviation of internal control and will be reported to management. Meanwhile the auditor is checking a larger selection of personal files, and will report back on whether this is an isolated lapse or symptomatic of a breakdown in this control.

PAYMENTS OVER £5,000

No further errors found.

TRAVEL AND SUBSISTENCE CLAIMS

Population value – £20,000

Value sampled (five officers):

	£
Officer 1	2,404
Officer 2	3,004
Officer 3	4,610
Officer 4	3,800
Officer 5	3,002
	£16,820

Total number of transactions – 20.

Errors:

All twenty claims show exaggerations of mileages on journeys mainly to conferences and courses. Most of the exaggerations were small, and for Officers, 1, 2 and 5 was within a 10% tolerance set as an unofficial guideline by Internal Audit. But Officers 3 and 4 are 25% and 28% over the accurate amount due. These two officers both maintain that they only entered a rough estimate of each claim mileage and assumed that administrative staff would measure the distance on a map and make any necessary adjustments. They also maintain that they never bother to check what is actually paid.

HEAT, LIGHT, CLEANING

and

MATERIALS, EQUIPMENT, FUEL, CLOTHING

Population value (50.4 + 50.7) – £46,960

Total number of transactions – 352, per records kept by budget holders.

Sample number – 16

Sample value – £1,526

Errors:

1. An overpayment of £5 – arithmetical error of measurement not spotted during invoice checking.
2. An underpayment of £1.50 – one extra box of light bulbs than ordered or invoiced.
3. An invoice (for £63.20) was not stamped 'paid' after payment. This deviation in control will give rise to a similar action as the failure to complete a letter of appointment (see p. 209).

Limitations of judgemental selection

The Chief Internal Auditor now faces one of the most difficult tasks following judgemental selections. He has to evaluate the errors found and to estimate their likely significance, if any, for the population from which they were drawn. As the selections were judgemental, any extrapolation of the results will be far more crude and prone to inaccuracy than is usual for statistical samples. This is one of the main disadvantages of judgemental selection, and the validity of such rough extrapolations is always likely to be dubious. Take, for example, Salaries and Wages. The members might be told that:

> The Chief Internal Auditor is aware of errors totalling £4.80 brought to light by recent test checks of payrolls. On the basis of the limited evidence available he feels it is likely that similar errors would not amount to more than £500, and that no more than 1% of payments will contain errors.
>
> The Chief Internal Auditor obtained his estimations as follows:

$$\frac{£4.80}{£39.80} \times £4,000 = £482.41, \text{ say } £500$$

Possible error rate if one pay slip in 74 as in error is 1.35%, say 1.5% (see p. 208).

In fact, apart from the known error of £4.80 the estimations are little better than guesses. Without statistical sampling it is not possible to make a more precise statement.

Conclusion

The lengthy judgemental selections by the Chief Internal Auditor provide little more than reasonable assurance that horrendous events, such as complete failure of internal controls over payment processing or widespread fraud, have not occurred. They have, nevertheless, provided a fairly rapid response to members' genuine concerns, and the results will provide useful pointers to further audit investigations.

These judgemental selections will usually be necessary when indications of fraud, serious errors and similar problems come to light. But such selections will need to be supplemented by representative audit samples, as illustrated in Case studies 8.1 to 8.3, before an opinion can be formed on the operational reliability of internal controls or the presentation of a set of figures.

CONCLUDING POINTS

This chapter has covered a fast developing area of public sector audit. It has introduced the auditor to techniques that can greatly improve the quality of his work in some of the most important areas of audit testing.

Much of the chapter is revolutionary compared to traditional audit-testing methods. Auditors used to following well-trodden audit trails may require a little extra effort in planning their work and evaluating the results. The rewards will be great, not least in the service provided to the client and the confidence the auditor has in his results.

9 Fraud and corruption

INTRODUCTION

Fraud and corruption are areas about which a wide divergence in perception often exists between the auditor and the auditee. The subjects of fraud and corruption are normally at the periphery of the auditor's day-to-day role whereas they are often perceived to be his main or only function by client staff. Most staff do not have frequent contact with an auditor and their opinions of his work have been formed largely by reports in the press relating to fraud. More recent press reports have included value for money reports by the National Audit Office and the Audit Commission but fraud reports still tend to grab the wider public attention. As auditors we have a duty to inform officers of the nature of our audit in general terms and if appropriate the reasons for specific enquiries. This is simply good manners and improves our professional image. Perhaps it is partly a reflection on our lack of manners that auditees tend to retain an outdated perception of our role.

This chapter is mostly concerned with measures to prevent or at least to guard against fraud and corruption. Fraud investigation should not normally account for a very significant proportion of audit effort and a well planned audit should manage to uncover any major risk of fraud. However, some guidance is offered for the auditor placed in the position of an investigating officer.

Unlike errors and system deviations each fraud tends to be treated in isolation. Because fraud cases are both complex and infrequent each one is usually seen as unique by the investigating auditor. This is unfortunate, because although many cases are unusual, common aspects can be discerned, and these can help the auditor detect or prevent similar cases. This chapter will cover some useful common measures to guard against fraud.

WHAT ARE FRAUD AND CORRUPTION?

Unlike many terms encountered in audit, legal definitions exist. Fraud as covered by the Theft Act 1968 effectively includes a wide variety of offences involving intentional deceit, falsification of accounts, corrupt practices, embezzlement, corruption, etc., and can be summed up by saying a fraud occurs where a person obtains property or pecuniary advantage by deception. This implies an element of deliberate intent and thus excludes negligence. The Act excludes forgery which is dealt with separately in the 1913 Forgery Act as the making of a false document in order that it may be used as genuine with the intent to defraud or, simply, to deceive. Thus an act of forgery can be committed even before the forged document has been used.

Corruption in public life is further covered under the requirements of the Prevention of Corruption Acts 1889, 1906 and 1916 and in the 1972 Local Government Act. Basically corruption relates to rewards or inducements such as bribes. Often many parties are involved and corruption can become widespread affecting many aspects of an organization's structure and the attitudes of officers towards their work. It is such widespread corruption involving numerous and repeated frauds that have characterized cases of public scandal, such as the Poulson affair which resulted in the Department of the Environment drawing up a National Code of Local Government Conduct in 1975.

THE SIZE OF THE PROBLEM

It is impossible to give definite figures for the number or value of frauds perpetrated in the public, or for that matter the private, sector. Most cases probably go undetected and those reported are often difficult to measure.

The Audit Commission conducts national surveys of computer fraud covering both the public and private sector. So far these have been published at three-yearly intervals, 1981, 1984 and 1987, and reveal a steady increase in the number of incidents and money involved. The Commission also publishes brief summaries of reported frauds in local authorities. Although the frequency varies between 50 and 150 per annum the most interesting and useful facet of the Commission's surveys is the case-by-case summary of the causes and outcome of each fraud. Not all cases can be fully costed in terms of losses to the organizations and numerous petty housing benefit frauds are excluded.

In 1987–88, 187 cases of government fraud were reported totalling £2½m known gross loss, though in 22 cases the amounts involved could not be determined. No reliable figures for other areas of the public sector are available, though in London the private sector frauds dealt with by the police are estimated to total over £3 billion!

THE AUDITOR'S ROLE

The auditor's role is often summed up by saying he is a 'watchdog rather than a bloodhound'. He should, it seems, he mindful of the possibility of fraud and take steps to investigate where he has grounds for suspicion, rather than deliberately setting out to hunt for fraud in areas where no obvious likelihood exists. This attitude stems from judgements dating from the Kingston Cotton Mills case in 1896 and is one that has evolved to meet the needs of the private sector external auditor, particularly in relation to stock valuation.

In the public sector the auditor seems in a similar position except that he is expected to be a slightly more diligent watchdog. He should be not just mindful of the possibility but prepared to review specific measures taken to guard against fraud – usually as part of his wider evaluation of internal controls.

The Audit Commission Code of Local Government Audit Practice sets out auditors' duties when auditing local authorities and specifies the need to consider the possibility or risk of fraud when planning the audit and when reviewing internal controls. The Code also pays special attention to corrupt practices and the authorities' 'duty' to take steps to limit the possibility of corruption.

CIPFA statements of Internal Audit Practice (now replaced by the APC auditing guideline — Guidance for Internal Auditors) mention the need for the auditor to consider the risk of fraud and the adequacy of controls to prevent fraud and irregularities. The CIPFA statement also mentions that he should be 'alert to the possibility of corruption'. The APC's auditing guideline is less specific, mentioning the need to 'have regard to the possibility of malpractice', i.e. back to the private sector's less diligent watchdog.

In general, public sector auditors have found it necessary to have a more involved (though still mainly advisory) role than their private sector colleagues. This is unlikely to change, if only because of their clients' expectations which reflect the wider moral issues when **public** money is lost through fraud.

GUARDING AGAINST FRAUD AND CORRUPTION

So far we have considered general aspects of this type of audit. We will now consider specific audit work.

Systems based approach

Ironically, perhaps, much of what has already been described under the systems based approach to audit in Chapter 6, is directly relevant to guarding against fraud and corruption. Auditors who follow the systems based approach are doing much to ensure that their organization has adequate measures to guard against fraud and corruption as this is one of the main purposes of sound internal control.

All the internal controls mentioned in Chapter 6 are to some extent helpful in preventing fraud and corruption. The documentation stage can help highlight obvious weaknesses. If the auditor finds it difficult to find out exactly what is happening, what procedures are undertaken and by whom, then an environment conducive to fraud may already exist. Lack of defined responsibilities and regular procedures enables unusual practices to go unchallenged and any discrepancies to be covered up by a hotchpotch of buck-passing.

Selected key internal controls

Circumstances will obviously differ greatly between different organizations but some key controls are particularly useful in preventing fraud and corruption, as opposed to merely reducing errors and waste.

Controls involving more than one officer

(a) **Separation of duties** – so that no single person can control the entire processing of a transaction, or the accounting for a branch or local office. In general, whenever the risk of fraud, especially misappropriation, is evident, duties should involve two or more officers, for example post opening and cashier duties.

(b) **Direct supervision** – reduces the chances and temptation to commit a fraud. Staff left alone for long periods or predictable times may be subject to greater temptation specially if they are in charge of valuable and portable assets, including valuable information. Stock-checking should usually be supervised for example.

Controls involving independent reconciliations

Bank reconciliations are the obvious category but **independent** reconciliations of at least two sets of records often deter or detect frauds as no party has access to all records. Often the very performance of a reconciliation, even if it would not 'spot' a fraud, may deter one because officers who prepare one set of records are not usually aware of the details of the other set(s) or of details of the reconciliations. Reconciliations of staff in post to personnel records, reconciliations of time sheets to charge-out totals and of computer output to input are further examples.

Controls involving signatures

Potential fraudsters are often deterred if they are required to put their signature to their work. Evidence of who did the work is often an impetus to achieve good quality and reliability. The signed transfer of cash between officers is a frequent example as are time sheets and signatures to record authorizations.

Physical controls

Locks on doors, combination safes and securely fenced goods yards are obvious examples that help to deter petty theft. Physical control generally helps to minimize risks and temptations.

Registers of declared interests

These should be compiled for both politicians and officers who have an interest in works awarded by their organizations.

Activities prone to fraud

Activities will vary from one organization to another but some of the more common ones with regard to expenditure are:

(a) Benefit claims and grant claims.
(b) Contract payments, especially building work and defence contracts.
(c) Stocks, including valuable office inventory items.
(d) Employee loans, for cars, etc.
(e) Bonuses, overtime payments and allowances.
(f) Travel and subsistence claims.
(g) Property of those in residential homes, prison inmates, hospital patients, etc.
(h) Petty cash expenses.
(i) 'Unofficial funds' for charity, club, etc.
(j) Hourly paid casual employees.

Some common activities prone to fraud with regard to income are:

(a) Cash kiosks and other unsupervised cash points.
(b) Route based cash collections, e.g. rents, car parks, etc.

(c) Fees and fines for licences, minor offences, etc.
(d) Tokens for travel, etc.
(e) Loan repayments for mortgages, industrial development loans, etc.
(f) Cheques made payable to 'initials', such as A.B.C for Aberfluke Borough Council, which can be easily amended to, say, A.B. Carter.
(g) Irregular lettings, including advertising hoardings.

Activities prone to corruption

In addition to the more common frauds certain activities can become particularly susceptible to widespread corruption, for example:

(a) Tendering, awarding and settlement of contracts, hiring consultants, or temporary staff from agencies.
(b) Pressure selling, where goods or free holidays, etc., are offered with the order.
(c) Hospitality.
(d) Awarding permissions, licences, etc., for planning or trading.
(e) Purchasing goods for delivery direct to building sites rather than to stores.
(f) Conflict of interests that arise when politicians or officers (or their family and friends) have a pecuniary interest in work awarded by a public body.
(g) The use of specialized equipment such as computers or vehicles for personal work.
(h) The destruction or disposal of obsolete stocks, furniture and equipment.

Possible indications of fraud

After the fraud, it is very easy to see the signs that were missed. Before the fraud it is dangerous to read too much into such 'signs'. Nevertheless, we attempt below to list some of the more common reasons for arousing suspicions, in no order of priority:

(a) Inability to arrange meetings with key client staff.
(b) Inability to locate documentation.
(c) Altered documents, especially if photocopied or 'Tipp-Exed', unless clearly recognized signatures accompany the alteration and the items crossed through can still be identified.
(d) Long-standing suspensed items or unexplained balances in the books.
(e) Reluctance of officers to take leave (many frauds are uncovered when the perpetrator is taken ill).
(f) Unsupportable lifestyles.

(g) Unusually frequent visits to or from contractors.
(h) Reluctance to have another person present during or when checking cash-handling duties such as overnight banking.
(i) Persistent offers to choose information, such as samples of transactions, for the auditor.
(j) Offers of exceptional hospitality, especially if these could later be construed as bribes.
(k) The computer is always 'down' when the visiting auditor expects to be able to use it.
(l) Unnecessarily spiteful allegations (whether true or not) that may be an attempt to divert the auditor's attention to an innocent third party.

One could go further. Any one of the above is unlikely to arouse suspicion; the convergance of several **should** be noticed.

Fraud checklists

Despite the likelihood that a well planned and documented systems based audit will cover all the main controls, including those particularly useful for preventing or detecting fraud, many auditors find it useful to produce a separate 'Fraud and Corruption' test programme or checklist. Apart from making sure that the main points have been covered, this measure enables the auditor to extract papers readily, showing his coverage of fraud and corruption in the event of any major cases coming unexpectedly to light.

Such checklists must be designed to suit each individual organization and would include specific tests such as:

(a) Agreeing the Register of Members' interests to Council Minutes.
(b) Re-performing bank reconciliations.
(c) Circularization of banks and main debtors/creditors.
(d) Checking the physical security of stores.
(e) Surprise cash counts and stock checks or valuable stationery and other high value stocks.
(f) Detailed reviews of standing orders and financial regulations.
(g) Physical verification of valuable/portable assets.
(h) Visits to construction sites to verify purchases and architects'/surveyors' certificates.

(b), (c) and (e) are particularly useful in detecting teeming and lading whereby officers may expropriate income and hide the shortfall. A shortfall in, say, yesterday's bankings can be made up with today's takings or by using the float or personal cash. The most famous case of such a practice led to the winding-up of Gray's Building Society – where the expropriations had been used for gambling. The Government Inspector's Report criticized the auditors and makes very interesting reading.

The possibilities for fraud checklists are almost limitless. It is important to realize that the testing should be part of the wider compliance or substantive testing designed to satisfy planned audit objectives. This is because fraud detection and prevention is usually a secondary objective at the planning stage (see Chapter 4).

Computer related fraud

This is a fast developing specialist area. Over a hundred interesting cases are described in the Audit Commission's *Survey of Computer Fraud and Abuse* (HMSO, 1987) to which the reader is directed.

Two related features seem to pose particular problems for the auditor.

(a) The perpetrators of such frauds are often 'experts' (even when using relatively familiar technology) in the sense that they understand both the input and output involved and the ramifications of their malpractice. This means they can often cover their tracks.
(b) There is an element of 'challenge' or satisfaction at manipulating very complex technical systems.

The auditor is often dealing with trusted officers (from junior operators to senior analysts) with a high level of specialist expertise; only very rarely are any outsiders involved.

Computer fraud is seldom held in contempt or disdain to the same degree as petty theft of, say, benefit cheques or patients' savings. In some respects it is almost socially acceptable, particularly if it is 'only' the organization's processing time and equipment that is stolen for personal use. This means that officers are less likely to voice their misgivings or offer the auditor their full co-operation. Controls over the integrity of computerized systems are considered in Chapter 11, and help greatly in reducing the risk of fraud.

CONDUCTING INVESTIGATIONS

The boundary between a normal audit enquiry and fraud investigation is very blurred. To some extent it depends upon the auditor's own attitude. Some would call in the police at the earliest suspicion; others, while they might alert senior management, would be reluctant to call in the police until they have overwhelming evidence.

It is a regrettable fact that many organizations are reluctant to involve the police and risk a prosecution with all the attendant adverse publicity. Some feel this would undermine public confidence, others that any prosecution is likely to harm staff morale. We feel that such arguments are against any responsible public spirit and may even undermine the support for the rule of law that has characterized British public bodies.

Whatever the auditor's feelings on this matter certain procedures must be followed:

(a) Audit papers and notes should be kept and initialled and dated. This is in any case the usual professional practice. The sources of evidence should be clearly stated even if this is an anonymous tip-off.

(b) The papers should be adequate for an intelligent layman to follow the auditor's facts and reasoning to see how he reached his conclusions. In this respect they may need to be more detailed than normal papers which need only be sufficient for another auditor not familiar with the case. All documentary evidence from the clients, or other papers, should be held in original form rather than be copied. Evidence will be indexed and filed so that its purpose and its source can be clearly identified. No original document that may be required as court evidence should remain in use. Copies may be made for the client's purposes.

(c) Interviews should be very carefully conducted. At this point it is worth considering calling in the police. They have far more experience of interviewing suspected fraudsters than do auditors. Even so, interviews may be conducted by auditors, perhaps because of the need for urgency or because, originally, fraud was not suspected.

(d) The provisions of the Police and Criminal Evidence Act 1984 should be adhered to. No promises or inducements should be made. Suspects **must** be cautioned along the lines of: 'You do not have to say anything unless you wish to do so, but what you say may be given in evidence.'

(e) The interviewee must be told he or she is not under arrest, is not obliged to remain with the interviewer and that if they do remain they may obtain legal advice if they wish to.

(f) Interviewing should be conducted with at least two auditors present, at least one of whom should be of the same sex as the suspect. Notes should be made during the course of the interview, stating the place and time of commencement and termination. The names of those present should also be recorded.

(g) At the conclusion of the interview the interviewee should be allowed to read the record made and record any points of disagreement he/she has.

(h) If a person wishes to write his own statement or record, he or she should be asked to write and sign and date the following prior to making their written statement: 'I make this statement of my own free will. I understand that I need not say anything unless I wish to do so and that what I say may be given as evidence.'

(i) In all but the most exceptional circumstances auditors will have been able to call upon the assistance of the police prior to conducting such an interview.

CONCLUDING POINTS

This chapter has briefly considered one of the most controversial areas of audit, and yet one least discussed by the profession. It is hoped that an appreciation at least of the complexity of fraud and corruption is conveyed. No examples are given for this chapter. Numerous case summaries are published by the Audit Commission in the updates to *Local Government Auditor* and by CIPFA in *Public Finance and Accountancy* and *Audit View-Point* which give a flavour of the circumstances surrounding fraud and corruption.

10 Value-for-money audit

INTRODUCTION

The chapter provides an introduction to value-for-money work. First we point out that valuable VFM work can be obtained as a 'by-product' to other types of audit work. This is followed by a discussion of the management techniques clients will be using if they are obtaining good value for money. Auditors can assess the nature and adequacy of these techniques by way of an 'arrangements review'. Where management is clearly sub-optimal the auditor can usefully report this to clients. The next stage involves an objective assessment of actual value for money achieved – 'performance review'. A list of useful publications which provide the data necessary to carry out performance review is given. Lastly we discuss how the auditor can help improve an organization's VFM after he has submitted his reports. Throughout the chapter VFM audit is discussed in terms of the essential audit process. Just as for more traditional types of audit, VFM audit starts with the setting of objectives, followed by planning, testing, opinion forming and finally reporting.

WHAT IS 'VALUE FOR MONEY'?

Value for money is achieved when a public body carries out its duties to **high standards** at **low cost**. This can be summarized colloquially by saying that a good job is being done.

Slightly more technically, value for money is achieved when administration and service provision is 'economic, efficient and effective'. These three concepts are interrelated. Economy and efficiency are similar: both relate to saving resources. Economy ensures that input costs are minimized. Efficiency ensures that maximum output is achieved at the minimum level of input cost sufficient to be effective. Efficiency, therefore, subsumes economy. A body cannot be efficient and uneconomic, but it may be both economic (i.e. cheap) and inefficient. Effectiveness is a far more positive idea. Effectiveness means that a service provided properly caters for a real need. For example, a health authority might provide substantial facilities for ulcer operations. However, most doctors and patients may opt instead for new effective drug treatment for which there is, in consequence, a long waiting list. Such a health authority would not be providing an effective service since patients are not being treated and cured.

This positive, action-orientated view of value for money is stressed in this chapter. The auditor is encouraged to go out and look for more effective ways of providing services and to report his findings to the management. Efficiency will be considered, but the auditor's work will be largely wasted if a service he helps to make more efficient turns out to be ineffective.

BACKGROUND

The value-for-money audit function is not new. Traditionally, auditors have raised issues of this nature. Usually these points have referred to economy and efficiency. Slow cash banking or slow collection of debts are still favourite points for auditors to raise. However, lack of effectiveness is also a common audit point. A poor computer system may be hindering the development of a public body. Auditors will normally raise such issues with the management as a professional duty. This type of VFM work will always be done since it forms a natural by-product of traditional audit work.

However, the public sector needs more than this relatively informal approach to value-for-money issues. This is because it does not have profitability as an ultimate control over performance. A refuse disposal company will go into liquidation if income does not, at least, match outgoings. A traditional local authority refuse disposal department did not have such a simple sink-or-swim principle by which to order its affairs. Consequently many were shown to be relatively poor value for money for year after year. Government services, many of necessity a monopoly such as defence, will always suffer from this lack of natural yardsticks. Value-for-money audit is one imperfect, but useful, method of instituting a formal control over achievement.

THE AUDITOR'S ROLE

The auditor is well placed to carry out much value-for-money work. This is because:

(a) He has access to all financial information.
(b) He has access to all management information.
(c) He is independent.
(d) He has a professional training.
(e) He is available.

The main weakness in the auditor's capacity to do value-for-money work is his lack of specialization in many of the services being provided. However, the benefits the auditor has normally outweigh the lack of specialization. Where specialization is needed this can usually be obtained as required from experts. Again this delegation is a skill auditors have traditionally nurtured.

There are three broad categories of VFM work. The simplest type of work as mentioned above is value-for-money work done as a secondary objective to some more important work. This is the type of VFM work auditors have traditionally done. The second type of work involves checking that an organization has the necessary structure and information to be able to achieve good value for money. The last category of VFM work is often the most interesting. It involves injecting new ideas and even attitudes into a management by providing details of the nature and benefits of best practice in a given field. These three types of work are laid out in Checklist 10.1 and are discussed in more detail below. A further 'follow-up' review may form a fourth category.

Checklist 10.1 Types of value-for-money audit work

1. **'By-product' VFM work.** This type of work is a by-product of audit assignments carried out for other reasons. It is normally a less structured approach than 2 and 3 below.
2. **An 'arrangements review'.** VFM work of this type is done to ensure clients have the necessary administrative arrangements to enable them to achieve value for money.
3. **Performance review.** Performance review aims to assess objectively the value for money achieved by a client when compared to past performance, agreed targets or the performance of other similar organizations.
4. **Follow-up review.** Follow-up reviews are done between major assignments. The auditor assesses the extent to which the client is implementing past review recommendations and is improving his value for money.

BY-PRODUCT VFM WORK

This type of work normally seeks to quantify the savings available to a management by minor changes in working practices. The change may be small, but often the cost benefit is substantial.

In Case study 4.2 from Chapter 4 a plan detailing work on purchases and payments was given. VFM considerations were given as a secondary objective. If, during the audit work, it was found that advantageous quick settlement discounts were not being taken, the saving available could be usefully quantified and given in the report when it was issued. In the past an auditor would probably only report on such matters if substantial sums were being lost. With a much more cost-conscious attitude being given to audit work, auditors should always seek to find areas where costs can be

---

Checklist 10.2 Likely areas for the identification of audit by-product savings

---

1. **Cashflow.** Revenue and capital receipts should be collected and banked with the minimum delay, e.g. Rates/community charge, sundry debtors, capital receipts for sale of properties. Sensible payment of creditors taking advantage of quick settlement discounts where appropriate should be encouraged.
2. **Stock turnover.** If stock does not move quickly then unnecessary holding costs are incurred and increased obsolescence and write-off are inevitable.
3. **Insurance costs/own risks.** A public body may insure items which it could easily afford to replace without insurance aid, e.g. local authority garages.
4. **Rent/buy.** Assets may be purchased that will not be used on a continuous basis. Rental would be a more economic alternative. Conversely, rents might be paid for items constantly used, e.g. small works vans could fall into either category.
5. **Rent opportunity costs.** Buildings or other assets may be owned but not used efficiently. For instance, large imposing offices may be used for storage. A better use might be to rent the asset out to a better suited user and rent a cheaper alternative when required.
6. **Overtime payment.** Where high levels of overtime are consistently paid staffing is almost certainly inefficient.
7. **Work practices.** Some work practices clearly waste resources. The likely cost of this can be estimated. For example:
   (a) near-permanent use of outside consultants or agency staff;
   (b) bonus or incentive schemes that come into operation at 'normal' levels of work;
   (c) itineraries and travel schedules for mobile staff should minimize non-productive time;
   (d) internal controls should be designed to be cost effective as well as provide an internal control.
8. **Staffing levels.** These need regular review especially after major technological or administrative change.
9. **Disposal of assets.** Obsolete stock, surplus equipment and furniture and even waste paper and other waste should be sold at a 'sensible' price rather than being auctioned or dumped.

---

cut. It is therefore useful to outline some of the areas where savings can be made. This is done in Checklist 10.2.

Ideas for savings obtained from audit work primarily done for another reason are, by their nature, likely to be superficial. This does not matter as long as this is made clear in the report. Managers then have the opportunity to investigate further and make changes as seen fit.

Having warned his client of possible cost savings and administrative deficiencies, the auditor must consider whether he can usefully carry out further, more specific work.

ARRANGEMENTS REVIEW

Normally a complex service can only be provided economically, efficiently and effectively if formal arrangements are made to control and direct the use of resources. The auditor can check the existence and assess the likely value of these arrangements. Where he finds deficiencies, he can very usefully report these to management.

This type of audit work will be done for one of the following reasons:

(a) It may form the background to performance review work.
(b) It can form an end in itself as a relatively short review of a particular service. It will provide a useful insight into the likely VFM of the service without the cost of a full review.

This second objective for an 'arrangements' review is often apt since in many public sector organizations management and accountancy information is not available in sufficient quantities to ensure value for money is achieved. Because this is a general problem in public bodies, it is worth discussing the issue further.

Management and accounting information

Public sector bodies are set up as a result of political initiatives. They are not primarily designed to make or conserve money. A corollary of this is that management and accounting information in the public sector is often considerably less comprehensive than that expected in a similar sized organization exposed to the free market. A brief comparison of the likely output from a local authority, a central government department and a good medium sized public company is instructive. This is presented in Table 10.1.

Commercial organizations are generally in a state of flux. They need to

Table 10.1 Financial and management information generally available in local government, central government and public companies

Local authority	Central government department	Public company
Accounting		
1. Both cash and accruals based accounting.	Cash accounting.	Accruals accounting.
2. Revenue accounts and balance sheets prepared.	Receipts and payments accounts.	Revenue accounts and balance sheets prepared.
3. Historic cost valuations of fixed assets.	No accounting for fixed assets.	Historic cost accounting normally with revaluation of land and buildings.
4. Revenue accounts charged with debt repayment.	No accounting for use of fixed assets.	Depreciation charged to the revenue account.
Budgets		
5. Detailed revenue and capital budget revised once during year.	Detailed receipts and payments by vote prepared once in the year.	Detailed revenue balance sheet and cash budget regularly revised throughout the year
6. Strict yearly expenditure allocations.	Strict yearly cash allocations.	Flexible expenditure allocations.
Management accounts		
7. Accumulated receipts and payments figures on relevant account codes available to managers.	Cash figures available to managers.	Monthly management accounts prepared on an accruals basis.
8. Actual expenditure and income compared to the budget at year-end.	Vote monitoring on a cash basis during the year.	Budget figures compared to management accounts on a monthly basis.
9. Budget variation analysis mainly at the year-end.	Budget variation analysis mainly at the year-end.	Monthly calculations of variances.
10. Little formal analysis of budget variances.	Little detailed analysis of budget variances.	Detailed analysis of variances at monthly management meetings chaired by senior executives.
11. Little unit costing.	Little unit costing.	Detailed unit costing with emphasis on marginal costs.

be informed on this flux at regular intervals so as to continue actively serving a market. In contrast, public bodies can reliably establish their income for some years ahead on the basis of very small quantities of information. Spending is then monitored to ensure it does not exceed available resources. In general, 'line-item' budgeting techniques are used with yearly increments for inflation. However, this stability is increasingly under threat and in any event does not obviate the need for management information.

It is sometimes difficult to know how much a public body would benefit from more detailed data on its activities. Many organizations have provided a service with very little reliance on management accounts and data which has been accepted by the public for many years. As an example, highways authorities have traditionally had only the barest information on the mileage and condition of roads for which they were responsible. However, it is not from the examples of past service provision that the effect of good management information can be seen. It is where effective management information systems have been implemented that benefits have arisen. Examples of dramatic improvement are readily available. Some local authorities have obtained detailed information on refuse disposal. This included accurate statistics on tonnes of rubbish collected, length of collection routes and technical details of available collection and disposal equipment. Using this information in conjunction with cost data from previous years, services have been improved and costs reduced at some authorities by up to a third. This represents savings of perhaps £300,000 a year for a typical shire district council.

In cases where dramatic savings and service improvements have been made, good management information has been a tool aiding achievement. Management information is not an end in itself, just a means. Examples of really dramatic change fostered by use of management data usually go hand in hand with a rapid and powerful change in attitudes by the management. Unfortunately, much of this change in attitude results from external threats to the organization concerned. This aspect of VFM is considered later.

Absence of management data

Any public service should be able to show:

(a) What it is obtained with public money, and
(b) How much public money is being used.

This sounds so straightforward that, at first, it is difficult to see how this information could not be available. However, a brief example will clearly illustrate the point. The Department of Transport and local government, often acting as agencies, will be responsible for the upkeep of many thousands of miles of road throughout the country. Every year they will spend very substantial sums of money on repairs. Management information is required which will give perhaps:

(a) The road stock condition at the beginning and end of the year.
(b) The number of miles of resurfacing, new Cat's-eyes, white lines, etc., achieved in the year.
(c) The cost in the year of each of the above activities:
    (i) in total;
    (ii) per unit.

For the vast majority of roads in Britain, management information at this basic level is not available. Public bodies throughout the country on a wide variety of services do not know what such basic provisions cost.

For some services it is difficult to define output and measure achievement. Social services provide a good example. However, for most public services useful measures of achievement can be formulated (this is discussed in the section on performance review on pp. 237–38).

Evidence of inadequate information

A number of signs of lack of management information give immediate indication of poor management control. These are listed in Checklist 10.3. In these situations an organization is incapable of monitoring its own actions. The auditor need be in little doubt that economy, efficiency and effectiveness can all be improved substantially.

Within public bodies it is common to see low spending in the summer and autumn, and substantial expenditure in the winter and spring. For such services as social security this is generally due to seasonal job prospects in

Checklist 10.3 Existence of inadequate management information

1. **No readily available information** on:
   (a) Costs incurred in total and per unit;
   (b) The result of spending programmes.
2. **Inefficient spending patterns.** Spending is not spread evenly over a budget period, but tends to accumulate over the last few months of the year.
3. **Projects are behind schedule:**
   (a) Projects are seriously overspent, delaying other projects.
   (b) Budgets are seriously underspent, signifying:
       (i)   fear of overspending due to lack of reliable cost data;
       (ii) a lack of timely cost information;
       (iii) insufficient staff to manage projects and control costs.

summer and a return to government-assisted income in winter. However, for services that are not normally demand-led, such as equipment provision for the armed forces or property maintenance, this spending pattern is clear evidence of poor management data and poor management control. Managers are waiting until the year-end before using expenditure allocations. They are doing this because, earlier in the year, they feared that they would run out of money before April and they were not able accurately to monitor spending. The results of this lack of control are clear. If most roads are repaired around March then the prices contractors charge will be unreasonably high. If construction works are undertaken when there is frost at night and working days are lost, costs will be high and safety will be impaired. Economy, efficiency and effectiveness are all severely hit. Managers know this, but cannot change the situation without dramatically improved information.

If projects are left to the end of the year, some will not be carried out in the budget period at all. Over the last few years it has been very common for local authorities to have capital spending projects designed to use funds up to the legal maximum for the year. Many authorities have failed to meet their capital budgets and substantial underspends have been observed. In these situations it is likely that insufficient management information was available to control the projects in question. In addition there has been an inability to estimate future associated revenue costs. There is a fear of current – and, to a lesser extent, future – overspending, as discussed already, and there is a lack of information on the resources needed to manage the project. Similarly, many completed projects have been heavily overspent. Cost control systems were probably either never in place, had broken down, or cost data used for budgeting was inadequate.

The cost of management data

Many managers within public bodies will readily admit that they do not have sufficient management information. They point out that obtaining information on the services they provide and the costs incurred is expensive and that the cost cannot be borne at the present. This may be the case where budgets are strained and spending is at sub-optimal levels. However, two points are worth making in this respect. First, managers who talk in this way see management information as a luxury – an expensive luxury. If this were not so they would have it already or would have moved to a different job. Secondly, when good information that can actively be used to make decisions is obtained, work practices will change so that full use is made of such information. The cost of obtaining the information will almost always be recouped through improved value for money. Even if a service does not cost less its effectiveness should be enhanced.

The auditor's contribution

We have discussed the nature and benefits of management information at some length. We have said that adequate management information is necessary to ensure that there are 'satisfactory arrangements' to ensure that value for money has been achieved. The auditor must now make his contribution.

The auditor must be 'concerned for action'. Unlike other audit functions where a negative report may assist users of accounts even if no action is taken, a negative VFM report without specific and detailed recommendations for action will assist nobody. We have said that a report on the lack of arrangements to ensure VFM is likely to be effective only in situations where change is actively sought; to make useful suggestions the auditor will need a reasonable understanding of basic management accounting as well as a proper comprehension of the public service concerned.

CARRING OUT AN ARRANGEMENTS REVIEW

When a review of a public service department's arrangements to secure VFM is carried out, the work can be divided into five phases. These phases can be referred to as:

(a) Instruction stage;
(b) Planning stage;
(c) The policy and management objectives stage;
(d) The management procedures stage; and
(e) The auditor's reporting stage.

This is summarized in Fig. 10.1.

The instruction stage

Auditors may be specifically requested to carry out work on a particular subject. Politicians, client management or the Audit Commission and public accounts committees may all commission work. Alternatively the auditor may be in a position to decide for himself where to direct his work. In any event he must clarify his audit objectives very early on so that he can effectively plan.

The planning stage

As with all audit work the auditor needs to plan his work before the detailed field work begins. After he has been directed or has decided for

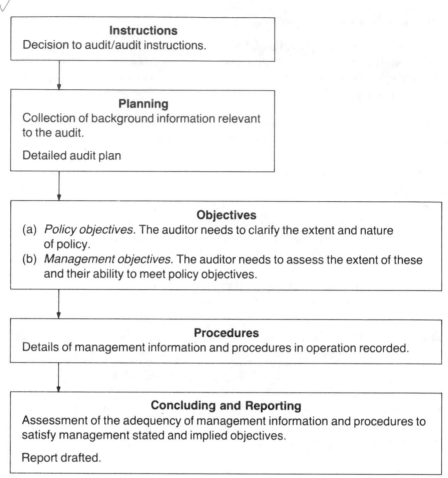

Fig. 10.1 'Arrangement' audit–an overview.

himself which area he is to review, he must obtain some background information on the subject he is to work at. A useful starting point, as with all audit work, is the accounts for the department or organization for recent periods. The auditor needs to know the materiality of his account area compared to the organization as a whole and other clients as described in Chapter 3. He can then judge the relative importance of his work and the depths of review appropriate. He should then obtain further background data from relevant legislation, departmental circulars and published data so that he understands the basis of his subject. Once all this information has been gathered he will produce a detailed audit plan outlining audit objectives, main areas of investigation, manpower, etc. (see Chapters 3 and 4).

The policy and management objectives stage

Public bodies are generally under the control of politicians accountable to the public. These politicians have policies which they use to ensure their election. The auditor has to consider these policies before he can comment on value-for-money issues. He will also need to understand the management objectives set by civil servants and local government officers which they have set to achieve the politician's objectives.

This relationship between policy and management objectives can be shown in an example. The Home Secretary may have formulated a policy on combating drug abuse. This policy could be very straightforward, such as a statement in Parliament, recorded in Hansard, to the effect that: 'This government is committed to the reduction of drug abuse in our major cities.' It is now up to the civil servants to set management objectives to carry out this policy. Such an objective might be to 'reduce the number of known drug addicts by 10% a year'.

In theory there is a strong distinction between a policy and a management objective. In practice many policy objectives are unstated or are largely set out in statutes. In these situations management objectives will cover both the policy and its implementation. As an example, policy objectives on property maintenance will almost certainly be implied and management objectives will be needed to lay out maintenance standards.

When the auditor starts his field work, as with most audit work he starts by introducing himself to the chief officer involved and discusses in outline the nature of his work. It is at this stage that he is able to obtain the essential information he requires on the policy and management objectives in that department.

The auditor needs to know the objectives of the department he is auditing for a number of reasons:

(a) He needs to ensure management objectives are designed to meet policy objectives.
(b) He needs to know management objectives so that he can assess the adequacy of the procedures and management information used.
(c) If management objectives are not clearly stated, he will use this as evidence of poor arrangements to ensure VFM within the department.

At the end of this objectives stage, the auditor must be able to prepare a list of the management's clearly stated objectives and a further list of the implied objectives of the department. He will also record those areas where there are no objectives either stated or implied. To illustrate this, consider a maintenance department for an education authority which might have a clearly stated objective that all emergency repairs are responded to within 24 hours. This would be a stated objective. There might be an implied objective that, say, schools were rewired on a regular basis consistent with high safety standards. This would imply, perhaps, that rewiring was carried out every 25 years. There would probably be no education committee minute supporting this, nor is it likely that the chief officer would be able to produce clear instructions to this effect issued to his staff. However, it would be clear to the auditor from his discussions and work that, say, high electrical safety standards were expected from maintenance staff and that wiring should be up to date. However, there would be no management objective, either stated or implied, if the auditor discovered that interior decoration of schools was carried out only on the basis of available funds.

From his lists of categorized objectives, the auditor now knows a substantial amount about the nature of the department under review. It is an exceptional organization that has detailed objectives set out in writing but which achieves none of them. Similarly, outstanding results are seldom obtained by departments which are incapable of communicating any of their management objectives to an auditor.

Management procedures

Now that the auditor understands the objectives of his client, he can look with an informed eye at the **data** and **procedures** used by the client in pursuit of those objectives.

Departmental procedures

The auditor will need a record of departmental procedures, information about which he will obtain from a number of different sources. Often system flowcharts and notes of procedures involving finance will already be held by the auditor. These records will show how income is recorded and collected, how purchases are made and paid for and how fixed assets are requisitioned and obtained. The auditor will have used these records in previous systems and attestation work, and will be familiar with their contents.

Records on information processing will not normally be held by the auditor. He will need to compile records for his use during the audit work. Often narrative notes will be sufficient for this purpose. However, if the system is complex, flowcharts or the use of internal control questionnaires will provide the best records.

Information processing relates to how non-financial records are controlled and updated. For instance, a highways authority will need to know when street-lamp light bulbs fail. Once it has been ascertained, the authority will need to arrange for bulbs to be replaced cyclically or on demand. This information will not appear on systems records prepared for the purposes of more traditional audit work: much of the work of a VFM 'arrangements' review is concerned with collecting and recording this type of data.

Management data and information

An authority may have a procedure for replacing light bulbs that work adequately. There are few complaints and it is thought effective. But does it have the necessary management information to ensure that it is efficient? Should light bulbs be replaced cyclically or *ad hoc*? The auditor needs to discover what accounting information is available to his client. He also needs to know what data is available showing the use to which the money was put. The importance of the idea that departments should know what they spend and what they get for their money has already been discussed. Using the example of street-lamp bulbs, the auditor would wish to know whether the management knows at least the following information:

(a) Costs:
    (i) How much in total was spent in a period on repairing reported street-lamp bulb failures;
    (ii) Of this total cost how much was a:
        (1) variable cost depending on the number of lamps broken;
        (2) fixed cost independent of the actual number of failures in the period.
(b) Units:
    (i) The type of bulbs breaking;
    (ii) The number of bulbs breaking.

Note it is whether the management has and uses this information that is important at this stage of the audit. If the information is available, but not used, managers are clearly hoping the system will run itself.

Often the management information required to monitor the cost of achieving objectives is complex. Sometimes it is not possible to obtain clear-cut data on what particular expenditure has achieved. An instance already mentioned is social work where spending on a policy may produce results that are very hard to monitor in the short term. However, the most efficient and effective clients will have produced the best possible methods of measuring what they achieved. As an example, a public body may provide capital grants to aid industry to assist product design. Some projects financed will be commercially successful whilst others will not. In addition, once a company has been introduced to an industrial designer further collaboration may ensue unfunded by the government which may be highly successful.

Monitoring the result of spending is clearly complex for this type of
service. However, useful statistics can be produced, for example the
following data:

(a) Number of grants given each year;
(b) Average size of grant;
(c) Administrative costs for each grant on average;
(d) Industry sector to which grants are given.

This is very basic but instructive data. If grant numbers dropped, for
instance, policy effectiveness would clearly be low. However, much more
information is available. Companies assisted could be categorized under
size. Using information from Companies House, future growth rates of
companies could be monitored. If grant monies were targeted, say on
consumer goods, the percentage input penetration in various sectors of
the market could be monitored. Similarly, the success of the design firms
used in the scheme could be monitored using design industry statistics.
Using this type of information it might be possible to state that companies
in a particular industry, making use of the scheme, on average grew by
20% each year for the last three years as compared to the industry average
of 10% a year. Clearly this type of information is of great assistance to
managers. Grants could be effectively targeted to successful areas.

Some clients will inevitably not have comprehensive data on costs and
achievements. In these cases the auditor will need to consider possible
methods of monitoring so that the inadequacy of the client's approach can
be overcome.

Reporting

Having recorded the client's objectives and the procedures and data used
to satisfy them, the auditor needs to assess the adequacy of these objectives, procedures and data so that he can report. First, the auditor must
assess the client's objectives. He will normally take the view that objectives
are best clearly stated so that staff providing the service learn what is
expected of them. Where there is an absence of objectives this is prima
facie evidence of neglect. Efficiency and/or effectiveness are almost certain
to suffer.

Where objectives are clearly stated but lead in the auditor's opinion to a
reduction in potential value for money, the auditor may consider factually
raising the issue in his report. However, he should not give a preference
himself. At this point he is beginning to move into the realm of politics and
his opinions are not called for.

The auditor should now consider the procedures used by the management to achieve their objectives. The auditor will highlight, in his report,

the procedures that lead to poor efficiency and effectiveness. For instance, the auditor might raise the issue that orders for street-lamp repairs are written out by hand for each broken bulb, when a cheap computerized system is available that sends orders directly to contractors using the telephone lines.

Lastly the auditor should consider the management information available to the client. He assesses the adequacy of this information to meet not only the management's stated and implied objectives, but also to meet those unstated, but commonly held, objectives which the client ought reasonably to have. This last point is important. Many public bodies produce management information to satisfy important unstated objectives traditional to that body. For example, information will be available in an accounts department on outstanding debtors not because it is a management objective, but just because it is necessary if proper accounting procedures are to be followed.

DETAILED VFM PERFORMANCE REVIEW

So far we have looked at by-product VFM work and at the arrangements made to ensure value for money. We have concluded and made a report, including any specific recommendations for restructuring or other improvements. It is perfectly reasonable for the auditor to finish his work at this point. He has achieved a tangible result which should be acted upon by management. However, further useful work is possible. At this stage we may refer to the work not as an 'arrangements review', but rather as a full 'project' or 'performance review'.

Performance review involves comparing the achievements of a client to valid comparators. Evidence is obtained mainly in the form of performance measures to demonstrate how the client compares **either** to the outside world **or** to its own view of satisfactory achievement – or both. Whereas in an arrangements review the auditor was looking to see if the client was likely to be good value for money, with performance review he is attempting to find out whether value is in fact obtained.

Externally chosen comparative data

The essence of performance review is very straightforward. The auditor is trying to establish that his client, say Department A, spends, for example, twice as much per unit of work done as Department B, when both departments do similar work.

For the auditor's purpose standard statistics on all types of public sector work are required. (How the auditor may obtain information on public sector work is discussed further below – see p. 243.)

Internally set objective standards

Clients which have effective arrangements for ensuring value for money will often produce their own list of objective standards with which to compare their actual results. A department handling application forms from the public may decide for a variety of reasons that it should process 300 a day. This would be an 'objective standard' by which to judge actual achievement. The Audit Commission publishes a useful volume entitled *Performance Review in Local Government – Data Supplement*. This provides 50 pages of up-to-date objective standard statistics relevant to local government. Below, examples are given for a number of different services:

Typical target age of replacement for light vans:	5 years
Average purchase discount on new vehicles:	18%
Upper quartile average for school meals produced per kitchen employee in shire counties per year:	6,698
Upper quartile average revenue surplus per 1,000 of the population for car parks in London boroughs:	£163

Both the auditor and his client should be involved in assessing the actual achievement and assessing the reasonableness of the criteria used to set the standard.

Internally set objective standards are a useful management tool and an alternative often worth consideration even when comparative data can be obtained by the auditor.

CARRYING OUT A PERFORMANCE REVIEW PROJECT

As stated, performance review follows naturally from the arrangements review. The findings obtained from looking at management objectives, procedures and management information are all needed in the assessment of actual performance, although the level of detail can be varied. At the planning stage work is required to isolate the comparative data available. At the objectives stage full details of any objective standards set by the client should be obtained. This is summarized in Fig. 10.2.

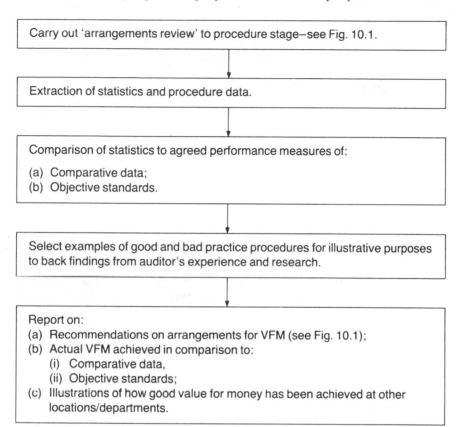

Fig. 10.2 Performance review—an overview.

Extraction of statistics

Having recorded details of the management information available within a client department as part of his 'arrangements review', the auditor is in a good position to extract and generate data for comparison.

In the arrangement review work we stressed that the auditor has to record the data **used** by the management rather than that which is simply available. For performance review purposes the auditor is not concerned about whether it is used. He needs to use it himself to make vital comparisons.

As a brief example the auditor might wish to know the ratio of planned maintenance of buildings to day-to-day maintenance since he wishes to compare his client to a good-practice bench-mark of 60% planned maintenance, 40% responsive maintenance. Clearly he would extract costs from his client's records so as to be able to make this comparison, namely:

	Responsive £000	*Planned* £000
Direct staff costs	170	185
Contractor's costs	2,372	3,151
Sundry direct expenditure	101	202
	2,643	3,538
Percentage	43%	57%

The actual statistics required by the auditor depend on what he intends to compare them to. The process of extraction and, later, comparison is illustrated further in Case study 10.2.

Comparison of statistics

Having obtained statistics in a format similar to that of his comparators the auditor can begin to assess the VFM of his client. At its simplest level comparison is straightforward. If Department A spends £100 in processing an application form from the public and Department B spends £200 doing similar work, then prima facie Department B is more expensive. However, the auditor cannot stop his work at this point. He must discover the reason for the difference in spending. Ideally he should be able to quantify the differences in spending totalling them to the variance observed. For example:

	£	£
Department A cost per form		100
Add: Additional central establishment charges in Department B	50	
Add: Additional processing staff cost at Department B	70	120
Less: Reduced stationery costs at Department B		(20)
Department B cost per form		£200

Even at this stage it may not be totally clear that Department A is the better value for money. Department B may be housed in a listed building with high maintenance costs pushing up the central establishment charges. The building will have to be repaired whoever uses it. Secondly, staff costs per application may be high due to a different mix of application type as compared to Department A. There is evidence from stationery usage that staff at B may be more careful workers than at A where stationery usage is considerably higher. This should be considered when looking at the reason for the staff costs difference.

The auditor can only discover whether value for money is being obtained at Department B by:

(a) Understanding the Department's objectives and procedures; and
(b) Informed discussion with Department B staff.

It is here that the arrangements work becomes important to performance review. If the auditor knows that Department A has defined management objectives, good procedures and relevant management information where as Department B does not, then he is unlikely to believe the high staff cost at B to be totally due to case mix. Further, in his report he can use the evidence of poor procedures to back his point that staff costs are unreasonably high.

Performance review is not easy. Care in preparation and analysis pays off and earns the respect of the client.

Selection of examples of 'good practice' procedure

When carrying out performance review work it is not sufficient just to compare extracted figures with comparators before reporting. The auditor should obtain concrete examples of tried and tested good practice procedures. These examples provide supporting evidence for his conclusions and provide persuasive precedent for his clients.

For example, work may be done on improvement grants at a district council. Two neighbouring authorities may provide very different standards of service. One may categorize all grants given so that at the year's end the number of new roofs, rewirings and damp-proof courses provided could be reported to members accompanied by unit cost figures. The other may produce none of this management data. The auditor can use the example of the good authority, even if its exact identity is suppressed, to make a very powerful point to its neighbour. In addition, the auditor has details of how such work can be done and has proof of its feasibility. This is an immense advantage to the auditor who is pushing for beneficial change.

Internal auditors will find obtaining examples of good practice procedures more difficult than external auditors. Full use of practices in different parts of the same authority and from the past can be used: service quality may be variable or have declined. In addition, contacts with external auditors and internal auditors at other organizations will be of help.

Reporting

Having made his comparisons and analysed the variances and obtained illustrated cases, the auditor is ready to draft his report. The report should cover both the arrangements work and the performance review.

Evidence of poor arrangements can be reported as fact. Even the wiliest client cannot claim he has detailed management information when he has none. The only point of possible dispute relates to the usefulness of missing procedures and data. This is covered in large measure by the performance review work.

In reporting on the performance review results the auditor is normally on weaker ground. Managers are very well aware that reports of poor value for money may be taken to mean that they are 'lazy, wasteful and semi-competent'. They will answer by asserting that they are in fact 'heroes struggling with totally inadequate resources in near impossible conditions'.

The auditor will wish to steer away from both stereotypes so as to be seen as a caring individual doing his best to assist. The auditor is genuinely concerned for action. He must make his point cogently and self-confidently, but he must not alienate the very people he relies on for a change for the better.

Checklist 10.4 Sources of comparative VFM data

Central government
1. **Government statistical services.** Central government departmental statistics.
2. **Audit Commission.** From 1991 the Audit Commission will carry out VFM studies on district health authorities. Value-for-money studies will also be published on health service issues.
3. **CIPFA management department services.** Health authorities' VFM handbook.
4. **National Audit Office.** Value-for-money studies on a number of areas of central government have been published.
5. **Central government departments.** These publish appropriation accounts every year through HMSO.
6. **Health authorities.** These publish budgets and accounts every year which can be obtained from the authorities themselves.
7. *Pink* **and** *Blue Books.* These are published by HMSO on economic statistics for public bodies.

Local government
1. **Audit Commission**
   (a) Local authority profiles;
   (b) Local authority cost trees;
   (c) Value-for-money studies on most important areas within local authorities;
   (d) Audit Commission handbook on economy, efficiency and effectiveness;
   (e) Audit Commission performance review manual.
2. **District Auditors' Society Statistics Panel Publication.**
3. **CIPFA statistical information service.**
4. **CIPFA management information service.** Local government VFM handbook.
5. **Government statistical service.** Local government financial statistics.
6. **The budgets and published accounts** of all local authorities are available on request from the authorities themselves.

SOURCES OF COMPARATIVE FIGURES

Within public services there are many sources of statistics which can be used in value-for-money work – see Checklist 10.4. Figures available in local authorities are generally more detailed than those for central government. This is largely due to the differences in public access to information between the two.

Many aspects of local government are duplicated in central government. Both maintain premises and vehicles, are involved in payment of benefits, make substantial revenue and capital purchases, provide catering facilities and heat and clean buildings. Much of the data available concerning local government will have a use in central government VFM performance review. For example, a local government vehicle fleet can be compared to that of other public bodies.

Where an auditor is doing a number of VFM studies at similar organizations he can compile his own statistics for the bodies he is involved with and make comparisons between them. This method of performance review has the weakness that all bodies looked at may perform sub-optimally. The benefit is that information can be prepared by the auditor in a totally comparable format. This is a great benefit allowing far more positive conclusions and reporting by the auditor.

FOLLOW-UP WORK AFTER VFM ASSIGNMENTS

Arrangements and performance reviews are major pieces of audit work. They cannot be carried out every financial year – nor do they need to be. However, if audit coverage is to be maintained between reviews some work is needed.

The follow-up review is designed to give an opinion on whether the recommendations made in the arrangements and performance reviews have been implemented. A simple analysis is made of procedures, costs and key statistics so that the effects of any changes can be monitored.

At the end of the work the auditor forms an opinion on whether value for money is improving. He reports this opinion to the client.

Follow-up procedures

The follow-up review starts with the formulation of a brief plan. This states the objectives and scope of the work in the same way as assignment plans for other types of audit work. Planning will include discussions with management – the auditor needs to know the problems the organization had in implementing the auditor's original recommendations.

The next requirement is data. The auditor can obtain this himself or he can ask the client for assistance. Bear in mind, however, that if the recommendations made in the arrangements review have been accepted the client will have direct access to the management accounts and statistics the auditor is likely to want. This aspect of the follow-up review is therefore unlikely to be unduly time-consuming. The auditor will know fairly quickly whether his original recommendations have been accepted and properly implemented.

Analysis of data follows. The analysis will be very similar to that done in the original review. The auditor will not need to carry out any original research; he will just slot his figures into the calculations laid out in the performance review. Again a client who has unreservedly accepted the performance review recommendations will probably monitor his own efficiency and effectiveness. The auditor will have access to the results of this monitoring.

Lastly the auditor needs to form his opinion and make his report. The auditor decides the extent to which the client is improving performance and will also isolate the main problems handicapping progress towards implementing the points set down in the original reports.

VFM follow-up work is in essence brief. It does not take long to discover whether the client is actively improving value for money and the auditor's job is to report on recent achievements or the lack of them. Client and auditor need to know whether procedures are improving and whether improved procedures are actually resulting in improved value for money.

OTHER VFM ROLES OF THE AUDITOR

The auditor is often called upon for advice by his client. Consequently his VFM role is not limited to arrangements and performance reviews. There are two areas where the auditor can assist:

(a) Promotion of organizational skills;
(b) Advice on modern attitudes to work.

The auditor who is genuinely concerned for action will wish to influence both the technical competence and the attitudes to work of his clients.

Organizational skills

In considering arrangements reviews we discussed the problems associated with inadequate management information. However, it is not only management accounting which the auditor should review. There are other areas where auditor involvement can be highly productive.

Checklist 10.5 Modern organizational skills

1. **Management:**
   (a) Management is a skill which can be taught.
   (b) Good management makes the most of available resources.
2. **Personnel.** People are the greatest asset a public body has. Emphasis on recruitment training and retention of high quality staff has a rapid and beneficial effect on the whole organization.
3. **Accountancy:**
   (a) Up-to-date methods of accounting provide much of the information managers need to manage.
   (b) Highly efficient and effective methods of accounting in conjunction with computer back-up are now available.
4. **Data processing and information technology:**
   (a) Computers assist processing and monitoring of information.
   (b) Carefully chosen software and hardware can be obtained to provide targeted management information.
5. **Market research and marketing:**
   (a) Needs must be understood and services must be publicized.
   (b) Hard work is wasted if its purpose is misunderstood or service uptake is low (e.g. tower blocks were not wanted).
   (c) Marketing is required to obtain efficient and effective use of public services.

There are a number of skills associated with running a modern organization which are required almost irrespective of its function – see Checklist 10.5. These attributes are very different from the practical competence required to build a sewer or steer an aircraft carrier, but in a complex world such organizational skills are becoming near essential. Traditionally, public bodies have not seen business management as an important area of concern. For instance, firemen sliding down poles represent the essence of the fire service. The efficiency, accountability of the provision and the marketing of fire prevention advice are still very secondary issues. Such a Victorian view of public service is now sadly out of date. The competence of the organization is now very much allied to the competence of the managers, marketing men and others who now form the backbone of the organization.

Public attitudes

To the surprise of many outside the public service sector the vast majority of those working in public service have a genuine wish to serve the community. Where circumstances conspire to limit service to the public this is often seen as unreasonableness on the part of those who finance those services.

This viewpoint assumes that the only variable affecting service provision is money. Quite clearly this is far from the case. Lack of skilled staff, poor administration and bad planning are just a few of the many other possibilities. A direct relationship between finance and service provisions has been drummed into our heads via the mass media.

To some extent the simplistic methods of financial reporting used by central government have helped reinforce the dogma. Poor management accounting throughout the public sector is another reason, as is weak budgeting. Whatever the historical reasons for this unrealistic attitude to service provision its persistence is extremely common and damaging.

How the auditor can help

Staff administering, say, housing benefit all day may tend to think in terms of immediate housing benefit problems. The same type of constrictions apply to most public servants. However, the auditor is to some extent outside this humdrum day-to-day routine. This gives him the chance to plan and investigate new ideas in a way that others find difficult. This area of audit work can be extremely rewarding since it involves creative thought followed by persuasion of senior management and finally monitoring of improved services.

The points made in Chapter 5 concerning audit credence are very relevant to the auditor in this role. He must be seen to have studied in depth the issues raised by his suggestions. Similarly, he must not overstep the bounds of his position as auditor. His role is to assist managers by virtue of his professional training and independent objective viewpoint. He must not be seen as an enthusiastic amateur attempting to specialize in someone else's field.

Pursuing change

The auditor can further change in a number of ways. He can:

(a) Include detailed recommendations in his arrangements and perform-
    ance review reports;
(b) Provide specific advice to clients who have asked for guidance;
(c) Promote the formation of management structures dedicated to im-
    proved performance.

The first two methods of influencing the way services are carried out are generally accepted practice. The third is more complex. Public services are run by senior officers who often consider they are there to provide a single service in pursuit of regulations or statutes. Despite the recommendations of the Bains Report and moves towards a more corporate approach, particularly in local government, management structures still tend to isolate one service from another although both may be the responsibility of one organization. Beneficial change almost always requires a broader view of service provision. In the formation of that wider viewpoint the issues of efficiency and effectiveness are paramount.

In order to promote what are in fact stronger and more vigorous management structures, the auditor has to demonstrate to senior officers the benefits of modern management techniques and the limitations of the old working practices. In local government the co-operation of the chief executive is essential. There are a number of areas which the auditor should stress, as laid out in Checklist 10.6.

Written management objectives

As we discussed under arrangements reviews, objectives are essential to strong management. The auditor should stress that it is important that the public body as a whole promotes the setting of objectives in all its different departments.

Checklist 10.6 Effective operational management

Positive thinking managers need to be accountable to the management as a whole. To do this there needs to be:

1. **Written management objectives.** These should cover all activities of the public body.
2. **Strong budget setting procedures.** Some form of zero based budgeting should be used whenever possible.
3. **Budget review and variance analysis.** Budget/actual achievement variances should be calculated on a regular basis, ideally once a month. The reasons for variances should be highlighted.
4. **Regular senior management meetings.** Senior management will be:
   (a) accountable for budget variances;
   (b) able to discuss and implement policies on a corporate basis to improve value for money.

Strong budget setting

Value for money depends on strong budgeting. Consequently, budgets must reflect income and expenditure at realistic levels associated with efficient and effective service provision. Public bodies spend substantial amounts of time producing budgets which are often really little more than last year's budget plus a percentage for inflation. This form of budgeting may be adequate as a basis for wider political debates, but not for detailed operational management. 'Zero based budgeting' or 'planned programme budgeting' should be employed wherever it is practical so that the budget represents a positive action plan rather than a continuation of the status quo.

Budget review and variance analysis

Having set a budget many public sector bodies make only one formal comparison of actual results achieved with the budget. A much more rigorous probe into budget variances is required if value for money is to be achieved. Managers should be provided with variances on their budgets once a month or at the worst once a quarter. The auditor should promote internal reporting structures so that this information is available.

Senior management meetings

Once managers have obtained operating variances for their departments they need to account for major differences to their peers. The view that money wasted by one department is money that would have been available for other departments to use should be stressed. Managers will take a far more active interest in the management of the organization as a whole if they believe that poor management, say in the police, is adversely affecting fire services. Monthly management meetings coinciding with the production of budget variances act as a very strong stimulus to corporate and departmental efficiency and effectiveness.

Management meetings will not only consider budgets and past achievements. They will also discuss and implement new procedures for improving services. One of their first activities will be the setting of objective standards for all aspects of the public body's activities. This process will continue so that improvements are continually being considered while subject to scrutiny by all departmental managers that may be involved.

All auditors should strongly recommend senior management meetings as a method of promoting value for money. This can be done as part of a review of overall arrangements a client might use to ensure value for money.

Internal auditors can usefully take a more direct role in setting up the appropriate reporting and management structures. Internal auditors could usefully sit in on senior management meetings using them as an important opportunity to inform managers of the possibilities available to them.

SUMMARY

Value-for-money audit is an expanding and exciting area for auditors, who are naturally well placed to provide this service. The auditor should consider value-for-money points in all his work. He should carry out reviews of individual services to ensure that there are proper arrangements for ensuring value for money. He should carry out performance review work to make objective comparisons of services to external and internal criteria. The auditor should seek to promote managerial and organizational best practice, and should inform his clients of the benefits of effective accountability of senior managers to their peers and political members.

Both cases studies which follow are based upon assignment plans given in Case studies 4.2 and 4.3 in Chapter 4. Key working papers have been illustrated. These exemplify the circumstance of, first, a by-product value for money and, secondly, a major value-for-money project covering both arrangements and performance:

(a) **Case study 10.1.** Most auditors will recognize the type of audit points raised, but it requires further consideration to single out the value-for-money issues, and to recognize the opportunity of presenting at least a management letter if not an audit report to the client body.
(b) **Case study 10.2.** This presents a major reporting situation based on detailed arrangements and performance review work.

The examples have been kept to an absolute minimum. It should be borne in mind throughout that a major VFM study would include far more detail than it is practical to include here as a case study.

CASE STUDY 10.1 RIBSTONE DISTRICT HEALTH AUTHORITY

Extract from Internal Audit Report on Purchases and Creditor Payments System: Value for money.

Settlement discounts

6.1. A number of suppliers have recently introduced discounts to encourage quicker settlement of their accounts.
6.2. There are three major suppliers who have offered 2½% discount if invoices are paid within 2 weeks. The Health Authority is now taking over 2 months to settle most creditors' accounts, and no discount is taken.
6.3. The authority could make worthwhile savings by isolating invoices for the few suppliers offering discounts and paying them early. The probable savings available have been quantified below. It can be seen that they are sufficient to cover the salary of one junior member of staff.

6.4. Potential available savings for discounts:

Supplier	Annual estimated turnover £	2½% discount £	Interest loss (10%) £	Saving £
Smith's Taxi & Car Rental	103,000	2,575	1,188	1,387
T.E. Heating Oils Ltd	417,000	10,425	4,812	5,613
Brooms Cleaning Services	251,000	6,275	2,896	3,379
				£10,379

6.5. Finance staff should consider taking settlement discounts where they are offered. The benefit of the discount does need to be set against the cashflow advantages of normal payout procedures before a decision is taken.

Opportunity cost of office space

7.1. The creditors' payments department is situated in a large Victorian building in Ribstone. Recently this area of the town has seen a substantial increase in property rents. Most of the adjoining properties are now used by firms of solicitors and accountants.

7.2. Rents paid by professional practices for such accommodation are now at £15 a square foot. Rents for office space nearer the main hospitals in the district are about £7 a square foot.

7.3. A substantial saving could be made by transferring the creditor section to available space near to Ribstone Hospital, leaving their present accommodation open to rent or sale.

7.4. Saving available from vacation of present property:

Floor area	4,000 sq. ft.
Probable open market rent 4,000 × £15	£60,000 p.a.
Probable replacement rent 4,000 × £7	£28,000 p.a.
Potential saving	£32,000 p.a.

7.5. The benefits and likely costs involved in relocating the department need full consideration. However, significant savings do appear to be available.

CASE STUDY 10.2 URBAN POLLUTION INSPECTORATE

VFM work on building maintenance at the Urban Pollution Inspectorate has been carried out. Extracts from a few of the working papers from the project are given.

The report on the work has yet to be written. The important points that will be made will include the following:

(a) **Arrangements:**
   (i)   The management objectives of the inspectorate are not clearly stated, particularly with regard to emergency repairs.
   (ii) Where objectives are set in detail no monitoring occurs to ensure that they are complied with.
   (iii) Management information is generally 'thin' and little use is made of it.
   (iv) Budget/actual performance comparisons suggest that poor management information is preventing achievement of planned maintenance budgets.
(b) **Performance review:**
   (i)   The level of emergency maintenance to planned maintenance is severely sub-optimal.
   (ii) Efficient and effective property maintenance requires a high level of planned maintenance. This is not being achieved at the Inspectorate.

Arrangements to secure VFM

Building repair policy

The Inspectorate has a general policy noted in its operations booklet that all assets owned or used by the Inspectorate must be kept in good working order.

Management objectives

The Inspectorate has a Buildings Repair Manager who is responsible for the maintenance of all offices, testing stations and depots. He is in charge of both day-to-day management of repairs as well as the longer-term management policy.

The repairs manager has the following management objectives:

A. Routine maintenance
1. Written objectives issued as desk instructions to staff:

		Repairs cycle
(a)	Painting – Exterior joinery	5 years
	– Exterior masonry	5 years
(b)	Floor finishes – Testing areas	4 years
(c)	Heating systems overhaul	5 years

2. Objectives implied by procedures undertaken:

    (d) Replacement of windows   about 40 years

3. The Inspectorate has no management objectives for:

    (e) Re-roofing

    (f) Rewiring

    (g) Re-plumbing

    (h) Interior redecoration.

B. Emergency maintenance

1. The Inspectorate has no written management objectives covering emergency maintenance.
2. Objectives implied by procedures undertaken:

    (a) Response time – as soon as possible.

    (b) Type of repair – most repairs can be classed as an emergency.

Management procedures

Not recorded here.

Management information

Background

Management information on the state of repair of buildings stock is not recorded.

Data on work carried out during the year is reasonably comprehensive. Details of numbers of windows painted and areas of roofing replaced, for instance, are kept. However, the information is used to calculate estimated costs of works by which may be judged the reasonability of new contractors' prices. A comparison of expected maintenance achievement and actual achievement in terms of unit costs is not carried out.

Generally both jobbing and planned maintenance outturns are monitored only financially. Little measurement of physical output or calculation of budget variances on a unit basis is attempted.

Arrangements/performance review

Budget outturns in recent years:

	19X0–X1		19X1–X2	
	Budget £000	*Actual* £000	*Budget* £000	*Actual* £000
Salaries and administration expenses	295	318	321	342
Routine repairs	1,200	1,101	1,200	1,093
Emergency repairs	1,450	1,702	1,600	1,806
Other expenses	52	56	55	61
	£2,997	£3,177	£3,176	£3,302

An analysis of the 10 largest routine maintenance contracts and their budgets is given:

	Budget £	*Actual* £
Derby depot repainting	98	120
New heating in Norwich offices	105	115
Redecoration of London office	45	47
New roof to Newcastle testing station	112	–
Refurbish Bristol WCs	21	24
Liverpool depot repainting	85	41
Reclad Leeds testing station	75	134
Rewire and plumb Birmingham testing station and office	107	105
New roofing and refurbishing Manchester depot	145	47
New flooring at Norwich testing station	57	49
Other	350	411
	£1,200	£1,093

Performance review

Objective standard – ratios of planned to emergency work

A best practice 'bench-mark' by which to judge ratios of planned to emergency building maintenance work is 60% to 40%. It has been found that even higher levels of planned maintenance to emergency are efficient, e.g. 70 : 30.

Calculation of ratio at the Inspectorate

	Routine £000		*Emergency* £000
Total costs per accounts		1,327	1,975
Less: Fixed costs			
– Other fixed expenses	(49)		(12)

	Routine		*Emergency*
– Overheads absorbed within administrative expenses (41% on cost rate)	£000 (54)	£000 (46)	
	(103)		(58)
Actual ratio	£1,224	'	£1,917
Bench-mark	39%		61%
	60%		40%

CONCLUDING POINTS

No single chapter could do full justice to a subject so extensive and in such a state of flux as value-for-money auditing. However, if the reader appreciates the nature of the different types of value-for-money audit and the need to approach value for money in the spirit of a unified audit approach, this chapter will have achieved its objectives.

The auditor can develop wide value-for-money skills by attempting value-for-money projects and reading the value-for-money reports of other auditors. The National Audit Office and the Audit Commission publish extensive, often controversial, value-for-money reports. These exemplify the best current practice and are recommended for further reading.

11 An overview of computer audit

INTRODUCTION

In this chapter we consider computer audit for the non-specialist. We intend to provide a framework for such audit work and an appreciation of the main techniques encountered as part of normal audit assignments. Figure 11.1 shows the main areas of computer audit.

Most auditors should be familiar with what computers are and do, though not usually how they do it. They should realize that computer audit is not a distinct sub-type of audit like, say, contract audit. Contract auditors audit contracts, or at the very least the contractors' final accounts. No one should seek to 'audit' a computer in the same sense as one might a contract. It is not the computers that matter; it is the way they are used by the clients or the use to which they can be put by the auditor.

THE ROLE OF COMPUTER AUDITORS

All auditors will need to be computer auditors for some of their work in all but the smallest organizations. Nowadays it is rarely feasible or efficient to call out specialist computer auditors every time computerized procedures are encountered during audit work. Three broad types of work are undertaken:

(a) Technical reviews of a proposed or existing computer development. This, the traditional type of work, generally accounts for a decreasing proportion of time as demand for (b) and (c) below increases.
(b) Advice to other audit staff regarding individual controls and weaknesses related to specific computer hardware or software.
(c) The use of computers to assist general audit work.

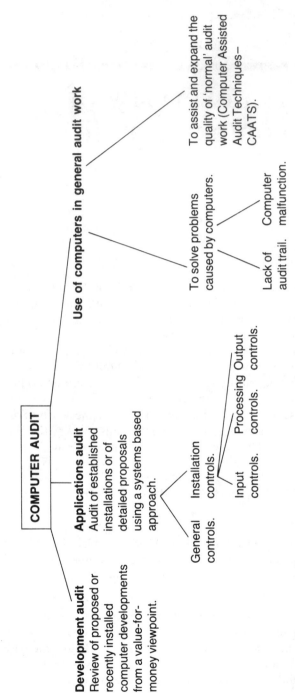

Fig. 11.1 Computer audit.

All three types of work can be usefully carried out by a non-specialist, depending on the complexity of the system being looked at. Where substantial computer expertise is required a full-time computer auditor should be called upon.

We will not describe all the likely duties a specialist computer auditor will encounter. Instead we will tackle the main aspects of computer audit, generally sufficient for the non-specialist auditor, with further indications where appropriate when specialist work is required.

One of the interesting features of computer audit is the emphasis on combining VFM review with wider aspects of systems based audit. Quite often the review of an installation can conveniently include the system development controls and the application controls, designed to ensure both VFM and the completeness and accuracy of transaction updating. This exemplifies the way in which VFM issues rise to the forefront of audit when very large sums are involved.

SYSTEMS DEVELOPMENT AUDIT

This is computer audit from a value-for-money viewpoint. Basically, the auditor needs to form an opinion around the following key questions:

(a) **The approval stage.** Is there a system of controls that ensures no development can be approved before the need for it has been assessed and documented?

(b) **The costing stage** or **cost-benefit stage.** Are all approved developments fully costed with detailed cost-benefit analysis of capital and revenue implications?

(c) **The planning stage.** Are all approved developments subject to a project planning stage? This should lay down standards of control, user requirements, amendment procedures, the implementation times of each stage of development, and any other planning considerations relevant to the particular organization and development.

(d) **The post-implementation review stage.** Are there control arrangements to ensure post-implementation review from the moment the system goes live?

In practice, the first three stages usually overlap. Approval may be withheld until the main costs and benefits have been assessed; costs may not become clear until user requirements are fully understood.

The approval stage

This often involves the preparation of a documented development plan and/or fairly detailed report outlining the departmental computer requirements, workload estimates, estimated cost at least in terms of maximum likely figures, and other information to justify the need. In most organizations, a head of branch, chief officer or other senior level manager should give his approval for the project. Even relatively small projects can, if they go badly wrong or need specialist assistance, end up being far more costly than at first anticipated. For this reason, the chief financial officer should be required to 'vet' the costings of all new projects over a very low *de minimus* level.

It is important to employ a separation of duties in project approval that goes beyond the normal requirement for two single officers to be involved in a transaction. We have already mentioned the need for a financial and other senior official to be involved but in many cases it is the finance department which wishes to implement a new development. As a general rule, no single department should have the power to approve major new developments. In most cases a 'computer development group' or similar body with representation of all departments can be set up, or the chief executive, minister or other relatively independent figure can be asked to give approval. This will help ensure that no one department dominates development, perhaps because of its existing expertise in computer development rather than its comparative need. Computer developments are usually costly and can offer so many opportunities and pitfalls that, whatever detailed stages are involved, the needs of the body corporate must be seen to take precedence over those of any one department or branch.

The cost-benefit stage

This should consist of at least two stages of review. The initial costings/benefits are supplied on behalf of the main instigator of the development. The final costing stage prior to certification by the chief financial officer is presented for the approval of an inter-departmental group. In practice, this latter stage may be very brief for small developments which can usually be costed in detail by a relatively junior accountant.

The auditor will usually need to test approvals in detail to form an opinion on the level and detail of cost-benefit analysis. Is a simple payback period calculation sufficient? Should calculation of the net present value of future costs and benefits be undertaken? Is approval of low cost schemes becoming a 'rubber stamp' exercise? In the current public sector climate these types of questions can form the basis of a value-for-money exercise.

The planning stage

This stage will include some of the foregoing aspects outlined under the approval and cost-benefit stages, but planning involves far more than deciding the project will be of net benefit to the organization and does not conflict with the priorities of other departments. Arrangements should be set up to ensure that users formally agree to the system specification. This may have to be rewritten or 'dejargonized' for more complex systems. Even a relatively simple application involving a desk-top microcomputer, perhaps to perform a job scheduling or time-recording function, should at least have documented user requirements agreed in writing by the user and a systems analyst, or on the contract with a software package supplier. In practice, many micros are relatively powerful machines compared to mainframes over ten years old and the user, in conjunction with in-house computer section expertise if necessary, should ensure he is fully aware of his machine's potential. Perhaps a cheaper model would suffice.

A detailed planning stage should also ensure that systems are not unnecessarily duplicated. Each plan once approved by the inter-departmental group should be summarized and categorized to enable periodic review of resources by audit and management as a control to ensure that unnecessary duplication of development, particularly micros, can be spotted and prevented.

Planning should incorporate resource requirements in manpower and building space terms as well as cash terms. Target dates should be clearly set out. Standards of internal control (these will be mentioned later in detail) should be agreed with internal auditors. Procedures to deal with unforeseen difficulties should also be agreed. The ability to retain the old system in the event of major systems failure in the early stages of live running is particularly important.

Overall it is more important for the auditor to ensure that adequate formal project planning procedures along the lines discussed are implemented than to become involved in the assessment of detailed planning himself. He should not usurp the role of management.

Post-implementation review

This stage is usually the most difficult and least popular stage of system development review. Woe betide the auditor who reports that a multi-million pound data processing system, installed and running for the past three years, is quite ineffective in meeting its policy objectives of, say, halving a claims waiting list. This is especially the case if he is able to point out the management's own shortcomings in not recognizing that the policy objectives could easily have been met by a slight amendment to administrative regulations governing the claim.

Obviously, the auditor would have to present any such report with the maximum of tact. In such cases, the auditor may well be the subject of justifiable criticism if he had not checked to ensure management had adequate controls over the implementation stages of the project (stages (a)–(c) above).

If the worst case occurs the auditor may simply have to accept some degree of unpopularity with management. It will normally be short-lived and more than offset by the long-term impact he can achieve.

Sometimes the auditor is able to carry out detailed post-implementation reviews as part of his VFM programme. He should pay particular attention to the effectiveness of projects in meeting agreed user requirements. If the requirements are not stated in terms of management and policy objectives the auditor will need to ensure that the user requirements are indeed compatible with such objectives. User requirements should in any case have been reviewed in auditing stages (a) to (c) but such requirements are often subject to alteration as the project develops, for example at initial testing of the new system.

If, as is usually the case, the auditor does not have resources to conduct his own post-implementation review of all projects, he should ensure that arrangements exist, and are adequately recorded, for management's own review. This should be undertaken by senior management not directly involved in the implementation if it is to have a reasonable degree of credibility and independence.

APPLICATIONS AUDIT

This involves the auditor in reviewing the procedures and controls set up to input, process and output data. In most situations applications audit will form part of one or more wider systems based audits.

Sometimes it is convenient to carry out the 'computer application audit' as a separate exercise, particularly if related to several processing systems. At other times it can be conveniently integrated into the wider system audit.

Input controls

Input controls should ensure that input data is complete prior to input and that all data has been accurately and completely input to the processing unit. For large-scale batch processing systems still commonly employed, a high degree of control can usually be exercised. Some frequent examples follow:

(a) Batch header slips should record at least the batch total value, number of documents, date and signatures of officers responsible for transferring the batch from the preparation to the data entry staff.

(b) Upon input, batch totals should be agreed to input totals retained on hard copy printout or written onto the header slips.

(c) Input can be punched into the system and verified by separate officers who sign and date 'punched by' and 'verified by' boxes on an input control sheet.

(d) Input totals should be agreed directly to output totals whenever possible.

For on-line systems different controls are required. These are often direct on-line systems updating live data and are usually operated from a network of visual display units (VDUs). Sometimes the on-line VDUs are used indirectly to update transaction files which are themselves used to update a master file at the end of the day's work. In either case similar controls are required, for example:

(a) Sufficient separation of duties of ensure that no single operator can process an entire transaction.

(b) Password controls over access to data. These may be different for different levels of access to the data, e.g. Password A – Read only; Password B – Read and update amounts only; Password C – Read and update amounts and standing data. Individual passwords may apply for different personnel.

(c) Random selection of transactions output for checking back to source documents, by supervisory staff without input duties.

The situation for stand-alone micros and workstations is similar to on-line input. Slightly more risks to input are likely as supervision is more difficult. The most important controls may be controls ensuring that access to the microcomputer is restricted by, say, a key and that no transaction processing can be undertaken, i.e. the machine can only be used for management information and data analysis.

Processing controls

Unlike input controls processing controls can be the same for very different hardware systems. A variety of controls are incorporated into the computer program to ensure that data is processed completely and accurately. This usually means that the input transaction data is correctly used to update a master file, e.g. commercial rates payments are used to update each commercial property account. In some cases, the input data may be subject to manipulation by a computer program for other purposes such as preparing a statistical analysis. Typical controls might include:

(a) **Format checks** whereby the program compares the alpha-numeric or other format of key input fields to a predetermined format.

(b) **'Reasonableness'** checks of the type and value of input records, e.g. that payments cannot be above a maximum as refunds of fees are within a maximum and minimum range. Age limits of applicants, stock line types might also be programmed for comparison to 'transaction' data.

(c) **'Matching'** of transaction data fields to key fields in the master file such as names and postcodes on input data being matched to suppliers' names and postcodes prior to updating a creditors' file.

(d) **Run-to-run** totals are often produced, as transaction data is used to update one or more standing files to ensure the complete number and value of records have been processed.

(e) **Exception reports** are sometimes automatically produced and sent to key managers to identify unusual transactions by size and type.

(f) **'Validity checks'** like (b) above often compare input data as updated values to valid codes or other tables of valid parameters held on the program.

(g) **'Check digits'** are key characters usually punched into the end of a data field that allow the program to test the validity of the field compared to a pre-set formula and reject any incorrect fields.

(h) **Sequence controls** ensure that data is processed in a predetermined order, e.g. that property rent charges are not updated before the latest tenant changes.

Output controls

These must satisfy the auditor that output data is complete and accurate and in most cases that it is timely and securely distributed (especially since the Data Protection Act 1984) and acted upon. As with input controls output controls have a large clerical component, selected examples are:

(a) **Direct comparison of input to output.** This can seldom be done manually for every transaction – why use the computer if every transaction can be conveniently rechecked manually? Usually it is important to check input for totals of transactions processed, by number or value, or for selected characteristics of all transactions such as details of age, income etc. Such direct comparisons give assurance of both completeness and accuracy.

(b) **'Reasonableness' checks** of output can be included to compare calculations done by the computer program to pre-set parameters such as maximum weekly wage or salary or maximum totals of payment to individual suppliers' credit ratings.

(c) **User recipient should be specified** on the hard copy printout. Users should be required to sign for sensitive output.

(d) **Error correction and exception reports** may be separately logged and the logs reviewed by senior management to ensure this particular category of output has been actioned.

(e) **General control schedules** can be used to monitor expected output against actual output.

For on-line VDU and stand-alone systems much output may be via screen display without hard copy backups. However, when file records are altered hard copy may need to be produced, authorized and evidenced by the officers responsible. For rent, community charge, taxes and general charges, for example, notification should be sent to tenants, chargepayers, etc. This output should be authorized independently from the officers responsible for inputting the change details to lessen the risk of fraudulent changes.

The examples of input, processing and output controls mentioned above are merely the more common ones from among the large number and variety found in practice. If specialist controls are required or the detailed programming of these controls is to be examined, then programming expertise will often be required. This, given the development of high level languages, is becoming ever more a feasible option for the auditor.

General organizational controls

The variety of possible general controls is enormous. These controls are designed to safeguard the computer hardware and software and ensure their validity and value for many day-to-day operations. Examples of general controls include:

(a) **Separation of duties** between programming, including system design staff and computer operations staff. This should reduce the risk of unauthorized program amendments. Other separations between management and staff for purposes of reviewing operations logs (see below) and between operational and error correction work should also be considered, resources permitting.

(b) **Management controls** to ensure periodic review of computer 'logs' that record the details of system amendments and in many cases master file updates should be undertaken and recorded to detect any unauthorized program amendments or suspicious file amendments.

(c) **Backup copies** of all master files should be retained at remote locations from the main computer installations. Depending upon the difficulty of recovery from fire, flood, theft, etc., it may be necessary to keep copies of all transaction files too. In general at least two 'generations' of data should be kept, and three or more is not uncommon.

(d) **File libraries** in the larger installations should record all the files held or in use and each officer requesting disks or tapes should sign and date an issue-returns register as appropriate. Smaller installations may need to keep a similar record.

(e) **The physical safeguards** against dust, heat, vibration, etc., should be checked by qualified experts and certified at least once per year.

(f) **A disaster recovery plan** or procedure should be designed, agreed by senior management and tested at regular intervals.

(g) **Terminal locations** should be planned to minimize the risk of unauthorized use or vision of sensitive screen displays.

(h) **Terminal keys** should be issued and recorded if access is to be restricted to designated users.

(i) **Software controls** over unauthorized entry to the system include passwords (see above) with a limitation on the number of attempts at password entry and encription of particularly sensitive data so that it must be decoded before it can be read.

(j) **Insurance** against disaster and theft should be regularly reviewed.

COMMON DATABASES

Many organizations are starting to employ common databases. This means that the data is held separately and is commonly accessible for different applications. Audit implications can be varied but particular attention must be paid to ensuring that any commonly held sensitive data cannot be accessed by unauthorized officers. The vulnerability of data will usually be increased, and any loss is more likely to affect the whole organization. The requirements of the Data Protection Act 1984 may be difficult to meet. In general, common databases are only justifiable in terms of cost and risk if frequent need to share data occurs between different users.

USE OF COMPUTERS IN GENERAL AUDIT WORK

As any user of a computer will know computers are often a mixed blessing. Their phenomenal processing power is a great benefit. By contrast computers can also cause enormous problems when their software or hardware is deficient. Because computers of different types and sizes are now so common the auditor needs to consider both the benefits and problems of computers during much of his general work.

Computer interrogation of a client's machine will allow the auditor direct access to records in a highly efficient manner. This may be of assistance to the audit both when computerization is causing problems and when it is successful.

Problems caused by computers

There are two types of problem associated with computerization which the auditor may have to consider.

(a) Lack of audit trail;
(b) Computer malfunction.

Both these cause the auditor problems since they make audit testing difficult.

Lack of audit trail

In a manual system it is usually relatively simple to trace a transaction from start to finish through a client's records. Normally the same applies in a computerized system. For instance, it is seldom difficult to trace a purchase from an order through to a record in the books of account. This is the case whether the system is manual or computerized. Each stage of the transaction is normally fully documented. Problems arise, though, when a computer does not document all the stages of its work. When this happens the auditor may not be able to trace a transaction from its source.

A common example of a lack of audit trail caused by a computer is a stock recording system. Many stock systems value each stock line at the price paid for the last stock item purchased. A consequence of this is that the cost of stock is usually different to its valuation in the books. The difference is written to the revenue accounts in a double-entry book-keeping system as a valuation adjustment. An auditor wishing to check the composition of the adjustment would need to check the aggregate of all the many revaluations of all stock lines over the period. The problem is that:

(a) The computer will normally keep no record of the individual revaluations;
(b) The number of revaluations will be very large.

What then does the auditor do?

Manual re-performance

The simplest method of overcoming a lack of audit trail is extremely tedious but in some cases may be the most effective. The auditor can manually re-perform the work of the computer to ensure that it gives the correct answer.

In the situation of stock revaluation the auditor may perhaps manually recalculate the change in stock adjustment over a week. If he agrees the computer calculation for a small period he may consider that the revaluation computer program is working properly.

In most cases manual re-performance is the least satisfactory and most expensive audit solution to a lack of audit trail.

Test pack

A better method of dealing with the problem involves the use of test data. The auditor can run a pack of test data through a computer program. He can then compare the output from the computer to his own precalculated results. The benefit of this audit method is that the pack can be designed to incorporate a large variety of non-standard transactions which may highlight weaknesses in the software. Another significant benefit is that the test pack can be used more than once. Repeated use can provide rapid and therefore cheap audit evidence. There are, however, problems with audit evidence from test packs. The evidence obtained is indirect; no evidence is obtained about live transactions. Another disadvantage is the substantial time needed to write new packs.

Desk check

In the example of the stock revaluation system it may be that the auditor would not wish to check the system manually or use a test pack. He may wish to use a 'desk check'.

A desk check involves analysis of computer programs by an auditor who is skilled in programming computers. By following the logic of the program through the auditor can form an opinion on whether it will produce in practice the expected output.

Amendments to programs

Since a lack of audit trail is caused by a lack of documentation, the best method of audit is to remedy this lack and then carry out normal procedures.

With the audit of historic data the recreation of documentation may not be possible. But often data is available within the computer but is not available in hard copy or on a VDU screen because no reporting program has been written. The auditor therefore needs to obtain such a reporting program either by writing it himself if he has the expertise or more usually by seeking expert assistance.

Where an auditor wishes to provide an audit trail for future work he will have to convince client management of its importance so that programs can be obtained and run so that the information the auditor needs is available.

Computer malfunction

When a computer does not work properly the auditor can be faced with serious problems. If he is to report usefully and positively he and the client will need to co-operate in solving these problems. Normally the client will carry out most of the routine work. The auditor will give advice and check results.

Computer malfunction causes similar problems to a lack of audit trail. However, these problems are of a more serious nature and the risk of error is clearly much more significant.

As with a lack of audit trail the auditor's first option is manual re-performance of the work. Often the auditor arranges for his client to do this work for their mutual benefit. Client and auditor will also need specialist assistance. This should normally be provided free of charge by the providers of the faulty programs.

Lastly the auditor may consider interrogation of data held in the faulty system by use of another computer program. Data can be test checked to discover the stage within the system that gives rise to the errors. In the simplest of cases this type of audit work may highlight that a report listing in alphabetical order is correct but that a similar report in account code order is flawed.

Where computer malfunction occurs the auditor needs to use all his intelligence and ingenuity to solve the resulting problems without excessive expense.

COMPUTER ASSISTED AUDIT TECHNIQUES

As computers improve and become more flexible the auditor's work tends to become less laborious. Reporting packages can provide data for the auditor that was never formally available. Interrogation packages can sort vast quantities of transactions into meaningful lists. The auditor needs to be aware of the capabilities of his client's software. He also needs to know what software is available that auditors can purchase for their own use.

Use of computer software to assist audit is known as 'computer assisted audit techniques' or CAATs. The first CAATs programs were developed in the 1960s. A few of the large accounting firms began to use them in conjunction with a statistical sampling approach to audit sampling – a use for which CAATs are highly suited. These days computer programs are available covering a number of functions as discussed below.

Test data

The most basic but one of the most useful computer programs to assist audit is one that can be used to select samples for audit testing. Computers are ideal for providing random or monetary unit samples. These days all auditors should arrange for such programs to be run at all their major clients.

Analytical review data

Computer programs can process data into an ideal format for comparison with other imformation. For instance, a computer could provide a list of stock lines which have not moved for over a year. This listing could be compared with previous years' figures and to known statistics on stock obsolescence. Many modern accounts packages have reporting functions that allow the production of exception reports, perhaps comparing actual figures with budget figures. These can be useful to auditors especially when reporting parameters can be set to isolate only material differences. The auditor needs to consider his requirements for analytical data and make arrangements with his clients for such data to be available.

Permanent audit routines

Permanent programs can be 'embedded' into the client's software to provide audit samples or to carry out audit tests. Permanent audit routines can be particularly helpful to internal auditors. An embedded sampling package can produce a sample print for each transaction's update run. The auditor is then in a good position promptly to alert client departments should errors be found.

Portable computers

It is becoming increasingly feasible for auditors to carry portable computers to clients' premises and to download client data for audit analysis. This exciting development will in time radically change day-to-day audit practice. It is important to keep track of developments in this field so that efficient up-to-date audit can be employed.

SUMMARY

This chapter has covered an area where the number and variety of audit situations and techniques are constantly changing. Nevertheless the basic audit approach is the same: objectives are still to verify the accuracy of figures or the adequacy of internal system controls (including those to ensure VFM). Computer audit fits into the overall approach to audit oulined in Chapter 2 and utilized throughout this book.

The following case studies illustrate situations in a large and a small computerized site:

(a) **Case study 11.1** exemplifies an all too familiar situation of lack of control over project appraisal and subsequent implementation.
(b) **Case study 11.2** presents the summarized working papers and auditor's opinion for a large data processing mainframe site with on-line and batch processing facilities. It represents a more complex situation but one often faced by the auditor of even relatively small public bodies.

CASE STUDY 11.1 NATIONAL ART MUSEUM – COMPUTERIZED INVENTORY RECORDS

The external auditor arrives at the National Art Museum to find that the inventory records have been computerized since his last visit. He received no notification through the usual channels of this change in procedure. His visit, part of the audit of the larger Head Office published accounts, usually involves compliance testing of the inventory control system and a sample of the inventory for direct substantive testing by verifying the existence and valuation of a sample of 'items'. No material income is received by the Museum and all expenditure is controlled as part of the wider control of Head Office purchases and creditors' arrangements. The auditor knows that his organization's computer auditor examines the purchasing and suitability of all new computer installations. On enquiry he finds that the installation, a stand-alone minicomputer called Zipit-250 with VDUs and line printer, cannot be fitted into the computer auditor's schedule for another six months.

After amending his audit plan to take account of the new development the auditor decides on a course of action to include the following:

(a) Document any manual controls that have changed since the introduction of Zipit and evaluate any weaknesses.
(b) Compliance test any controls upon which he still intends to place reliance. Examine any potential weaknesses in detail, reporting to management if appropriate.
(c) Attempt to verify the completeness of original data transfer from the manual records to the computerized records.
(d) Document the controls over the computerized records and compliance

test any upon which he intends to place reliance. Examine any potential weaknesses, reporting to management if appropriate.
(e) Copy his final working papers and any report to the computer auditor for further action.
(f) Undertake substantive testing as for previous visits.

His findings can be summarized as follows:

(a) The pre-computerized system has remained largely intact, the computer acting mainly as a larger and more versatile register. A significant weakness involves the interface with the purchasing system. In the past all purchase orders were 'crossed' and signed by the curator upon satisfactory receipt of goods. Today orders are simply retained at Head Office and a floppy disk is forwarded monthly from the accounts department with details of all purchases, including exhibits, for updating onto Zipit.
(b) Compliance testing of other controls in the manual system proves satisfactory. The auditor drafts a paragraph for his report to management outlining the need for orders to be agreed as in the past or for discussion of some other acceptable confirmation of the curator's checking role.
(c) The auditor's own working papers from his previous audit state that 10,520 exhibits existed at 31/3/X1, total estimated value £425,001,000. Zipit, he discovers, was purchased on 10/9/X1 and the inventory was initially input over the weekend 3/11/X1 to 4/11/X1. He is able to reconcile the total of items transferred as follows:

	No.	Value £000
Balance 31/3/X1 – audited	10,520	425,001
Purchases, exhibits as per purchase orders:		
8/4/X1–1/5/X1	200	500
2/6/X1	10	42
23/8/X1	10	105
3/9/X1–24/9/X1	220	325
Disposal 31/7/X1 as per Committee Minute	(10)	(5)
Items donated 5/7/X1	30	30
	10,980	£425,998
Initial inventory printout confirmed by stocktake by an independent manager	10,980	

(d) Controls over computerized records appear weak. With regard to application controls read-out only access is available but without a password. The value of some items is considered relatively high – three dating from 1800 are valued at £4m, £5m and £6m. Such information could be put to misuse in criminal hands.

Although a password is required for inputting record changes, this password has not been amended since the Zipit was installed. The terminal location is in a general office and the VDU can easily be viewed by the visiting public.

Despite the line printer very little hard copy output is produced. Reliance upon magnetic data is almost complete but no master copies are kept at a secure location and no contingency plans exist to deal with any emergency.

The auditor would not expect a relatively simple system such as this to display a great many application controls but controls over access to the data and to ensure that records are safeguarded in an emergency are the least one would expect.

(e) With regard to development and VFM controls, no development plan or cost-benefit analysis appears to have been undertaken. The computer appears to have been purchased as part of a general upgrading of office equipment. A national policy statement on the need to bring the office systems into line with technology of the 19X0s seems to have been the impetus for this (and possibly, other) purchases. During interviews with senior management the fact that until 19X1 the Museum was, in their opinion, the only significant museum site without a computer was mentioned as a likely justification for the purchase.

The auditor can see no readily apparent savings of the present system over the previous system as an inventory record for just over 10,000 items.

(f) Substantive testing of 180 items chosen judgementally to cover £399,000,000 by estimated value reveals two minor errors in revaluation where the incorrect multiplier had been used. Total error of mis-statement, £42,000, is not material to the accounts.

In summarizing, it can be said that elements of this scenario are likely to occur in the audit of many installations. Many are not formally justified by a cost-benefit analysis – a system such as this could well cost from £5,000 to £50,000 and may not be fully utilized. Operating staff whose past duties may have incorporated internal control are rarely briefed on the need for security and control in a computerized system. Small installations usually have few of the possible controls, even those selected in the narrative of the chapter, and generally present a serious potential risk.

CASE STUDY 11.2 LAND DEVELOPMENT COMMISSION – EVALUATION OF APPLICATION CONTROLS

The Internal Auditor of the Land Development Commission wishes to evaluate the application controls of the Commission's recently installed mainframe computer. This evaluation will form a 'common system element' of several manual 'feeder' systems. The installation includes a network configuration with direct on-line access for 12 terminals with VDUs. All hard copy printouts are produced centrally in the computer installation room. The network terminals are used to update land sales, changes of use, valuation and site visit records. Some of this information is of a commercially valuable and hence confidential nature.

Most other data is input by batch processing and consists of wages, salaries and other expenses on a cash basis. No accrual accounts are prepared and the only income is a single cash limited grant. Monthly outturn statements are produced on a code-by-code basis for budgeting purposes.

The Auditor has summarized his working papers as follows:

Batch processing   *On-line*

Input controls

Batch processing	On-line
1. Batch headers recording number and value of transactions are agreed as 'punched by' and 'verified by' different signatories.	1. Strict password-only access for all functions. Each user has a defined password known only to him or her. Each password has a well defined level of access. Passwords are changed: (a) on staff changes, or (b) every four months.
	2. Managers select a random sample of record changes revealed by the computer log and check these back to land and property files.
	3. Input cannot be accepted until a 'cursor check' of all field entries displayed on the VDU has been completed. **Note:** although the inputting officer has to wait for the cursor check to be completed, there is no guarantee that he/she is actually paying attention to the screen details.

Batch processing   *On-line*

Input weaknesses

2. No attempt is made to agree input headers to totals received from 'feeder' system.
3. No attempt is made to agree total input for any function to output totals, except for wages and salaries.

Processing controls

4. Reasonableness checks produce automatic exception reports for the given sizes of transaction for all codes of expenditure.
5. Run-to-run totals are checked on each file update.

4. The system is subject to a series of 'data vet' checks that scrutinize format of data:
    (a) Values are in money terms;
    (b) Names and address and land use are in alpha characters for given fields;
    (c) Site records must have key fields completed including the visiting officer's initials.
    Data vet checks must be completed before input.
5. Reasonableness checks over size and value of land and property records are programmed to output exception reports to inputting officer and his/her line manager.

Processing weaknesses

6. No action is evidenced over exception reports. Managers interviewed were 'vague' over the action they were expected to take.

Output controls

7. A general control schedule exists for the expected timing of output and its normal distribution to users. No evidence that the

6. Control (2) above is performed in conjunction with a general selection of output reports by managers. These appear chosen

Batch processing	On-line
schedule is followed is retained. Users reported three cases of misdirected output over the past month.	haphazardly but agreement to input data on files is documented by each manager. This record is used in staff assessment procedures.

Weaknesses

8. No comparison back to input
   except as per (3) above for
   wages.

General controls

These appear limited to review of the computer log for occasional exception reports and an annual inspection of the installation by the Fire Prevention Officer. In particular the auditor notes serious weaknesses in control caused by lack of separation of duties between programming and operational staff, lack of copies of master and transaction files and lack of insurance cover or any disaster planning.

Summary

The Auditor is of the opinion that control over batch processing is generally inadequate and that for both batch processing and for on-line networks the output and general controls are also inadequate. The auditor's findings, conclusions and recommendations will be detailed in a report to the Computer Manager. One of the auditor's recommendations is that a specialist computer auditor be invited to assess further the level of risk and make detailed recommendations for control procedures as well as advising the auditor on test data and retrieval software packages.

CONCLUDING POINTS

Computer audit is a specialist area. We have in this chapter attempted to provide a brief guide to the non-specialist auditor. Computers are in use with virtually every public sector organization and the auditor has come to accept them and their involvement in most systems as second nature. It is hoped that this chapter has provided both a starting point for the relatively inexperienced auditor, and an overview for the more experienced.

12 Forming final opinions and reporting

INTRODUCTION

Having planned the audit and completed the field work, the auditor has two remaining tasks:

(a) To decide for himself what is the true picture of events;
(b) To communicate effectively the true picture of events and any recommended actions to his clients.

The first task involves the auditor forming his **opinion**, the second **reporting** his opinion. This chapter therefore covers the final stages of the 'essential audit process' from test conclusions through to delivering the report.

In the private sector the responsibility the auditor holds towards his clients and certain third parties is periodically impressed upon the practitioner by substantial claims for damages. In the public sector auditors are less likely to be subject to the same penalty of public exposure and financial loss. However, this protection from full public accountability should not influence the rigorousness of audit methods and the opinion forming process.

It is interesting to note that where audit cases have come before the courts or have become the subject of Department of Trade investigations, it is at the opinion forming and reporting stages that most major shortcomings appear to have occurred.

AUDITING STANDARDS AND GUIDELINES

It was as a direct consequence of the bad publicity that auditors received from a number of financial scandals that the **Auditing Practices Committee**, which includes CIPFA, was set up. The Committee's first published output included the **Auditing Standards and Guidelines Explanatory Fore-word**, the **Auditor's Operational Standard** and the **Auditing Guidelines** directly supporting the Standard. All were issued in April 1980.

As CIPFA is a member of the Auditing Practices Committee, CIPFA members are bound by these Standards and Guidelines. The Audit Guide-line, 'Guidance for Internal Auditors', requires that it should be read in conjunction with the Explanatory Foreword to Auditing Standards and Guidelines and hence all the Standards and Guidelines. The Code of Local Government Audit Practice, which has been laid before Parliament, incorporates the Auditor's Operational Standard.

Much of this book has concentrated on applying the Standards and Guidelines in an up-to-date manner appropriate to the public sector. The guidance they give on how to carry out audit work of all types is simple, but strong. From beginning to end the auditor must work logically and with care, exercising good judgement. Nowhere is this more appropriate than when completing an audit since this represents the last chance to correct errors.

OPINION FORMING

Chapter 6 discussed the bases on which audit evidence is obtained. Chapter 8 discussed how much evidence was needed by looking at statistical sampling methods which are directly related to levels of audit assurance. Once audit evidence has been obtained conclusions and opinions are required. When VFM work is done an opinion is similarly required before reporting takes place.

Systems and attestation audit requires a clear statement of opinion, such as that a set of accounts is 'fairly presented' or that an internal control operates reliably. VFM work is by its nature less rigid since normally opinions are given on the basis of sub-optimal levels of evidence. It is relatively simple to prove that an internal control is failing. Deviations in a randomly selected sample can provide statistically valid evidence. To prove that a service is provided in a less efficient and effective manner than it could be or than in the average department requires research on a far larger number of variables. This has been discussed in Chapter 10 on value for money.

Substantive testing

The basic processes in opinion forming can be explained using as an example an audit of a list of debtor's balances.

Let us assume that a list of ten debts owed to a public body has been audited for overstatement by a full circularization of all debtors. To ensure the reliability of replies the auditor has checked that all the debts have been paid off over the last few weeks. He has received his ten replies and is about to form his opinion. He may conclude that all the replies agree to the list. He may also conclude that the evidence of after-date payment is consistent with the list. Now, by taking these two conclusions and by ensuring that they are consistent with one another he may then conclude that the list of ten debtors is not overstated.

The point to understand is that all the test conclusions available to the auditor are assessed in the light of the audit objective before the audit opinion is known. This is the fundamental audit process outlined in Fig. 2.1. In the example above, little audit judgement is required. However, in many audit situations considerable skill, judgement and experience is needed for the following reasons:

(a) A large number of figures are involved;
(b) Test sampling has been employed;
(c) Compliance evidence has been relied upon.

Compliance testing

When compliance evidence is used to support substantive test evidence an extra stage is introduced into the opinion forming process. So that errors are not made in forming the opinion, it is important that the process is clearly broken down into its constituent parts. This is illustrated in Fig. 12.1.

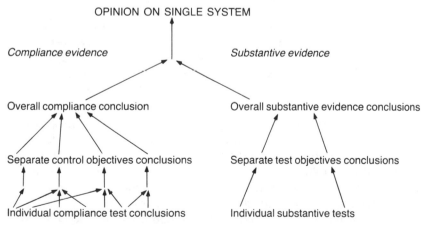

Fig. 12.1 Opinion forming and the systems based approach.

Good layout of working papers when carrying out compliance testing greatly assists opinion formation since many individual compliance test results will have to be categorized under control objectives before further conclusions can be drawn. If less than perfect compliance evidence is obtained, valid opinions will only be given if the nature of deviations and their effect on control objectives is clearly understood.

Poor results

In the ideal situation, the client has all the internal controls he could be expected to have, and on testing all these controls they are found to operate effectively. In fact a client will not usually have instituted all the controls he should have and in some cases controls in place will be found to fail. Chapter 8 discusses how to move audit assurance from compliance testing to substantive testing by increasing substantive testing sample sizes. This process is essentially one of judgement. Judgement is exercised at the planning stage of the audit, during testing and finally at the opinion forming stage. Before the opinion is formed the auditor checks again whether he was correct to place the level of assurance he did on the internal control structure.

When the auditor has carried out his testing, he may find controls do not in fact operate; he must then decide the effect this has on his opinions. Let us assume that in an audit of payroll a reliability factor of 1.5 has been ascribed to internal controls out of a total of 2.3, or 90% confidence. On testing, the auditor discovers that one particular internal control did not operate in 10 out of the 40 cases he sampled. Statistically this control clearly does not operate. But what is the effect on his 1.5 reliability factor for internal control?

The failed control will have been designed to satisfy a control objective. It is possible that other controls which the auditor has also tested and found to operate will cover the control which does not. In this case, assuming the other compliance testing gave good results, the auditor would probably ignore the errors he found. More commonly, as with the above example, a failed control will weaken a control objective. The auditor cannot now accept his original reliability factor for internal control of 1.5. He must reduce it. This in turn increases the reliability factor for substantive testing with the consequence that more substantive test work will be needed. It is up to the auditor to judge the reduced reliance on internal control in the same way as he originally agreed the original reliability factor. A failed control may affect more than one control objective. In this situation one would expect the reduction in reliability factors to be greater reflecting this.

Combining compliance and substantive evidence conclusions

Where compliance test results give an overall compliance conclusion within expectations and where substantive evidence results are good, the opinion can be given with relative ease. Both sources of evidence are consistent and support the planned audit approach. We have discussed the position when compliance errors arise. We must now consider the effect of substantive test results.

Normally, if compliance testing reveals no errors the substantive testing will also be error-free. This is the case for two quite different reasons. First, if controls really are effective we would not expect errors. Secondly, it is normal to combine compliance and substantive testing in a single sample. Internal controls clearly are not effective if a substantive error is found in a transaction used to test compliance results.

Where substantive errors do occur the reliability of the evidence given by the testing must be evaluated using the techniques described in Chapter 8. Where acceptable levels of error are found, the compliance and substantive evidence conclusions are combined to give the overall conclusions. Where unacceptable substantive errors occur no opinion can be given until further work on the cause, nature and extent of the errors found is carried out. Normally this is done by increasing substantive sample sizes and by using analytical review to check that figures appear to be consistent with one another and with previous years. Clearly, when the auditor is 'reduced' to these methods of obtaining evidence no reliance can be placed on internal controls; they are clearly ineffective.

MORE COMPLEX OPINIONS

When an auditor is asked to report on a single system, concluding on the reliability of internal controls and of the output of the system, this is relatively straightforward. Where an opinion is requested on a set of accounts or on controls in a number of interrelated systems or on VFM work, another level of audit work is required. This is the **final review**.

The importance of the final review can be illustrated. Figure 12.2 shows how the review pulls together evidence from different sources so that a complete picture is obtained before the opinion is given. This complete picture focuses on four main areas as laid out in the Audit Guideline 'Review of Financial Statements':

(a) General review;
(b) Accounting policies;
(c) Presentation and disclosure;
(d) Compliance with regulations – regularity.

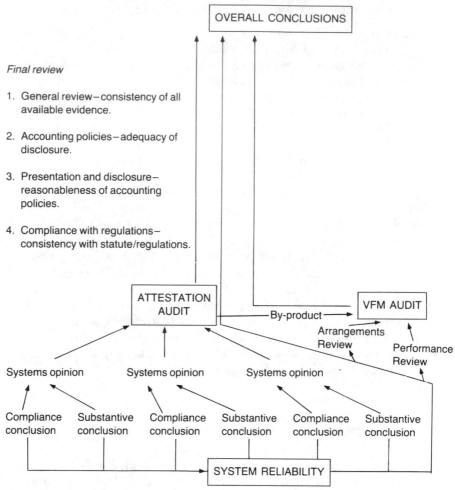

Fig. 12.2 Opinion forming on a set of accounts, inter-related systems or VFM work.

Final review

Final reviews have a number of functions:

(a) Conclusions and evidence from **different sources** are finally brought together.
(b) The **technical adequacy** of the accounts and systems are reviewed.
(c) The **regularity** of the accounts and services they represent is checked.
(d) Responsibility for the final opinion is **formally** taken.

We will look at the importance of each of these functions separately. In the public sector regularity takes on a special significance. This is because deviations from the objects for which a public body was set up can be politically important. For this reason special emphasis is given to this aspect of the subject.

Evidence from different sources

Although all the individual audit tests, systems results and VFM conclusions may be thoroughly checked, the auditor must also check that when all the evidence is brought together there are no obvious inconsistencies. As an example, revenue accounts showing a substantial increase in property running costs but no balance sheet increase in freehold and leasehold buildings would appear suspect. Similarly for VFM work indications of poor value for money regarding, say, the mix of planned building maintenance to responsive maintenance would have to be considered in the light of actual value for money achieved.

Auditors need to consider all the results in the light of all the other evidence available. Thus evidence obtained directly from the audit is augmented by knowledge obtained from wider experience. Table 12.1 lays out the procedures required for attestation, systems reliability and VFM work.

The auditor needs to record this work. The level of detail of recording will vary depending on the results. When evidence is clearly consistent, few records will be needed. Where apparent or real inconsistencies are found, a full record of the nature of the inconsistency and how it has been resolved is necessary. Case study 12.1 at the end of the chapter shows how this might be done.

Subjective evaluation

At the end of an audit when all the evidence obtained is assessed, before the opinion is formed, some work will be subjective in nature.

Audit work can be usefully divided into work that can be said to have an objective conclusion and that where subjective conclusions are required. Chapter 8 on sampling mostly discussed objective audit evidence where the conclusion was governed by statistical rules. This type of work gives the auditor little trouble since he either is or is not confident of the results. However, much audit work is not so easily concluded upon. It is not possible to test statistically a bad debt provision. Nor is it possible objectively to judge whether a change in the law affecting value for money will occur. In the same way the importance of internal controls can only be judged subjectively.

In the public sector subjective judgements on the audit of sets of accounts

Table 12.1 Review of evidence from different sources

Attestation work	Systems reliability	VFM
1. Evidence from the audit:		
(a) **Completeness of evidence.** The auditor checks that his audit work has covered all figures in the account.	The auditor checks he has covered all the relevant controls to meet control objectives.	The auditor checks that he has obtained audit evidence for all relevant areas.
(b) **Consistency of evidence.** Evidence from different account areas is compared to ensure they are consistent.	Evidence on the level of control from different services is compared (e.g. control may in fact occur although it is not evidenced).	The auditor checks that evidence of good or bad VFM is supported by evidence from all the services he has looked at.
(c) **Audit strategy.** The evidence obtained is compared to the original audit plan to ensure that all important areas are given the correct coverage.	Evidence obtained on controls is compared to the original audit plan to ensure that the correct coverage has been given and that special issues have been addressed.	Evidence obtained is compared to the original audit plan to ensure that the planned coverage has been given.
2. Evidence from experience:		
(a) **Political circumstances.** The figures are checked to ensure that they are consistent with known changes in policy and the law.	Controls are reviewed to ensure that they take account of changes in policy and the law.	VFM is reviewed in the light of changes in the law and policy. This is particularly the case when comparisons used in performance review do not reflect recent legal changes.
(b) **Similar organizations.** Where similar organizations exist figures are compared to these to ensure that clear and unexplained differences are not present.	Where experience has been gained from the audit of similar organizations this is very useful for assessing the adequacy of internal controls.	This is clearly essential in both arrangements and performance review.
(c) **Value-for-money work/other audit work.** The auditor ensures that figures are consistent with knowledge gained from relevant VFM work.	The auditor considers the input of VFM on existing and possible additional controls.	VFM evidence should be compared to evidence obtained from other audit work.

are far less important than in the private sector. This is because obsolescence of highly material stock holdings and going-concern considerations are not normally relevant. This should make public sector attestation audit, using statistical sampling, a fairly exact science. The auditor can have an almost mathematical confidence in his opinion in a way not often shared by auditors of private sector concerns.

When the auditor is forming opinions on systems reliability and value for money, clearly much more subjectivity is involved. Systems testing results are clearly objective. The subjectivity enters when assessing the importance of the controls in place. The auditor has to rely upon his experience and apply accepted standards. For instance, a bank reconciliation may not be regularly undertaken. The importance of this control lapse can only be judged subjectively; however, it is accepted that bank accounts should be reconciled every month. Similar processes have to be brought to bear in more complex situations. Discussion of the problems with other audit staff and possibly with the client will help in arriving at a final conclusion.

The problem of assessing value for money has been discussed at some length in Chapter 10. At the end of the audit certain key issues will still need deciding upon. The auditor must use his skill and judgement in making what is a subjective decision, by considering all the evidence available to him as laid out in Table 12.1.

Technical adequacy

This part of the final review covers a number of presentational and accounting considerations which really only affect opinions on sets of accounts. The Audit Guideline 'Review of Financial Statements' considers the different aspects of accounting policies, and presentation and disclosure. External auditors will consider the technical quality of accounts at some length. Accounting policies and disclosure may be designed to mislead rather than inform. This is particularly the case where the regularity of accounting and policy is suspect or open to interpretation. Where

Checklist 12.1 Technical adequacy review

1. **Accounting policies:**
    (a) Compliance with best accounting practice, including SSAPs;
    (b) Consistent with previous accounting periods;
    (c) Consistently applied throughout the organization.
2. **Presentation and disclosure:**
    (a) That the accounts give a correct and complete impression of the organization to the reader;
    (b) That the accounts present material in a way uncoloured by possible management bias.

internal auditors become involved in attestation work on management information the technical adequacy of the material again comes under review. However, this time the emphasis is on the capacity of the accounts to inform the management rather than strict compliance with Statements of Standard Accounting Practice. In both situations this part of the final review is an important element of the audit of accounts. Checklist 12.1 sets out the main aspects of review for technical adequacy.

REGULARITY

Public bodies are formed to carry out functions, often laid down in statute, in a manner consistent with the law as a whole. Ensuring that public bodies behave legally is consequently of importance. A recent case involving the regularity of financial deals carried out by a London borough made headline news. Clearly the auditor cannot ignore this traditional aspect of his role.

The auditor's role

There are two types of situation in which regularity issues can arise. These can be described as:

(a) Legality of proposed future actions;
(b) Regularity of past actions.

The authors consider the former to be predominantly the work of lawyers and the latter of both auditors and lawyers. In the first situation a point of law is at issue – nothing else. The professions best suited to provide clarification are solicitors or barristers. In the second situation the actions have already occurred. Lawyers may or may not have been asked for legal opinions. Unless the auditor picks up the point it is now unlikely that, if the law has been broken, it will be complied with in future.

The auditor, then, has to be alert to the possibility of irregularity and actions that are *ultra vires*. The best time to check that past actions were legal is during an audit. This does not mean that if he knows illegal acts are contemplated he waits until they are perpetrated. Rather he advises during his audit work of the possibility of irregularities, suggesting that a lawyer be consulted as appropriate. As regards local government, some of the powers of the District Auditor are of a semi-judicial rather than audit nature. This dual role is due to historical quirk rather than a modern concept of the nature of audit.

Much regularity work is concerned with the law of the land. However, all binding regulations, both external and internal to the organization, can be the subject of audit. The nature of regularity issues are set out in Checklist 12.2.

Regularity audit work

Audit work, as always, starts with the audit plan. When any audit is considered, the broader regularity issues need to be isolated during the planning stage of the audit. This is particularly important when recent actions may be *ultra vires*.

Regularity issues are by their nature contentious: political problems will often be involved. For this reason regularity needs to be considered early on in the audit. Many problems relate to recent or proposed changes in the law. Consequently this often assists the isolation, if not the solution, of the problem. Checklist 12.2 provides an outline to the type of work required.

Checklist 12.2 Regularity work

Type of regulation to be complied with	*Role of professions*

1. External regulations:
  (a) The law:
    (i) Specific statutes;
    (ii) Common law;
    (iii) Statutory instruments;
  (b) Legal charter, code of practice, etc.;
  (c) Government regulations.
	Legal profession – clarification of legal position.

2. Internal regulations:
  (a) Financial regulations;
  (b) Ministerial memoranda;
  (c) Committee minutes;
  (d) 'Desk instructions'.
	Auditor:
	(a) **Prevention** of future irregularities;
	(b) **Disclosure** of irregularities;
	(c) **Accountability** of public body or individual for irregularities.

Although issues of regularity are under consideration during planning and through the detailed fieldwork, it is only at the final review stage that many of the issues raised are fully worked through and resolved. It is for this reason that regularity is considered here in the final chapter of the book.

At the beginning of the audit the auditor needs to be acquainted with the legislation and other external and internal regulations affecting his client. Copies of the relevant documents can normally be obtained from the client if the auditor does not possess them already. Where problems become apparent the auditor needs to discuss the issue with the client so that he can learn all the facts. The client is also warned of potential problems early on. This greatly helps the resolution of the irregularity.

Many irregularities are the result of a distortion of the law. Consequently it is not easy for the auditor to claim that the law has been broken. In these situations he has often to rely on persuasion rather than heavy-handedness to ensure that the spirit of the law is upheld. Only a small minority of cases will go to court and when this happens substantial publicity is involved. (Notorious examples include the 'Fares Fare' ruling regarding the GLC funding of London Transport and the Clay Cross affair in which councillors were actually sent to prison.)

At this final review stage of the audit, the auditor will seek to resolve any regularity issues isolated during the work. He will also review the audit work in some detail to ensure all potential regularity problems have been considered.

Auditor's responsibilities

Once an irregularity has been found, the auditor must consider the three aspects of the error highlighted in Checklist 12.2.

First, he must consider **prevention** of future irregularities. The auditor will discuss the matter with senior management. He will ensure that they are fully aware of the nature of the problem and he will agree a method to prevent future irregularity. The auditor should write a minute on the meeting at which the solution was agreed and send a copy to the appropriate level of management. In this way a formal conclusion is reached at an early stage.

If the auditor is responsible for an opinion on a set of accounts, **disclosure** of the irregularity may be necessary. The auditor will need to ask the client organization to amend the accounts and the notes to the accounts. As an example, an education authority may have exceeded its powers when making purchases. The auditor would need to ask the authority to show the expenditure under amounts for which another relevant power was held. Internal auditors discovering such an irregularity would ask for the accounting records to be adjusted for the error.

Lastly, the auditor needs to consider public **accountability** for the irregularity. Serious illegality will require a report. The audit report to a set of accounts is one report which may be used to provide accountability. Secondly, a special report may be issued by external auditors. For local government this could be a 'report in the public interest'. For central government the NAO could report to the Public Accounts Committee. Internal auditors would report to senior management, to elected members or to an appointed board on the irregularity so that they could take the matter further.

It is not the auditor's job to take legal action over irregularities (except in certain situations regarding District Auditors, as already mentioned). Normally, the auditor is not an interested party in a breach of statute or regulations. Consequently it is up to those that have the power to take action to do so. The auditor's duty is to ensure that irregularities are discovered so that they can be prevented, if possible, or dealt with if not.

FINAL OPINIONS

The final review is the last chance the auditor has to get his opinions 'right'. It is important then that the review is documented in such a way that responsibility for the actual opinion is taken coolly and logically and not rashly.

There are three areas which the auditor should document with special care. These are as follows:

(a) Significant subjective issues;
(b) Key factual findings of the audit;
(c) Events after the completion of work.

Significant subjective issues

The problem of subjectivity has already been discussed. However, so that a decision is rationally taken the most material issues must be noted down during the review. The list must be concise and should be laid out in such a way that the reason for the opinion actually formed can be noted on the sheet. For audits of accounts this list of significant issues should be drafted and placed at the front of the audit file. For system reliability and VFM work the first draft report properly cross-referenced to the working papers will serve.

Key factual findings

In any audit there will be objective or factual findings. These, too, must be summarized before an opinion is given. A number of small errors may in total become material. In addition, the client should be informed of errors found.

For systems reliability work summary sheets of results for each control objective may serve as the list of factual findings. Alternatively major systems weaknesses and failings should be briefly noted and placed at the front of the audit work. With VFM work, factual findings may represent lack of management procedures, data and key comparisons in performance review. Again a brief list of these, placed at the front of the file, will be of great use. Subjective issues will be decided on the basis of factual findings, as well as wider experience, so such summaries are important.

Post-audit events

Very often auditors find themselves forming an opinion on a situation that is no longer current. Systems work may be carried out on a year's transactions up to, perhaps, the end of March. The audit work may be done in June and the report received by the client in July or August. By late summer, system improvements may have been introduced, further work may have been done by other auditors or the law by which a department operates may have been amended. Before a final opinion is given, the effects of post-audit events must be taken into account. With VFM work the same considerations apply.

Accounts attestation work is affected to a far greater extent than either of the two areas discussed above. A VFM or systems opinion that is out of date should not be totally invalidated by changing events; an accounts opinion may be. If after the balance sheet date a material quantity of debtors go into liquidation the accounts of public bodies may be seriously misleading. Similarly, legal action or political changes in overseas countries may affect an audit opinion. The Audit Guideline 'Events after the Balance Sheet Date' lays down a number of procedures an auditor should carry out to ensure his opinion is up to date. Issues of 'going concern' are less relevant to the public sector than legal and political changes. Where the Guideline stresses the former, the public sector auditor will need to look at the latter; the rest of the Guideline is of direct relevance.

Summary

We have discussed in some detail how an auditor forms his final opinion on the work he has done. We have looked at how opinions are formed when substantive and compliance evidence is brought together. More complex opinions on complete sets of accounts, systems reliability and value-for-money work have then been considered. The importance of defined 'final review' procedures have been stressed together with the idea that this review represents the last chance to form the 'correct' opinion before the report is made.

REPORTING

Once the opinion is finally formed it must be reported. Reporting is the culmination of the audit and forms the 'product' for which the auditor is remunerated. It is vital, then, that reports effectively communicate the auditor's opinion to readers.

Types of report

There are a number of different reporting forms. Many are laid down in statute or other binding regulations. Others take the form the auditor considers most appropriate in the situation. The reporting forms used by the main groups of public sector auditors are discussed below.

External audit reports

Local government

The Code of Local Government Audit Practice for England and Wales sets out how the auditor should report on specific occasions. Three different types of report are laid down and a fourth type of report, the 'Memorandum to Chief Officers' is implied.

District Auditors can make a 'Report in the Public Interest'. This type of report is made where the auditor considers that any matter coming to his notice in the course of the audit should, in the public interest, be reported upon either to the body or to the public directly via a newspaper. The code suggests twelve occasions when such a report could be made. These include 'delayed preparation of accounts' and 'deficiencies in internal control arrangements'.

The second report is the 'Management Letter'. This is a report sent directly to the members or councillors of an authority every year informing them of significant matters that have arisen. Management letters of this prescribed type are a method of formally briefing elected members on the important points regarding stewardship, regularity and value for money that council officers are probably aware of, but from which members may have been 'protected'. A management letter puts on record issues for members to consider and possibly act upon.

The last report set down in the code is the 'Auditor's Certificate and Opinion'. This report is analogous to an audit report under the Companies Act 1985 on a set of financial accounts. However, this report also requires a certificate that the audit has been completed in accordance with the Local Government Finance Act 1982. The auditor is required to state whether or not in his opinion the accounts to which the opinion is attached 'presents fairly' the position of the authority. Examples of wordings for clear and qualified reports are given in the code.

The fourth 'non-statutory' form of reporting is the 'Memorandum to Chief Officers'. In practice this is by far the most common report form. It is used to inform, admonish and congratulate a management as is required. District Auditors will use memoranda to report value-for-money and systems reliability work. Minor errors in accounts and regularity issues may also be communicated in this way.

Central government

The National Audit Act 1983 sets out the reporting duties of the Comptroller and Auditor General. Unlike the Audit Commission the C&AG is not bound by a code of practice. Reporting is to the Public Accounts Committee alone in any form the C&AG considers fit.

In practice, yearly appropriation accounts from government departments are certified using a brief form of words which states:

> I certify that I have examined the above account in accordance with the Exchequer and Audit Department Acts 1866 and 1921 and the National Audit Office auditing standards.
>
> In my opinion the sums expended have been applied for the purposes authorized by Parliament and the account properly presents the expenditure and receipts of . . .

Reports on value for money and other financial issues are made to the Public Accounts Committee. These reports are narrative in style and extend to perhaps 20 or more pages. Management letters are also used to report significant findings to management, usually issues of a lower order of importance than those reported to the Public Accounts Committee.

Internal audit reports

Internal auditors are not generally bound by statutory reporting requirements. Rather they advise managers of their opinions through a range of reports and memoranda laying out their findings and recommendations for the future.

Forms of report

There are three general forms a report can take:

(a) Statutory report certifying accounts;
(b) Formal discussive report on a state of affairs;
(c) Consultative report.

Statutory report certifying accounts

Little more needs to be said on this type of report. Forms are laid down by various statutes and are consolidated by the Code of Local Government Audit Practice, the C&AG, and the Audit Practices Committee for local government, central government and companies respectively. All these reports are very similar in style. They all report **by exception**. By carrying out a substantial amount of work the auditor is able to state that the accounts are materially correct. This is a positive opinion.

Formal discussive report

Sometimes reports are required which set down a state of affairs for the benefit of the public, politicians or senior management. Reports in a similar style may also be used by internal auditors who wish to inform formally senior managers of a state of affairs. Reports of this nature should be as concise as possible, but need not skimp on detail where this is important. A statement of the likely consequences of the state of affairs reported upon is usually included.

A very simple example of this type of report is a written statement by an internal auditor to a chief officer that an important financial regulation has been broken. Perhaps stocks have not been subject to continuous stock-take as required. The auditor would simply state that the regulation had been broken and that control over valuable stocks was consequently lost.

Formal discussive reports are used to report serious internal control and value-for-money failings. They normally follow a set structure as set out in Fig. 12.3.

Often it is useful to discuss a draft of such a report with managers. Not only is this conducive to more pleasant future working relations, but it allows the auditor to check his facts one last time. Clearly, where the management's view is included in a report this will have to be canvassed after discussion of report findings and recommendations.

Consultative report

Formal discussive reports are often inappropriate methods of giving audit opinions. This is because they are not designed to give direct assistance to managers to bring about service improvements; rather they encourage enforced change from above.

Required in every report
{
1. **Introduction/summary.** The nature and importance of the subject of the report is explained. A summary of the remainder of the report may be included.

2. **Details of findings.** The report gives the state of affairs found during the audit.

3. **Auditor's opinion.** The auditor states whether or not he considers the audit findings acceptable.

4. **Consequences.** The auditor states the likely consequences of inaction by the public body.
}

Optional elements of report
{
5. **Recommendations.** The auditor may recommend a number of improvements designed to reduce the consequences of inaction.

6. **The management view.** The auditor may record the views of the management concerning both his findings and his recommendations.
}

Fig. 12.3 Formal discussive report structure.

Most audit reports are consultative reports to managers. They are normally sent to the managers who must implement any changes. Other senior managers are informed of the auditor's opinions for reference purposes. The results of most systems reliability and VFM work are reported in consultative reports. Minor errors and omissions from accounts attestation audits are also often reported in this manner. Although the contents of a consultative report are little different from a formal report, the structure emphasizes recommendations. This is shown in Fig. 12.4.

Considerable skill is required to write a good consultative report. The auditor needs to make his points unambiguously whilst encouraging a hard pressed manager to improve his operation. Full discussion of draft reports is needed to ensure that managers are won over to the auditor's viewpoint. Auditors should, however, realize that managers see such discussion as their opportunity to win the auditor over to the management line. Consequently, auditors, particularly internal auditors, must take care to protect their independence and impartiality. The best of these types of report accept the management's view where this is appropriate and use it to support the audit recommendations. This process is aided by the fact

---

1. **Introduction.** The nature and importance of the subject of the report is explained.

2. **Scope of audit work.** The audit objectives are briefly given.

3. **Recommendations suggested.** Significant recommendations made by the auditor are listed and cross-referenced to the detail of the report.

4. **Detail of report:**
   (a) Audit findings;
   (b) Auditor's opinions.

   The auditor gives his findings and registers his opinion on them. Where applicable, the consequences of present procedures are given. Similarly, the managers' viewpoint may be given where this assists the auditor in making his point.

Fig. 12.4 Consultative report structure.

that normally both auditor and managers have a common goal in the improved operation of a department.

SUMMARY

Reporting is the process of communication of audit opinions to the public, Parliament and managers. Types of report may be governed by statute, codes of practice and Audit Guidelines. There are three common forms of report. The first is the statutory report used to certify a set of accounts. The second is a formal discussive document reporting a state of affairs. National Audit Office reports to the Public Accounts Committee are of this type as are District Auditor's Reports in the public interest. The most common form of report is the consultative report. This type of report aims to encourage management action whilst recording the auditor's opinions on areas of significant concern.

The case studies which follow continue the audit of JARDS, an extract of which was given in Case Study 8.3 of Chapter 8. The auditor here has the twin objectives of ensuring that:

(a) Figures in the accounts are a fair record of the activities of the operation – **attestation audit**;
(b) Effective controls exist and are in effective operation in the stock and purchases systems – **systems reliability audit**.

In the audit plan four main account areas were identified for testing – purchases, wages, stock, and plant and machinery. Substantive testing of purchases is illustrated in detail in the case study in Chapter 8. Compliance testing is also required but is not shown.

(a) **Case study 12.1.** This shows the opinion forming on the purchases system where compliance and substantive results are brought together. It shows part of the final review of the whole attestation audit.

(b) **Case study 12.2.** Due to concern over the poor stock system a report was written by the Chief Auditor on both the stocks and purchases systems. The study shows how the material is pulled together before the report is written. Some of the final review has been carried out already in the attestation audit and is not repeated in the systems reliability work. This would not be the case if the systems reliability work were carried out by itself. For instance, regularity issues might be raised concerning the powers of the constituent parties to JARDS in this work.

CASE STUDY 12.1 JARDS – FORMING AN OPINION ON THE PURCHASES SYSTEM

The documents shown below are as follows:

1. Report to Sponsors of JARDS;
2. Statement of Audit Opinion Checklist;
3. Final Review Notes;
4. List of Significant Subjective Issues;
5. List of Errors and Omissions;
6. List of Post-balance Sheet Events;
7. Extracts from Purchases Testing:
    (a) Overall purchases compliance testing conclusions;
    (b) Overall purchases substantive testing conclusions;
    (c) Overall conclusions on purchases testing;
    (d) Documentation for one Control Objective for purchases system work.

The first document is the actual report given. It is qualified because of the method used for accounting for plant. By reading through the working papers the reasoning for this qualification can be followed.

The final working paper is the Opinion Checklist. Here the audit manager and the person signing the report (the Chief Auditor) completed the assignment by positively answering some specific questions of general importance.

The Final Review Notes are the next working papers. The person who is to give the opinion makes a final review of the working papers. The queries he raises are answered by the audit manager or senior field staff. Note how the queries raised cover a wide range of audit objectives. Each has been specifically answered and cleared.

The third document lists 'Significant Subjective Issues'. These subjective and pertinent observations on the assignment are made so that the manager and the person giving the opinions can consider these subjective issues without having to find them in the main body of the working papers.

Next comes a list of Errors and Omissions found during the assignment. In this particular attestation audit, errors are most easily set out in journal form. Again, the person who is to give the opinion will find this summary of errors uncovered useful.

Before an opinion can be given, post-balance sheet or assignment events must be considered. A small list of the most important points prepared by senior field staff is useful.

Up until this point all the working papers for closing an assignment have been shown. What follows is a selection of the purchases system testing papers. First we have the conclusions given on the purchases system work – a conclusion on the compliance testing, and another one on the substantive testing. These are followed by the overall conclusions combining the two.

Below the overall conclusion is a sample of the documentation for one of the compliance control objectives. The other control objectives might have been that:

(a) All purchases were properly authorized on written orders;
(b) That all purchases are properly recorded in the books and records of JARDS.

The test programmes for the control objective shown is given, as are the conclusions resulting from that testing.

In this case we can follow the compliance and substantive testing through to conclusions. The subjective issues raised are recorded, as are errors found and post-balance sheet events. Lastly, the person signing the report carries out a final review and completes the Opinion Checklist. The report can then be given.

1. REPORT TO THE SPONSORS OF JARDS

I have completed the organization's audit for the year to 31 March 19X1.

The accounts do not make provision for the depreciation of plant and machinery. In my opinion fixed assets are overstated by £500,000 and the operating deficit for the year is understated by the same amount.

In view of the significant effect on the accounts of the failure to make such a provision, in my opinion the statement of accounts set out on pages . . . to . . . do not fairly present the financial position of the organization at 31 March 19X1.

Chief Auditor.

2. Statement of Audit Opinion

To be completed by the Audit Manager and Chief Auditor.

	√ or ×	Audit Manager	Chief Auditor
1. Have satisfactory conclusions been drawn on all audit work?	Except √	Fixed ABC	Assets CA
2. Has all audit work been properly reviewed by senior audit staff?	√	ABC	CA
3. Have all review points been satisfactorily answered by those carrying out the work?	√	ABC	CA
4. Has the Final Accounts Technical Checklist been completed?	√	ABC	CA
5. Have the terms of our audit brief been fully complied with?	√	ABC	CA

Client: JARDS	Year end: 31.3.X6	Schedule No.
Subject:	Prepared by: CA	Reviewed by:
	Date: 10.8.X6	Date:

REVIEW SHEET

Review Point	Cross ref.	Point clearance	Initials
3. Final Review Notes			
Evidence from different sources			
1. Can we be so sure on our purchases work if stock is subject to poor control?		The storekeeper was not responsible for signing GRNs. See N2.	
. . .			
4. The very low creditors' figure of £10,000 appears inconsistent with purchases of £2.5m revenue and £3.0m capital.		Little revenue purchasing in March due to high stock levels. See P3. Plants was purchased in October. See F10.	
5. We need to consider the effect of recent election at Ardshire CC. Will they continue to support the project? Clearly stock and plant will have a low realizable value.		Manifesto supports scheme.	
. . .			
Technical Adequacy			
11. A very large amount of plant and machinery has been purchased—£3.0m. Clearly no depreciation or other write-off is poor accountng. It will lead to major accounts mis-statements in future years.		Client will not agree to write down assets. Qualification may be necessary. See F3 for quantification.	
. . .			
Regularity			
17. We need to check that the various constituent bodies to JARDS have the necessary powers for this work. How do the various authorities show their working capital injections to JARDS in their accounts?		S.137 used by local authorities. NRO has a specific Parliamentary vote. See N2.	

Client: JARDS	Year end: 31.3.X6	Schedule No. 1.1
Subject: Final A/cs Audit	Prepared by: AB	Reviewed by: CA
	Date: 8.9.X6	Date: 10.9.X6

4. Significant Subjective Issues

1. This is the first year of JARDS operation. The organization has yet to settle down to routine working.

. . .

2. Stock
2.1 Problems have been encountered with the audit of stock. This is by far the largest figure in the balance sheet, excluding fixed assets.
2.2 Stock accounts for over 25% of supplies usage which amount to £1,902K.
2.3 No year-end stocktake was carried out. Our work traced purchases through to stock records.
2.4 A significant proportion of purchases did not enter stock records. In many cases this may have been due to direct usage by JARDs rather than omissions from stock.
2.5 There is evidence that stock has been over ordered. Obsolescence may be a problem. The real needs of JARDS will only become apparent as reclamation work progresses.
2.6 Written assurances from the management have been received that stock levels although high are reasonable. Management have made assurances that there will be little stock obsolescence.

See P6.

Client: JARDS	Year end: 31.3.X6	Schedule No. 1.2
Subject: Final A/cs Audit Completion	Prepared by: AB Date: 3.9.X6	Reviewed by: CA Date: 10.5.X6

5. Errors and Omissions

	Balance sheet		Revenue A/c	
	Dr	Cr	Dr	Cr
	£	£	£	£
1. Dr Stock	27,000			
Cr Supplies				27,000

Being purchases omitted in error from stock and found in the store building.

See P19.

2. Dr Stock	15,000			
Cr		15,000		

Being purchases recorded in error in the new year returned to the old.

See K41.

6. Post-balance Sheet Events
1. After the council elections Ardshire CC has changed political control.
2. At the last quarterly stock check by Ardshire Internal Audit stock levels were down to £200,000.

Client: JARDS	Year end: 31.3.X6	Schedule No. K3
Subject: Purchases	Prepared by: AB Date: 3.9.X6	Reviewed by: CA Date: 10.5.X6

SYSTEMS AUDIT CONCLUSION SHEET

7. Purchases System:

1. **Compliance testing:**
   All three control objectives identified have been satisfied.

   See K10/20/30.

2. **Substantive testing:**
   As per 'Results I' in Chapter 8, Case study 8.3 (see pp. 195–6), no errors were found.

3. **Overall conclusion:**
   In my opinion purchases are fairly stated in the accounts of the organization.

Client: JARDS	Year end: 31.3.X6	Schedule No. K10
Subject: Purchases	Prepared by: AB Date: 3.9.X6	Reviewed by: CA Date: 10.5.X6

7(d). Control objective
That all recorded purchases have been received.

Controls:

1. Invoices are matched to goods received notes for:
   (a) Description of goods;
   (b) Quantity received.
2. Prices are invoices are as agreed to suppliers' price list or orders.
3. Authorized personnel have signed for all goods received.

Weaknesses:

Test Procedures:

Using the sample selected for substantive testing purposes check that:

(a) Invoices have been properly matched to goods received notes;
(b) Prices have been checked;
(c) Goods received notes have been signed by authorized personnel.

Test paper reference	Checked by
K20	AB
K20	AB
K30	AB

Conclusion:
In my opinion control objective has been satisfied.

CASE STUDY 12.2 SYSTEMS RELIABILITY AUDIT OF PURCHASES AND STOCK

The documents shown below are as follows:

1. Final Review Notes;
2. List of Significant Subjective Issues;
3. List of Major Findings;
4. List of Post-assignment Changes to Systems;
5. Extracts from the Stock Systems Testing – paperwork for two Control Objectives.

This systems reliability audit is subject to a very similar opinion forming process to the attestation audit. The results of systems testing are summarized. Recent systems changes are listed and a final review is carried out by the person giving the opinion.

Client: JARDS	Year end: 31.3.X6	Schedule No. 1.1
Subject: Purchases and Stock Systems	Prepared by: CA	Reviewed by: —
	Date: 8.12.X6	Date: 20.12.X6

REVIEW SHEET			
Review Point	Cross ref.	Point clearance	Initials
1. Final Review 1. We should carry out a small stock check. It is not reasonable to rely on our year-end work this long after the audit. The results will put our control findings into perspective.		See C10.	AB
2. Now that all purchases are taken into stock we need to ensure that the purchases system is not 'imperiled'.		See B1.	AB
3. JARDS uses the Ardshire CC stock system. It would be useful to discuss briefly our results with their internal auditors before we report.		See 1.5.	AB

2. Significant Subjective Issues
1. Goods received notes are made out by the purchasing personnel before items are input into the stores systems. This is done because input into the stores system is a slow process due to:
   (a) Lack of staff;
   (b) Prices are awaited so that stores records
       can be updated in one process.

2. There was no year-end stocktake.

3. There is little continuous stocktaking. Some is done by the stores staff. But there is no independent checking.

4. There is little physical security for purchases which do not enter the stores.

Client: JARDS	Year end: 31.3.X6	Schedule No. 1.2
Subject: Purchases and Stock Systems	Prepared by: AB Date: 8.12.X6	Reviewed by: CA Date: 20.12.X6

3. Findings
1. Purchases system has strong controls and produces reliable output.

   See Final Audit Work.
2. (a) Stock system has adequate controls once items have entered the system. These controls have been tested and found to operate.

   See A1.
   (b) The stock system has no controls to ensure that items purchased are taken into stock.
   (c) Nil stocktakes have been carried out.
   (d) Year-end stock figures are materiality correct. They were substantively tested in the year-end audit of accounts.

   See A3.

4. Recent Changes in the System
1. All purchases are now processed through the stores.

Client: JARDS Subject: Stock System	Year end: 31.3.X6 Prepared by: AB Date: 3.9.X6	Schedule No. A10 Reviewed by: CA Date: 10.5.X6

CONTROL OBJECTIVE ANALYSIS SHEET

5. Control Objective I
That stock issues are completely and accurately recorded in the books of account and store records.

Controls:	Test Procedures	Ref.
1. The stores building has adequate physical security.		A14
2. Stores are only issued when the issue notes are signed by work's manager.	See Audit Programme A11.	A14
3. Issue notes are batched using headers with hash totals before input.		A15
Weaknesses:		
1. There is normally a long backlog of unprocessed issue notes.		A12

Conclusion:

Client: JARDS	Year end: 31.3.X6	Schedule No. A20
Subject: Stock System	Prepared by: AB Date: 6.12.X6	Reviewed by: CA Date: 20.12.X6

CONTROL OBJECTIVE ANALYSIS SHEET

5. Control Objective II
That new stock is completely and accurately recorded in the stock account and stock records.

Controls:	Test Procedures	Ref.
1. Delivery notes are batched using batch headers with hash totals before input.		A25
Weaknesses:	See Audit Programme A21	
1. Not all purchases are processed through stores.		A22
2. There is a long backlog of unprocessed stock deliveres. Some of these are awaiting prices when invoices arrive.		A22

Conclusion:

FINAL CONCLUDING POINTS

We are now at the end of the 'essential audit process'. The end product of the auditor's labours has been finally delivered to the client and the audit is over.

Was the final report accurate? Was it sufficiently hard hitting or was it unfair to some members of the client's staff? Does the client consider he got value for money from his auditor? After the report is delivered these questions often arise in the auditor's mind. It has been the ambition of this book to provide some general answers to such nagging doubts.

We have worked on the logical assumption that the best way to ensure a report is first rate and not merely 'glossy' is to carry out high quality work before the report is written. The work must be rational, consistent and orderly from beginning to end. Objectives must be set and plans made. Testing must be carefully designed to provide relevant reliable evidence. And the quantity of evidence must be carefully weighed in a rational manner. The sufficiency of audit evidence is crucial to the quality of the report given. In fact when using monetary unit sampling to decide the quantity of data required the factual quality of the report can be determined mathematically. A sample of 50 items may give 95% confidence of a material error. A sample of 38 items for the same test would give only 90% confidence.

And is the client happy with the audit? Does he give the report any credence or is it clear to him that the auditors never got to grips with the subject and the fee is a total waste of money? Or is the report acceptable but the fee or the time spent by the auditor on the work quite disproportionate to the value of the report? In this book we have given substantial guidance on how to audit efficiently. Planning gets the audit off to a good start by minimizing the time likely to be wasted. Systems based audit allows the auditor to avoid large substantive test samples. Directional testing and analytical review of physical and financial relationships allows the auditor to take valid short-cuts in his work. Monetary unit sampling gives the minimum sample sizes consistent with rational considerations of sufficiency of evidence. All these techniques mean that the client is likely to be happy with the result. The work will have been carefully controlled to provide an accurate report in the minimum period of time.

Every so often the auditor will make errors even when following best practice. Sometimes he will underestimate the strength of client feeling about a particular topic and his report may be unnecessarily insensitive in this respect. At other times the auditor will make a genuine error over a point of fact. By following a rational, consistent and orderly approach both problems will be kept to a minimum.

Audit is not an exact science. Considerable 'artistry' and judgement are required by the auditor if he is to do his job well. But that sense of professional judgement has to be combined with a solid appreciation of the technical nature of audit as represented by the essential audit process.

Specimen working papers

In this appendix we provide a specimen set of key working papers. Most audit organizations will have some standard forms. Internal audit sections frequently have standard test programmes, job sheets and routine forms for audit planning and control. It is probably fair to say that the average auditor has more forms at his disposal than he uses regularly and that a large proportion of those forms are of an administrative or semi-administrative nature – time sheets, job allocation sheets, requisition forms, file index sheets, etc. With perhaps the possible exception of standard audit programmes it is rare to find standard documentation that is actually used on all significant audit assignments.

Standard documentation for systems reliability and attestation audit greatly enhances the overall quality of the audit work. It makes for easier review of key findings and highlights the path the auditor has followed to arrive at his conclusions. These benefits are especially valuable for new staff and for those using a previous year's audit to assist new work. Standard documentation helps maintain a standard quality of audit service.

This collection of working papers provides key standard documentation for use throughout a systems reliability and attestation audit. It would be surprising if the reader could not suggest further refinements to suit the type of work and the 'house' style of his own organization. This is partly the point of the collection – to provide a skeleton that can be fleshed out to suit the needs of a wide range of audits.

(a) The **Assignment Plan Header Sheet** (1) provides an ideal opportunity to overview the plan of the audit assignment. It is a key index.
(b) The **Standard Working Paper** or **Schedule** (2) is used throughout for the basic documentation of an assignment.
(c) **Review Sheets** (3) would normally be found at the top of the file and at subsections of larger assignments. For instance, each main balance sheet figure of an attestation audit would require review as would a

major subsystem in a systems evaluation. For new staff written review is an invaluable training aid providing a record of shortcomings and corrective action needed.

(d) The **Assignment Summary Sheet** (4) is largely self-explanatory. It is important to provide a concise summary of objectives, results and conclusions to complete every assignment and to assist review of the work.

(e) The **Systems Flowcharting Sheet** (5) is standard to most assignments. It can be expanded to cover large systems by the use of 'follow-on' sheets. The sheet is divided into two so that the narrative describing each procedure can easily be associated with the document flow. Space has also been provided in columns for referencing key controls and weaknesses. We have found that such referencing greatly assists the auditor in the field to identify particular controls and weaknesses in a system.

(f) The **Internal Control Objectives Sheet** (6) forms a logical progression from the form listing the audit objectives, to the Assignment Summary Sheet. The control objectives for each system are listed.

(g) Each control objective listed on (6) should be the subject of a separate **Control Objective Analysis Sheet** (7). These are used to highlight the controls that satisfy the objectives, the compliance tests for each control and any significant weaknesses. The conclusion on the sheet should relate to the overall ability of the controls to meet the control objective. Thus we have a logical progression recorded as follows:

Audit objectives
↓
Internal control objectives (test objectives)
↓
Controls to be tested
↓
Tests to be undertaken

(h) Sheets (6) and (7) can be cross-referenced to any of the detailed working papers as necessary. However, it is often helpful in practice to have a single sheet with all the main control objectives, controls, tests and conclusions. We have chosen to use the **Compliance Test Programme Sheet** (8) for this purpose. Such a programme provides a convenient point for collating all such information. Usually the test programme is carried among the papers of the field auditor throughout the testing. The programme is thus geared towards the practical information required for testing.

(i) The **Substantive Test Programme Sheet** (9) is a general sheet to be used to record all substantive testing work. We have outlined two possible test objectives on the sheet. Other more specific test objectives should be annotated at the top of the test column.

(j) The **Systems Audit Conclusion Sheet** (10) forms the final stage of the systems audit. It should then be followed by filling in the Audit Assignment Summary Sheet (4).

(k) The **Systems Audit Progress Sheet** (11) is a useful control sheet to monitor the progress of systems based audit work. Details of who did the work together with the date it was done should be recorded in the columns provided. The assurance column (High, Medium, Low, Nil) is a subjective judgemental statement usually made by a senior reviewing auditor. It is possible from this to form a further judgement on the reliability factor to be assigned to internal controls as part of the exercise of determining any monetary unit samples.

(l) The MUS Forms 1 to 6 are used for determining the sample size (MUS 1), precision (MUS 2) and error extrapolation. These and the other MUS forms are fully explained in the Case studies in Chapter 8.

The following key summarizes the above overview of the standard audit documentation which follows.

Planning, recording and controlling:
1. Assignment Plan Header Sheet
2. Blank Working Paper
3. Review Sheet
4. Audit Assignment Summary Sheet

Systems based audit:
5. Systems Flowcharting Sheet
6. Control Objectives Sheet
7. Control Objectives Analysis Sheet
8. Test Programme Sheet – Compliance Testing
9. Test Programme Sheet – Substantive Testing (and continuation sheet)
10. Systems Audit Conclusion Sheet
11. Systems Audit Progress Sheet

Monetary unit sampling:
12. MUS Form 1
13. MUS Form 2
14. MUS Form 3
15. MUS Form 4
16. MUS Form 5
17. MUS Form 6

Client/Department: File Ref: Subject:	Year end: Prepared by: Date:	Schedule No: Reviewed by: Date:

ASSIGNMENT PLAN INDEX	

Heading
  1. Objectives
  2. Ranking of Objectives
  3. Reporting Format
  4. Audit Staffing
  5. Client Staffing
  6. Audit Timetable
  7. Important Points Specific to the Audit
  8. Figures under Audit
  9. Materiality
10. Detailed Audit Overview
	Page reference

1

Client/Department: File Ref: Subject:	Year end:	Schedule No:
	Prepared by:	Reviewed by:
	Date:	Date:

WORKING PAPER

Client/Department: File Ref: Subject:		Year end: Prepared by: Date:	Schedule No: Reviewed by: Date:

REVIEW SHEET

Review point	Cross ref.	Point clearance	Initials

Client/Department: File Ref: Subject:	Year end: Prepared by: Date:	Schedule No: Reviewed by: Date:

AUDIT ASSIGNMENT SUMMARY SHEET	Ref:

Audit objectives

Audit approach

Results

Conclusion

Client/Department:		Sheet of	Schedule No:
File Ref:			Encl. ref:
			File ref:

SYSTEM FLOWCHART

Title: _____

C = Control
KC = Key control
W = Weakness

Ref.	PROCEDURE	DOCUMENT FLOW	Comments and further notes

	Prepared	Revised	Revised	Revised

5

Client/Department: File Ref: Subject:	Year end: Prepared by: Date:	Schedule No: Reviewed by: Date:

INTERNAL CONTROL OBJECTIVES SHEET

System:

Objectives	Analysis sheet reference
1.	
2.	
3.	
4.	
5.	

Client/Department: File Ref: Subject:	Year end: Prepared by: Date:	Schedule No: Reviewed by: Date:

CONTROL OBJECTIVE ANALYSIS SHEET

Control objective:

Controls: Weaknesses:	Test procedures	Ref.

Conclusion:

COMPLIANCE TEST PROGRAMME	Schedule No:
Client/Department: **System:**	File Ref: Prepared by: Date:

Objective:

To discover whether or not the Internal Controls identified by our systems evaluation are operating effectively and can be relied upon when forming an audit opinion.

Note: System evaluation should be read before starting tests.

Control objective	Control	CT ref.	Test	WP ref.	Is the control working? Y/N	Initial and Date

Conclusion:

SUBSTANTIVE TEST PROGRAMME	Schedule No:
Client/Department: **System/audit area:** **Monetary Value fpa:**	File Ref: Prepared by: Date:

Objective:

Tick   1. To gain direct substantive evidence of accuracy, fairness and regularity of the above figures.

☐

Tick   2. To assess the impact of known weaknesses or failures in internal controls.

☐

Method of selection (tick box) Judgemental selection H.V.
                                      Other

Statistical sample
Analytical review

Cross-ref.

IC/W ref.	ST ref.	Test	WP ref.	Initials and date

Client/Department:				Schedule No: File Ref:	
		SUBSTANTIVE TEST PROGRAMME Continuation sheet			
System/audit area:					
IC/W ref.	ST ref.	Test		WP ref.	Initials and date

Client/Department: File Ref: Subject:	Year end: Prepared by: Date:	Schedule No: Reviewed by: Date:

SYSTEMS AUDIT CONCLUSION SHEET

1. Substantive testing conclusion:

2. Compliance testing conclusion:

Overall conclusion:

SYSTEMS RELIABILITY AUDIT
Progress Sheet

Instructions:
Complete in pencil and update as required.

File ref.	System M = Main system S = Sub-system	DOCUMENTATION					SYSTEM EVALUATION			TESTING		EVALUATION OF RESULTS		
		Narrative	Detailed flow chart	Key control chart	Examples of main docs.	Other, e.g. ICQ, depth test	IC and W identified	Compliance test prog.	Substantive test prog.	Testing (CT) (ST)	Extended testing (ST)	Memo report	Assurance HMLN	Comments inits.

IC Internal control
W   Weakness
CT Compliance test
ST Substantive test
H   High assurance
M   Medium assurance
L   Low assurance
N   No assurance

Form MUS 1			Schedule No: Prepared by:		
			Reviewed by:		
SAMPLE SIZE			Client/Dept:	Ref:	
Population					
1. Testing materiality £					
2. Population value £					
3. Reliability factor					
4. Sample size $\dfrac{(2) \times (3)}{(1)}$					
5. Sample interval £ $\dfrac{(2)}{(4)}$					
Notes:					

Form MUS 2		Schedule No: Prepared by:	
		Reviewed by:	
SAMPLE PRECISION AND ESTIMATED ADJUSTMENTS		Client/Dept:	Ref:

Account/overall materiality:
Basic precision:
Anticipated Adjustments:
    Anticipated Error
    Estimated Precision Gap Widening
Upper error limit Anticipated:			

Notes:			

Form MUS 3				Schedule No: Prepared by:			
				Reviewed by:			
ERROR PROJECTIONS (Book value less than sampling interval)				Client/Dept:		Ref:	
	Book value	Audit value	Error	Tainting error/BV	Rank T	Projected error (SI × T%)	Cross ref.
Overstatement errors: Understatement errors:	£	£	£	%	%	£	
Net value of errors				Net projected error			

Form MUS 4		Schedule No: Prepared by:	
		Reviewed by:	
ERRORS–HIGH VALUE AND KEY ITEMS		Client/Dept:	Ref:
Book value	Audit value	Difference	Cross-ref.
	Net total errors		

15

Form MUS 5		Schedule No: Prepared by:		
		Reviewed by:		
SAMPLE PRECISION AND PRECISION GAP WIDENING		Client/Dept:	Ref:	
Basic Precision				
	PGW Factor*	Tainting	Sampling interval	PGW**
Overstatements:		%		£
Understatements:				
Net total PGW				

* Calculated as per formula given with Fig. 8.3.
** PGW is the product of over/understatements, PGW factor, tainting % and sampling interval.

16

Form MUS 6		Schedule No: Prepared by:	
		Reviewed by:	
TOTAL ERRORS AND PRECISION		Client/Dept:	Ref:

1. Most likely error (net)
   (Forms MUS 3 and MUS 4)
 	
2. Basic precision
   (Form MUS 2)
 	
3. Precision gap widening
   (Form MUS 5)
 	
4. Upper error limit			

Notes:			

Bibliography

This is a short list of works that are useful to the public sector auditor.

GENERAL READING

Audit in the Public Sector, by R. Buttery and R. Simpson (1986), published by Woodhead Faulkner, provides a useful introductory text. A fairly detailed text specifically for internal audit, though aimed more at the private sector, is provided by *Internal Audit*, by J.S.R. Venables and K.W. Impey (1985), published by Butterworths. A lively and thought-provoking book with contributions covering diverse areas of audit, edited by D. Kent, M. Sherer and S. Turley (1985), is *Current Audit Issues*, published by Harper and Row.

AUDIT MANUALS

The Government Internal Audit Manual (2nd edition 1988), published by HMSO, concentrates heavily on the system-evaluation role of internal audit in central government. The larger private firms of external auditors have often published their audit manuals or adaptations thereof in which they discuss audit techniques in considerable detail. The reader is advised to consider two or three such manuals before attempting to adapt particular techniques to the public sector, as each firm tends to select and refine techniques most suited to its own range of clients. The effort, though time consuming, is usually worthwhile.

The Audit Commission publish a six-volume, regularly updated manual, *Local Government Auditor*, which includes their own working manual *The Audit Approach*. The National Audit Office have a useful and extensive audit manual, but neither this nor any adaptation is published.

STATISTICAL SAMPLING

Two notable works by H. Arkin, *Handbook of Sampling for Auditing and Accounting 1984* and *Sampling Methods for the Auditor: An Advanced Treatment*, published by McGraw-Hill, cover most of the basic and advanced techniques in readable detail. *Statistical Sampling for Audit and Control* by T.W. McRae, though currently out of print, is another major work in this area.

A classic work that brought monetary unit sampling techniques to the attention of many organizations is *Dollar Unit Sampling* by D.A. Leslie, A.D. Teitlebaum and R.J. Anderson (1980), published by Pitman Books.

The APC's draft audit guideline *Audit Sampling*, with its detailed explanations of some of the practical difficulties, appendices of models and worked examples, provides useful coverage. It should be read by all practising auditors.

VALUE-FOR-MONEY AUDIT

This is the one area of public sector audit with a reasonable coverage of specialist works. The Audit Commission have several published works in this area such as *Imposing Economy, Efficiency and Effectiveness in Local Government in England and Wales* and numerous *National Studies* on particular VFM issues in local authorities. We can expect similar national studies on the Health Service in the not too distant future. CIPFA has published several works in this area, such as its *Value for Money Handbook*.

Among the larger private firms, Price Waterhouse's *Value for Money Auditing Manual* (1983), published by Gee and Company and updated 1989, is also a useful text.

FRAUD AND CORRUPTION

The *Audit Information Circulars* provided by the Audit Commission provide regular updates on real cases. *Investigation of Fraud in the Public Sector* (1989), published by CIPFA, provides a useful work on the subject.

COMPUTER AUDIT

There are a great many texts on computer audit, but CIPFA's published work *Computer Audit Guide-lines* is probably one of the most useful for the public sector auditor.

Index